LIFE BEYOND FEAR

Life Beyond Fear

A UKRAINIAN WOMAN'S MEMOIR

Natalie Oceanheart

Potomac Books
An imprint of the University of Nebraska Press

© 2026 by Natalie Oceanheart

All rights reserved. Potomac Books is an imprint of the University of Nebraska Press.

For customers in the EU with safety/GPSR concerns, contact:
gpsr@mare-nostrum.co.uk
Mare Nostrum Group BV
Mauritskade 21D
1091 GC Amsterdam
The Netherlands

Library of Congress Cataloging-in-Publication Data can be found at search.catalog.loc.gov: ISBN 978-1-64012-687-9 (paperback)

Designed and set in Bulmer MT Std by Lacey Losh.

Some journeys begin with leaving,
but the hardest journeys lead us back—not to where we were,
but to who we truly are.

—Natalie Oceanheart

Contents

Author's Note ix

Part 1. Surviving the Frontlines (Ukraine, 2022)

1. Awakening to War 3
2. Steps of Hope amid Rising Danger 11
3. Between Fear and Purpose 21
4. The Burden of Unspoken Pain 29
5. Picking Up the Pieces 37
6. The Gift of Respite 47
7. A Heartbeat Away 53
8. Light in the Dark: Moments of Resilience 59
9. In the Grip of War: A Household of Dread 67
10. Shattered Roots: Escaping the Shadows of Home 75
11. A Last Embrace: On the Edge of Escape 85

Part 2. The Road to Safety (Europe)

12. A Fragile Peace: First Steps in Foreign Lands 95
13. The Atlantic Awaits: Letting Go and Looking Forward 105
14. Through European Crossroads: Balancing Hope and Fear 117

Part 3. The American Dream, Reimagined

15. Arrival in the Land of Dreams   127
16. Celebrating Freedom   135
17. Between Gratitude and Growing Pains   143
18. An Immigrant's Trial: From Dreams to Reality   151
19. Finding Comfort in Small Joys and Big Dreams   157
20. Freedom's Complex Landscape   165
21. Navigating Highs and Lows   171
22. The Price of Perseverance   177
23. The Burden of Uncertainty   183
24. Fighting for Peace and Place   189
25. The Hidden Cost of Dreams   193
26. Steps Forward, Glances Back   197
27. Crisis, Courage, and Continuance   203

Part 4. Roots of Resilience (Ukraine, 2014)

28. The Beginning of the End   211
29. Living Under Siege   221
30. Battling Fear and Finding Hope   227
31. Battles Within and Beyond   233
32. The Cycle Restarts   243

Author's Note

Dear Friend,

This book is both my heartfelt cry and a gentle whisper of hope for you. It stands as a testament to the resilience of the human spirit, revealing that, no matter how many times we fall, there is always a path to rise again. Here, I share my journey, marked by upheaval and uncertainty—bombardments, chaos, new beginnings, and the profound challenge of rediscovering oneself amid it all.

Through these pages, I recount not only trials and losses but also the moments of pure joy that sustained me. I tell the story of how my family and I endured the war in Ukraine, our forced departure from our homeland, our time in Europe, and eventually, our arrival in America. This story does not merely touch on the full-scale war that erupted in 2022 but also remembers how conflict first crept into our lives in 2014, changing them in ways we could never have anticipated.

With this book, I hope to connect with you, like children effortlessly finding new friends on a playground, unafraid of the unknown. That openness has inspired me through every trial—especially in the darkest hours.

Immigration is a journey like no other, shaking every sense of stability and safety. For some, it's a search for dreams; for others, a matter of survival. Yet we carry not only physical baggage but also emotional burdens that date back to childhood. Even so, it's often the smallest moments of joy that give us the strength to move forward.

This book is about a real person simply trying to find the meaning amid the surrounding madness, to break through the asphalt like a seedling.

A wise person learns from others' mistakes, and God knows I've made countless ones. There's much here for you to draw upon.

My story is a call not to give up. It's a reminder that every storm can be a source of strength. It's also an invitation, dear reader, to share these moments with me, so together we may find meaning in the struggle, joy in simple things, and peace in embracing ourselves as we are.

Another reason for writing this book was to relive everything—to understand what no longer hurts, even if a few scars remain. But as I wrote, I realized: It still does. Thank you for taking the time to get to know my story and for opening your heart to it.

Because I know with certainty: Life begins beyond the edge of fear.

LIFE BEYOND FEAR

Part 1

SURVIVING THE FRONTLINES

Ukraine, 2022

In the darkest hours, resilience is born—not from the absence of fear, but from the courage to face it.

1

Awakening to War

Thursday, 5 a.m., February 24, 2022. I am jolted awake by unsettling noises that terrify me, though I can't quite place them. There's something deadly about these sounds, a deep, instinctually felt warning that something significant is unfolding. The pale morning light spills through the balcony door, casting a grim glow on my husband's face, marked by fear and horror—a reflection of my own dread. Explosions chill the blood; their reality is undeniable and horrifying. As we lie in bed, our silent glances acknowledge the unknown trials ahead.

Our thoughts turn to our children, our two daughters aged ten and four, still asleep and dreaming of rainbows and unicorns, blissfully unaware of the stark reality intruding upon their dreams. The scene feels eerily reminiscent of Valentin Papko's chilling painting "Not Even Dreamed. June 22, 1941," which depicts the surreal calm before the storm of World War II. I never imagined facing a similar terror, a terror unfolding in the very heart of Ukraine, in the city of Dnipro. A terror that swept across the entire country that morning.

I feel helpless in the face of this looming danger, an ancient fear I can't protect them from. History, once confined to the pages of books or museum walls, is now painfully present, repeating in a way I could never have imagined, touching ordinary families like ours.

In a protective instinct, I wish to gather my children into our bed, to hold them close despite not understanding the full scope of what's happening. My husband, Artur, attempting to preserve their peace for a little longer, pleads with me not to wake them. So, I lie down with our younger daughter,

Dasha, holding her tight, while he does the same with her sister, Masha. We hold each other as the sounds of chaos eventually fade, but my mind races, trying to piece together the surreal events unfolding outside our home.

About an hour later, I rise to drink some water and, through the kitchen window, I witness a mass exodus. People are hastily packing their cars, an unmistakable sign of a dire situation. My mind races, overwhelmed by the sudden and surreal shift in our world. The silence in our home contrasts with the growing chaos outside, and I feel both an urge to act and a sense of disbelief, as if this can't possibly be real.

A call to my mother confirms my worst fears—she answers in tears, revealing that a war has started. The notion seems absurd, unimaginable in the twenty-first century, and my mind rebels against reality. War feels like a relic of history or a plot in a movie, not something that could invade our lives today.

And here I am again, grappling with this haunting thought. Just recently, I watched *Downton Abbey*, where the main character, Lady Mary Crawley, reacts with disbelief and indignation at the onset of war. How could such a thing happen in the early twentieth century? This same terrifying question weighs on me in the twenty-first century, and suddenly I realize how deeply I empathize with my beloved character. A wave of sincere compassion envelops me—I can feel her despair, the foreboding sense of horror that lies ahead. I know what awaits her: War, from which she cannot escape. This inevitable nightmare engulfs me, forcing me to recall the hopelessness Lady Mary once faced when confronted with the horrors of the First World War. The same darkness and despair wash over me again, making me ponder the grim parallels between our fates.

As the shock begins to settle, the grim reality sets in—we must face whatever comes. There's no hiding from it, and no running away. I stare out the window again at the half-empty parking lot, seeing the stark evidence of people fleeing. We need to comprehend, explain to our children, and adapt, making decisions moment by moment in a newly uncertain world.

Thank God for the internet, which allows us to quickly learn from social media and news outlets that war has indeed broken out. The headlines confirm my fears, but seeing the unfolding situation online pushes me into action. No longer just a tragic story far away, this is now personal. I realize we need to prepare, to secure what we can before supplies run out.

Russia has attacked us. Our city's airport, near where we live, along with all major airports in the country, has been targeted and bombed. Panic is palpable as people clog the roads attempting to escape, while others rush to stores, stockpiling essentials. My husband headed to an ATM, foreseeing the imminent necessity of cash over credit, but found the machines empty, the queues long and fraught with desperation.

It was a Friday morning—a day that was supposed to unfold like any other. Masha was meant to be getting ready for school. But that day, what was meant to be ordinary morphed into a nightmare. I chose not to send her to school. The parents' chat group was a flurry of confusion, everyone seeking guidance on what steps to take next. Eventually, the school communicated through the teacher that classes were canceled, a small relief amid escalating fears.

Artur, a software developer, worked from home, a blessing under these circumstances. The nursery Dasha attended also canceled its sessions. At that time, my role was managing our home. So, here we were, the four of us, confined to our modest two-bedroom apartment—not due to a pandemic this time, but to a war.

We had to discuss reality with our children. Concealing the truth was no longer an option; they deserved to be informed, not shielded from the truth under layers of deception. They sensed the gravity of the situation. We sat down and I explained things in terms they could grasp. Explaining the onset of war to your children is an agony I would not wish upon anyone—the danger lurking outside, the abrupt halt of everyday life, and the piercing realization that even home could not guarantee safety anymore.

I took a deep breath and looked at our daughters, their innocent faces filled with confusion.

"Girls," I began softly, trying to keep my voice steady, "there's something very serious happening right now. You might hear loud noises outside, and you might see people rushing to leave, but I need you to understand that there is a war starting."

Masha, our eldest, frowned and asked, "Like the ones in the history books?"

I nodded, feeling a lump form in my throat. "Yes, like that. But this time, it's happening here, in our city, in Dnipro."

Dasha, too young to fully grasp the concept, clung to her favorite stuffed unicorn. "Will it hurt us, Mama?" she asked in a small voice.

I reached out and held her close. "We're going to do everything we can to keep you safe. Dad and I will be here with you, no matter what." I glanced at Artur, who nodded in agreement, his eyes heavy with worry.

I had to tell them that their usual freedoms—school, playing outside, attending classes—were all suspended indefinitely. "We don't know when things will go back to normal," I said quietly. "For now, we need to stay together and stay safe. We might not be able to go outside like we used to, but we'll make sure you have everything you need right here at home."

Masha's eyes filled with concern, but she didn't protest, while Dasha simply held me tighter, sensing the weight of my words even if she didn't fully understand them.

It's a burden no parent should bear, the realization that our children's sense of security would forever be altered, that our lives would now be eternally split into "before" and "after."

The day was spent in a frantic search for food and essentials. Supermarkets were nearly barren, gas stations besieged, ATMs depleted of cash, as the city plunged into a frenzy resembling scenes from an apocalyptic film.

My heart raced as I navigated the aisles of the supermarket, desperately scanning for anything we could use. The shelves, once full, were now eerily empty. The sight was disorienting; familiar products had disappeared, replaced by gaps that spoke volumes about the panic that had swept through before us.

As I turned into another aisle, I felt a surge of panic rise in my chest at the sight of a lone packet of pasta. It was small, almost overlooked in the chaos, yet it seemed like a lifeline in that moment. I pushed my cart forward quickly, but before I could reach it, other shoppers spotted it too. A man and woman moved toward the packet, hands outstretched, their eyes locked on it like it was a precious treasure.

I froze as their voices rose. The woman grabbed it first, her grip tight as if she'd never let it go. The man protested, his face twisted in desperation. "I saw it first," he said, his voice edged with panic.

"Do you think I care?" she shot back, clutching the packet to her chest. "I have a family to feed, too!"

Their exchange escalated, as they pulled at the packet in a tug of war. My heart sank watching them—this wasn't just about pasta. It was about survival, about people pushed to the brink. I took a step back, shaken.

Outside the store, the chaos mirrored what I had just witnessed inside. The encounter felt surreal, like we were no longer in the city we knew, but in some nightmare from which we couldn't wake. Traffic choked the city's exits as those who remained scoured for the last remnants on store shelves—all of it accompanied by lines, disputes, and outright conflicts over mundane items.

With every honk of a horn, every raised voice, my anxiety grew. I kept thinking. How long will this last? How will we make it through? Caught in the tumult, we managed to secure some food and retreated home, weaving through the traffic. I remember gripping the steering wheel tightly, my knuckles white, as I tried to focus on the road, on getting us home safely.

Once home, we promptly prepared what we termed an "emergency suitcase"—a bag packed for those moments when every second counts. We filled it with essentials: identification documents, a small stash of food, water, and basic toiletries. For the children, we added a few familiar comforts, hoping these small items might offer them a sense of security if we had to leave in a hurry. For Masha, we packed her soft plush kitten, a companion that had been with her through countless nights and new experiences. Dasha chose her unicorn with rainbow hair, a bright symbol of innocence we so desperately wanted to protect.

With the suitcase by the door, our sense of control returned, even if only slightly. We couldn't guarantee our daughters' safety, but we could at least be ready for whatever came next.

Afterward, we turned to securing our small apartment. We rearranged furniture, moving our beds as far from the windows as possible. There's a belief that in the event of a blast, glass won't shatter beyond two walls, so placing two barriers between us and the windows could offer some protection. Though this would shield us from broken glass or debris, it was little comfort: we knew it couldn't guard against a direct missile strike: an ever-present threat in recent days.

As a final step, we decided to prepare the vestibule—the small space between our apartment and our neighbors'—as a makeshift shelter. Although our neighbors hadn't made any preparations, we were ready to share our provisions with them if it came to that. We placed chairs, food, water, and blankets there, creating a small haven in this narrow passageway. It wasn't much, but it was a place of quiet refuge, and in that moment, it felt like an act of defiance—an attempt to carve out a space of peace, however fleeting, in the midst of chaos.

My mind was reeling, desperate to make sense of it all and find some way out. It was agonizing to think of the children having to witness this nightmare. Poor kids. Their futures, their mental well-being, all overshadowed by the haunting question: "Why? What do they want from us?"

Every Ukrainian now carries their own tale of sorrow. War had invaded our peaceful lives, reaching our children. We didn't choose this life; we didn't choose this death.

The news provided no solace. We frantically looked for any indication that this nightmare would end soon, that perhaps in a day or two, life could somehow resume. We just wanted to keep living, to continue our lives. It felt like being thrust suddenly into an icy river's strong current—sheer shock.

But the enemy forces were advancing, moving toward the capital, and the fear of Kyiv falling was unbearable. Russian troops had already taken key positions in the north and were pressing forward relentlessly, while simultaneously advancing from the east, where the conflict had been ongoing for years. Their aim seemed clear: to capture the heart of the country—Kyiv. What next? For what purpose? Why was this happening to us?

Reports were filled with scenes of unbelievable traffic jams at the borders. People were fleeing—a natural response. Fight, flee, or freeze. We froze, just watching and waiting.

You know how there's often a north-south divide in many countries? It exists here too, not between north and south, but between the western and eastern parts of the country. We found ourselves in the center when war struck. Yet, the western part, especially cities like Lviv and Ivano-Frankivsk, untouched initially by the war, did not welcome us or anyone from the east warmly.

Instead, they exploited the situation—housing prices skyrocketed, fivefold, a hundredfold, as they wished. There was a frenzy, a desperation to survive. People fled to untouched areas and were welcomed with open arms—but only if they had substantial money to offer. And people in the west weren't ashamed of it. Not everyone could or wanted to flee the country; we had to manage somehow within our own borders. Yet, instead of offering help, our own people presented a burning hot poker—nothing personal, just survival and a stark lack of conscience.

After we obtained some supplies, a few hours passed as we tried to comprehend what was happening and to return to reality. People rushed to volunteer. Recruitment offices were overwhelmed with those eager to defend their home, their country, and their independence. The formation of territorial defense units began—a structure of volunteers, ready to fight, ready to resist. The government even started distributing weapons to civilians on the streets for city defense. This, personally, only heightened my fear—giving out weapons to everyone and anyone, indiscriminately.

Our unity eventually bore fruit—Ukrainian forces, volunteers, and ordinary citizens worked together, and through sheer determination and resistance, the Russians failed to take the capital. The Russian troops, despite their relentless assaults, were pushed back. It was a miracle, but one that came at the cost of thousands of lives. The war did not abate; the boundaries simply changed. The enemy controlled 27 percent of our territory. Everything was dire. Then they started the air raid sirens. The psychological pressure of that terrible wail signifying death was immense. During sirens and declared alerts, everything shut down—pharmacies empty, stores half-stocked. And no one knew when it would end. An alert could come at any moment. It was constant.

We were instructed to enforce blackouts from dusk till dawn, since it was winter and dark by 4 p.m. No lights outside or in homes, to prevent enemy planes from identifying a city below. To me, this seemed absurd. We live in the twenty-first century—who now identifies a city by the lights in its windows? What about modern technology, maps, and navigation? It felt like the authorities were driving us into panic deliberately, crushing us morally, intensifying our fear.

It was a nightmarish scenario. Winter, darkness by 4 p.m., the cold, the fear, and sitting in the dark with children under the wail of sirens—even without actual shelling, it was overwhelming.

In the unsettling calm of the early morning, I wrestled with the notion of keeping any semblance of normalcy amid the chaos. My beloved car, a blue Mazda 3 we affectionately called "the little bluebird," became a symbol of the life we had just two months before the war began. When my father bought his first car, I was thrilled. I couldn't believe that someone with a car could ever be unhappy. That car became a symbol of hope, of the life my father had built despite everything. I've loved cars ever since; they remind me of my father's strength, of how far he came from his troubled past, and now, they represented a precarious connection to that life we once had. Now, our little bluebird was parked on the street, vulnerable and exposed to the brutalities of war. Living in a city apartment meant we had no garage to shield it from potential damage—missile shrapnel, vandalism, or worse.

With the war entering its second day, the neighborhood was adapting as best as it could. People started equipping basements for safety, a luxury our building lacked. Many of our neighbors, along with their pets, would seek refuge there with every sounding siren, a stressful routine of fleeing back and forth. We chose to stay in our apartment, haunted by the thought that a direct hit could either bury us under rubble in the basement or send us plummeting from our fourth-floor home.

Driven by a need to maintain some routine, I decided to wash my car—a task I had planned in a time of peace just days before. There I was, alone at a self-service car wash in a deserted cityscape that felt like a set from a Hollywood war movie. But this act of washing my car, amid war and sirens, oddly calmed me. It was my way of grounding myself, a necessary respite to preserve my mental stability, which my family heavily depended on. Throughout the war, maintaining this routine helped me cope, each car wash synchronizing with the grim soundtrack of sirens.

2

Steps of Hope amid Rising Danger

I was born and raised in a modest family in the eastern part of Ukraine. My mother, Elena, a school nurse, grew up amid hardship, shaped by an unstable family life that instilled in her both strength and a relentless drive for order. My father, Anatoly, knew the struggles of poverty and the wounds of an abusive upbringing, yet he remained resilient and tried his best to be a strong role model for us. Despite everything, my parents' hardships bound them to their roles and each other, teaching my brother Danya and me resilience and the importance of family unity.

The news of an offensive in the eastern part of the country, where my parents and my eighteen-year-old brother lived, forced us into a difficult decision. Artur insisted that we bring them to join us, even though we only had a cramped four-hundred-square-foot apartment. He knew my profound bond with Danya and emphasized that his safety was more important than our comfort. I was initially resistant, worried about the practicality of our living situation. But after much persuasion, involving both my mother and me, Danya reluctantly agreed to leave. My father, however, chose to stay behind to protect our home from potential looters—a stark reality that had set in since the second day of the war.

Each of us was shaped by hardship and loss, and even as we gathered family close in the midst of war, the memories of our pasts continued to influence our lives. After talking it through, we came up with a plan that would require both courage and coordination. My father agreed to drive my mother and brother halfway to meet us, where I would be waiting. I would drive alone to pick them up—a task I was more suited to after eighteen years behind the wheel, unlike my husband, who was still a novice driver.

The thought of driving out there, with no assurance of safety, was terrifying. War was not just outside our door; it stretched across every path we might take. Yet, this drive felt like an essential mission, as if I were gearing up to enter a burning building to bring loved ones back to safety. The fear was palpable as I prepared to leave, knowing that this wasn't just an act of bravery but a necessary sacrifice.

As I sat in the car, ready to embark on this perilous journey, the weight of the situation pressed heavily on me. Fear, love, and determination mixed in a tumultuous storm of emotions. My husband's gaze, filled with love and fear, stayed with me as I started the engine. My hands and legs shook, and primal fear enveloped me. I was about to drive through a war zone, where the reality of being attacked was as likely as it was terrifying.

I started the engine and drove off, speeding down the highway faster than I had ever driven before. My hands ached from gripping the steering wheel too tightly, but I couldn't relax. Artur and my father, who was driving toward me, called frequently, heightening my anxiety. My father was anxious because I had left later than planned and he needed to return home after our meeting. Despite the urgency, my progress was hampered by new military checkpoints being set up on highways and at city entrances and exits, chilling me with the sight of weapons and military equipment.

Caught in a massive traffic jam, with only one lane open and guarded by military checkpoints, I felt the stress more and more acutely. Each car was scrutinized, and my father's anxious calls about my delay only heightened the tension. "Where are you now?" he asked anxiously during yet another call. "I'm stuck in traffic," I replied, trying to keep my voice steady despite the rising panic. Alone, surrounded by endless rows of cars and open fields, I felt trapped, unable to move in any direction.

Finally, my car was allowed through, and I sped toward the safety of my family. But fate had us miss each other initially. I slowed down, turned around, and there was my dad, who was fifty-two years old at the time, waiting by the roadside. He too turned back toward home. Out of his car stepped Danya, my tear-streaked mother holding our family cat, Sonya, and my father. I hugged my brother first, then my mother. They climbed into my car. My father and I shared a long look, a silent understanding that this might be our last goodbye as he was heading back toward the front lines. His eyes conveyed a mix of gratitude and sorrow. I struggled to hold back tears—a task I've never been good at—and hugged him tightly. He whispered that it was time to leave, and we parted ways. I watched him drive away, feeling a profound sense of loss and fear.

The drive back was somber. Danya asked to keep the conversation light, struggling with the day's events. We drove in silence, each lost in our thoughts. Desperate to be back with my children and Artur, I longed for the safety and comfort of home, not wanting to die far from them.

As we approached my city, we were met with a miles-long traffic jam at the checkpoint. Each vehicle and person was thoroughly searched, prolonging our wait. My father called to say he had reached home safely, surprised we were still on the road. Artur's increasingly worried calls echoed my father's concern. Night fell, and I was grateful for the bottle of water and some cookies I had in the car. The wait at the checkpoint stretched over five hours. Desperate for a restroom, I faced the embarrassing and difficult situation of having to manage on the roadside.

Finally, it was our turn at the checkpoint. Just as we were about to be cleared, a bold woman in a luxury SUV cut in front of us. Faced with the choice of a collision or yielding, I tried to intimidate her into backing down but ultimately had to let her go. The military thoroughly inspected our vehicle and belongings, causing chaos in our trunk. I had a brief exchange with a young soldier who hadn't slept in days, who warned us of the curfew and the risks of being out past it.

We raced home through the darkness, dodging police patrols. The fear of being stopped and not making it home was overwhelming. Fortunately, we arrived safely. Artur, who had been anxiously peering from our apartment window, rushed to embrace me. Masha and Dasha were awake, relieved to see me and excited about their uncle's arrival. That night, as we huddled together in our dark apartment, marked the beginning of a new chapter in our lives.

On the fourth day of the war, we marked a significant but somber occasion—Danya's nineteenth birthday. Amid the chaos and warnings about the risks outside, including landmines, I felt a strong need to celebrate. Surprisingly, I convinced my family to join me for a barbecue in the woods. It was not a deep forest but a beloved picnic park, the kind that many Ukrainians cherish for its simple pleasures—small groves of trees, gazebos, and a children's playground. The park was nestled by a gentle river, offering breathtaking natural views. The intoxicating scent of pine filled the air, a reminder of the world's enduring beauty.

The day was etched vividly in my memory. While we were there, I received a call from my neighbor, who was shocked to hear we were in the forest. "You're out there? In the middle of all this?" she exclaimed, her voice a mix of disbelief and concern. She thought me brave and reckless, but I calmly explained, "Now, more than ever, I cherish life and these precious moments with my family." My husband and Danya busied themselves grilling meat, my mother, feeling unwell, stayed in the car, and the kids and I watched the fire, finding solace in the simple act—a brief escape from the harsh reality.

Dinner was a quiet affair at the gazebo. We exchanged looks that carried a heavy sense of helplessness—a gnawing feeling that seemed to consume us from the inside. Observing Danya, whose adult life was just beginning amid the horrors of war, I felt the profound unfairness of it all. My heart ached for my children too; they were too young to be exposed to such grim realities. Once, my brother and I had debated about the most unbearable feeling. He believed it was helplessness. I had other thoughts then, but a renowned psychologist later confirmed his view, and I had to agree—helplessness cuts through the soul with unmatched severity.

Returning home, we faced a small but persistent challenge: My mother's British breed cat and our little rescue, Yubi, couldn't coexist peacefully. Each encounter added to our stress, a reminder that even the simplest routines were now complicated by the chaos of war.

By the fifth day, we had adjusted to life with near-empty shelves and the constant sound of air raid sirens. Everyone was glued to their phones, desperate for any shred of good news, clinging to the hope that good would eventually triumph over evil. Danya, in particular, was consumed with worry for our father, who remained in our increasingly endangered hometown of Bakhmut, a city in the east of the country. Our daily calls home were fraught with the background noise of bombings, which our father downplayed to ease our worries.

Despite his reassurances, the danger was palpable, and my brother struggled with guilt for not being there. I, too, couldn't shake the anxiety gnawing at me, the fear that something might happen to our father while we were helpless to protect him. Every time I tried persuading him to join us, his refusal felt like a personal blow. How could he choose to stay behind? I felt anger mixed with helplessness, and our conversations often turned into arguments, leaving me feeling torn between understanding his stubborn pride and the desperate need to keep him safe.

As the reality of war settled in, many stores and businesses closed. People either fled, leaving everything behind, or were too frightened to leave their homes. We lived on whatever savings we had, with only Artur working. His employer, the largest private bank in Ukraine, in a rare act of generosity, decided to pay salaries in full upfront during these turbulent times. However, this meant we would face a month without income once payments reverted to normal scheduling.

During this period, I often shopped not just for us but also for our neighbors, especially those without cars or those with infants, who found it nearly impossible to shop on their own. The constant air raid sirens made prolonged outings risky, and stocking up for a week's supplies was a challenge as we prepared for the possibility of heavier shelling or occupation. Every simple task was now a struggle, every small victory a significant relief.

Air raid sirens would sometimes catch us mid-shopping, leading to panic and confusion. Some stores would lock down with customers inside, refusing to let anyone leave until the air raid sirens ended, while others hurriedly pushed people out and locked the doors. This inconsistency was a stark display of human nature under stress, infuriating and upsetting in its unpredictability. You never knew what might happen during a trip to the half-empty store. Arriving only to have an air raid siren start could mean being left with nothing, unsure if the situation would resolve quickly or drag on for hours.

Another significant issue our city faced was the lack of drinkable tap water, which had been the case even before the war. People typically bought water from specialized kiosks or ordered twenty-liter bottles for home delivery. However, with the onset of the war, delivery services halted due to the danger, and we had to queue for hours to buy water on the streets. The threat of a bomb hitting the water station at any moment loomed over us, making every drop invaluable. War changes priorities and values dramatically—gold means little when you're dying of thirst.

The abandonment of pets was a dire issue as well. In their panic to flee, some people left their dogs tied up without any chance of survival. The internet overflowed with pleas to shelter these animals, with offers of even the most expensive breeds for free as kennels shut down. It was heartbreaking to see countless animals perish, innocent victims of human conflict and neglect.

Volunteers worked tirelessly to evacuate animals from conflict zones. While rescuing dogs was somewhat manageable, larger animals like cows presented far greater challenges. It was a grim reminder of how human conflicts devastate not just each other but also the animals and nature around us. We poison the soil with our hatred and the remnants of missile fuel, resulting in the deaths of countless birds, wildlife, and pets.

During this time, a neighbor from another building approached me with an offer of several expensive dog breeds. Her friend, who owned a kennel, was planning to flee the country and couldn't take the animals with her. Among the dogs were prized breeds such as Samoyeds, Chow Chows, Akita Inus, Corgis, and Pomeranians. Once treasured representatives of their breeds, these dogs were now as vulnerable as strays, abandoned once again by humans. We spoke at length in the stairwell about the situation. She told me how she and her three children would hide in a closet near their apartment door during every air raid siren. The horror of such moments was unimaginable.

She appreciated my calm and rational demeanor; in such times, having someone nearby who could maintain their composure was crucial. At thirty-three years old, and having just received my master's degree in psychology a month before the war began, I was able to offer reassurance and support to those around me. She wasn't the only one who sought me out for comfort; other neighbors also came to me, looking for a sense of security and someone to talk to.

Another neighbor, living on the top floor, was terrified by the ongoing conflict and stayed indoors with her two young children for months, afraid even to step outside. She believed the top floor was more likely to be targeted. I spent much time outside her door, trying to coax her outside to see that there was no immediate danger and that stepping out for some fresh air could bring some hope. Unfortunately, I couldn't persuade her to venture out more often. For her peace of mind, I even gave her the keys to my apartment so she could take refuge in the vestibule between my apartment and my neighbors' during shelling.

That was how the first week of the war passed. Authorities had promised us that the conflict would be resolved within a maximum of two weeks. But as weeks turned into a month, the conflict only escalated.

For a full week, we slept fully dressed, always ready to flee at a moment's notice. The thought of being caught unprepared during an attack, especially in winter, felt not only indecent but unsafe. If we had to run outside during shelling, the freezing cold would make it unbearable to be without proper clothing. Beyond the cold, there was also the embarrassment of being seen by neighbors in such a vulnerable state. Moreover, in the worst-case scenario—if our home was hit and we were trapped under rubble—being dressed warmly could increase our chances of survival, as warmth would be crucial while waiting for rescue in the winter cold.

Showering also became an operation timed between threats of shelling. The thought of having to suddenly flee to the street, exposed, or worse, being trapped under rubble without clothes, was terrifying. This fear made us take showers as quickly as possible, always aware that at any moment we might need to run for our lives. I was inspired by the story of an elderly woman who maintained her dignity meticulously: she showered daily, did her hair, manicured her nails, dressed in her best outfit, and went to bed prepared. Her philosophy was to face whatever came with grace, ensuring she would be found looking her best. Such stories of resilience under duress provided a small comfort.

However, the war also unleashed a torrent of harrowing tales that left deep emotional scars. One story, in particular, haunts me relentlessly. It involved a family just like any other, making do in the midst of chaos. One night, after the usual bedtime routine, a mother tucked her daughters into bed, shared a goodnight kiss, and retired to her room with her husband. Their lives, filled with love and everyday fears, continued despite the war. But that night was shattered by a deafening explosion. The parents rushed to their daughters' room, expecting to comfort them through the shock—only to find a gaping hole where their children's room had stood. The building was partially destroyed, and their girls were gone, swallowed by a chasm that opened several floors down to the ground. Only smoke, fire, and devastation remained.

This scenario, too horrific for any enemy to wish upon another, was a stark reminder of the brutal reality of war. As a mother, such stories shift your entire being. No longer were my thoughts preoccupied with my children's education or future ambitions. My only prayer was for their quick and painless end if shelling ever hit our home. The thought of them suffering a slow, agonizing death was unbearable. I wished for us to be taken together, for I could not fathom living without them. In my darkest moments, I imagined confronting the enemy myself, driven by despair. The most harrowing fear was not of potential death but of being trapped, helpless, watching my children suffer beside me.

These thoughts, looping endlessly in my mind, caused an overwhelming sense of shame. I felt reduced to the lowest form of life, grappling with thoughts no mother should ever have to entertain. The war had stripped us of normalcy and injected a relentless fear, eating away at my soul, leaving me feeling ashamed, terrified, and utterly desolate. What kind of mother did that make me? What had I become?

My oldest daughter, Masha, pleaded with us daily to leave our homeland. Tears streamed down her face as she begged; the trauma was overwhelming for her sensitive nature. Her friends had scattered across the globe, most seeking refuge abroad. Each bombardment left her trembling uncontrollably. The cold fear affected my younger daughter and me as well, and only warmth could mitigate the shivering that enveloped us. It was an agonizing way to live.

I had never seriously considered moving abroad before. The mere thought of leaving Ukraine terrified me. I had always been so scared of flying that I avoided even imagining a vacation in another country. So overwhelming was my fear of being in the air that I had never flown on a plane.

One evening, after another round of shelling, Masha's emotions reached their peak.

She burst into tears and screamed, "Mama, why are we still here? Why aren't we leaving like everyone else? I can't take it anymore!"

Her voice was filled with desperation and fear, and her sobs shook her entire body. "Please, Mama, let's go! Let's leave before it's too late!"

I took a deep breath, trying to steady my voice. "Masha, we could leave, but only without your father," I said softly, my heart aching with every word. "Men aren't allowed to leave the country right now. I can't just take you and your sister and leave him here. I'm not capable of that." Tears welled up in my eyes as I looked at her, my own pain mirroring hers.

"But why, Mama? Why can't we just go, like others?" she cried, her voice breaking.

I struggled to hold back the tears. "Because we don't have the money to live in another country," I whispered. "I can't just go and rely on another government to support us. I can't live as a burden on someone else's state. We're not in a position to do that." My voice cracked as the weight of the situation pressed down on me.

Masha looked at me, her face twisted in frustration and fear. "But I'm so scared, Mama! Why can't we just try?"

I couldn't take it anymore. My heart broke into pieces as I saw the desperation in her eyes. "I know, Masha. I know. And it's killing me inside. I want nothing more than to take you somewhere safe, but I can't leave your father. I'm torn apart. It hurts me so much that I can't do what you're asking, that I can't give you the safety you need." Tears flowed freely now, and I hugged her tightly, trying to hold back my own sobs.

I hugged her tightly, wishing I could somehow make everything right. The emotional toll of these conversations weighed heavily on me, and the strain was magnified by sleepless nights. The difficulty of falling asleep was exacerbated by the explosions, shelling, and the incessant wailing of sirens. At first, the sirens filled us with terror, then irritation, and eventually hatred. They were a constant reminder of death—a sound one never grows accustomed to. Each time we were on the brink of sleep, the sirens would erupt again.

One night, I finally drifted off just before dawn, but an explosion soon after jolted me awake. I raced to the kitchen, where my mother had been up early, watching the morning break. I looked out the window to see smoke billowing above our house and debris littering the area. Our car, though covered in dirt, was intact. My heart hammered uncontrollably as fear overwhelmed me. It took a long time to calm down. Eventually, a realization dawned on me—a clear, sharp understanding that I could not allow myself to succumb to panic or despair. It wasn't just about me; I had to stay strong.

As the Ukrainian forces liberated towns near the capital that had been under Russian control, the world saw the grim realities of war crimes. From the very start of the conflict, grave human rights violations came to light.

Journalists and organizations reported on mass civilian casualties, torture, and brutal acts in the regions once occupied by Russian troops. Mass graves were uncovered, and many of the bodies bore signs of torture, with victims found with bound hands.

Reports also surfaced of disappearances and widespread sexual violence. Along the roads, shot-up vehicles with women, children, and fleeing families painted a horrifying picture, evidence of the violence inflicted on innocent lives. Even from behind our screens—on TV, social media, and news sites—the horror was impossible to escape.

The fear of occupation haunted us deeply, knowing that wherever the enemy passed, life was shattered.

As the first month of the war dragged on, each day felt suspended in time, as if the world itself held its breath. In those days, I understood the urgency of supporting our soldiers and fellow citizens. We did all we could—donating clothes to the displaced, helping the homeless, finding ways to keep going. Our city became a refuge for those who had lost everything, and we gave freely, sharing whatever little we had left. In the face of so much loss, our compassion and resilience became our strength, a quiet defiance against the darkness that surrounded us.

3

Between Fear and Purpose

In the crucible of war, people needed support more than ever, and I wanted to be there for them, thinking that my psychology degree could help me make a real difference. I discovered a charity, supported by the Red Cross, that provided free psychological consultations to those struggling amid the war. Still, doubts crept in—would they even accept me? And even if they did, would my limited experience be enough in times as challenging as these? After a bit of soul-searching, I applied. When I saw my name added to their website's list of volunteers, a sense of purpose washed over me. I felt that for the first time in weeks, I had a role, a reason to keep moving forward.

Answering that first call was daunting. My hand shook slightly as I picked up the phone, trying to steady my voice. "Hello, how can I help you?" I said, hoping I sounded more confident than I felt. The silence on the other end lasted a few seconds before a quiet voice began speaking—a woman, struggling to talk through her guilt. She had left her elderly parents behind, fleeing for safety. And as I listened, my own fears faded into the background. At that moment, it was all about her, and I knew I was exactly where I needed to be.

Gradually, the work became central to my life. Each call added to a growing sense of purpose and a quiet, rewarding fulfillment. Though unpaid, the volunteer position became priceless as I encountered stories of grief, worry, and guilt. Many of the struggles were not directly tied to the war. Some people wrestled with long-standing issues intensified by the current crisis: a father of two felt helpless as his children became increasingly anxious with every shelling; another woman relived old grief, mourning a loved one she'd lost years before, the pain now resurfacing with renewed intensity. The war amplified these hidden traumas, and I could feel the toll it took on each person I spoke with. Divorces surged, as people found it increasingly hard to maintain relationships under so much strain.

Each story was unique. One client I'll never forget was a wealthy woman who had fled Kyiv for France, escaping with nothing but her tracksuit. I remember her voice, wavering with a mix of shock and disbelief as she recounted leaving behind her wardrobe full of elegant dresses. She even expressed guilt over missing her dresses at all, knowing so many had lost everything. And yet, her grief over leaving her life behind—the little luxuries she'd known—was real, raw, and human.

Another woman called with a voice that trembled as she described her nights in the basement of her apartment building, sheltering with neighbors to avoid the shelling. Her only companion was her parrot, and she struggled with panic attacks so intense that she sometimes couldn't breathe. She shared how, despite her fear, the simple fact of being surrounded by others who understood her struggle gave her a newfound strength. This sense of unity, even in fear, became her lifeline.

Some clients were profoundly grateful, and their gratitude buoyed my own spirits. There's truth in the saying, "If you're feeling down, help someone who's worse off." Other interactions were less warm; in one case, I called a woman who immediately lashed out at me — she was sheltering in a basement during an air raid alert and didn't appreciate the intrusion. When I asked where she was from, she named my own city — the one we were both in at that very moment. Her anger was understandable; she, like many, needed a place to direct her frustration, and a free counselor became an easy target.

This work brought me a deeper understanding of the quiet heroes beyond the battlefield. While soldiers stood at the front lines, countless others worked tirelessly behind the scenes—the rescue workers, firefighters, utility repair crews, and medical personnel risking their lives daily to keep our cities functioning. Even grocery store employees, drivers, and delivery workers continued, despite the risks, bringing supplies under fire. Their bravery—often unnoticed—created hope for all of us and reminded me why I wanted to be here, doing what I could to help.

Each story added to the intricate mosaic of my country in wartime. Everyone had a unique battle, including my younger brother, Danya. And while my role was small, it was clear that even the smallest acts of kindness could build resilience amid so much fear. Still, this new routine began to affect my family, adding tension to an already challenging time.

Working late into the night had become my norm, as I tried to balance responsibilities with the need to help others. However, this wasn't without its challenges. Artur often found these late hours difficult, spending long evenings alone with my mother, Elena, which sometimes created tension in the household.

One night, as I finished up a particularly exhausting call, I found Artur waiting for me in the kitchen. He stood by the counter, arms folded, his shoulders slumped in weariness. His eyes, usually so warm, were shadowed with fatigue and something deeper—an ache I hadn't fully seen until now. He looked up, his voice quiet but strained, holding a tenderness that only made the sadness in his words sharper.

"You're doing incredible work," he began, and I could hear him trying to mask his frustration, his voice gentle but wavering. "It's just . . . I miss us. I miss the evenings we used to have together." His gaze drifted away, as if lost in those memories for a moment. "And your mother's been asking . . ." he paused, the pain breaking through, "why you're always busy."

My heart tightened. I reached for his hand, holding it firmly. His skin was warm but tense under my touch. "Artur," I whispered, my voice soft, the weight of the past few weeks pressing down on me. "I know. I feel it too. This work . . . it's helping me stay steady, but I don't want it to come between us. Maybe I can pull back a little. Be with you more."

He held my gaze, a flash of relief and sadness mingling in his eyes. He squeezed my hand, his grip both reassuring and a bit desperate. "No, don't stop," he murmured, his voice thick with unspoken emotion. "Just . . . come back to me sometimes. Even if it's only for a little while."

In that moment, I felt the fragility of what we were holding on to. Yet, seeing Artur's vulnerability reminded me I wasn't alone in this struggle. In wartime, daily responsibilities and the care of loved ones were becoming a test of endurance, where both heroism and quiet suffering coexisted, often unacknowledged.

But the strain extended beyond our household interactions; the relentless scarcity of basic resources was adding to the burden on families like ours. Everyday life became a struggle for essentials, from food and medicine to fuel. The harsh reality of living with shortages meant that even the simplest tasks now required resilience and patience, and the stability we once took for granted felt further out of reach.

Not all situations we encountered during this time involved acts of resilience or heroism. The gasoline shortage brought out opportunists. Our bombed oil depots left severe fuel shortages, and certain stations exploited this by selling poor-quality gasoline at inflated prices. We learned this lesson firsthand when our car's engine light came on after refueling. Our mechanic confirmed it was a scam; we repaired the car and avoided that station in the future.

Securing basic necessities, particularly food and medicine, was becoming a challenge. I began stress-eating, often at odd hours, a poor coping mechanism amid the chaos. Artur even joked that I should start drinking since alcohol was easier to find than food in these circumstances.

In a moment of dark humor, I recalled hearing that ancient humans weren't plagued by depression because survival occupied their thoughts. Constantly hunting for food and evading danger left no room for existential concerns. Today, although we live with more comforts, the resulting overthinking and mental strain bring their own burdens. It's ironic how even comforts can present their own challenges.

The city around us was also undergoing profound changes, mirroring the internal and external chaos that had invaded our lives. Daily survival had become so intense that there was no space for deeper reflection. Every errand, every trip outside, felt dangerous. Existential questions took a backseat to the immediate need to make it through each day.

This summed up our first month of war—an intense period of adaptation and survival. Interestingly, despite the continuing pandemic, we noticed that stress seemed to stave off illness. Recovering from COVID and other ailments was surprisingly fast, almost as if adrenaline and survival instincts overpowered any susceptibility to sickness.

The city's transformation was haunting. Once-bustling streets were now empty, and homes that had teemed with life were deserted. The absence of people created an eerie silence, a stark contrast to the usual sounds of urban life. Just weeks prior, over a million residents animated this place; now, it felt abandoned.

As many fled, only a handful of families remained in our courtyard, too frightened to let their children play outside. The exodus continued at a slow pace, with roads congested and Ukrainians waiting days, even weeks, to cross borders. The checkpoints were crowded with pedestrians, elderly, and children alike, all braving the cold in a landscape that had shifted dramatically. Yet despite the fear and devastation, like spring flowers, glimmers of life began to emerge from the ruins.

As the second month approached, some residents reopened shops as their savings dwindled, and cafes gradually came back. Small routines, like entering a pizzeria to avoid cooking at home, brought a sense of normalcy. Slowly, the city revived, though many of its people remained scattered far from home.

We also started to adjust. I began taking Masha and Dasha to the playground in our courtyard each day, clinging to a routine we'd followed long before the war. Maintaining the routine became essential; these daily rituals grounded us and brought a small, reassuring rhythm to our lives.

Often, we had the playground to ourselves, as other families were too afraid to venture out, especially with their children. Masha, with her boundless energy, would run ahead, calling for Dasha to catch up, her laughter echoing in the quiet courtyard. Dasha, always the more cautious one, would linger close by, her wide eyes scanning the empty playground before deciding it was safe to join her sister. I could see how their personalities began to show themselves differently in these strange times—Masha, so determined to explore and play as if nothing had changed, and Dasha, hesitant, sometimes holding my hand a bit longer than she used to.

The silence of the once lively courtyard only emphasized how much life had changed. Yet, staying indoors—where constant news updates and the weight of my parents' worries filled every corner—was far from ideal for two little girls who craved fresh air and space to play, especially given the close quarters of our small apartment. These brief outings, in which we watched Masha create new games and Dasha occasionally asked if we could "go back home now," gave us all a chance to breathe amid the tension.

There's a saying about there only being one mistress in the kitchen, which anyone who has lived with parents can appreciate. No matter how good the relationship, cohabitation inevitably leads to friction. This was exacerbated by my mother's cat, which would incessantly chase my own, causing further discord. While my mother generally refrained from overt criticism, her dissatisfaction occasionally surfaced. And truly, nothing compares to the autonomy of living in one's own home.

It's curious how we tend to remember negative experiences more vividly than positive ones, how a single hurtful remark can haunt us for a lifetime, while joyful memories fade quickly. Why don't we visit psychologists to celebrate our happiest moments? Blaming our parents for life's unpleasantness has become a convenient trend.

As tensions escalated, my mother decided it was time to return to my father. The city was still intact, though the outskirts faced shelling. After a heated discussion, she found a driver willing to head toward the front lines. One morning, we loaded her and her cat into the car, and they departed for the once-glorious city that still stood.

We all breathed a sigh of relief, partly because our cat was finally at peace, and partly because the household tension eased. We all needed that break—both us and my mom. Gradually, despite the ongoing trials, an understanding dawned: in wartime, the significance of our usual concerns had changed drastically.

When life became a daily struggle to survive, all former routines and minor concerns faded into the background. The spotless house, completed homework, and carefully managed diets lost their importance. Confronted with the constant threat of loss, we gained a new clarity about what truly mattered—each precious, fragile moment we were still able to experience.

Survival, of course, remained paramount, but it was as if a veil had been lifted, revealing the illogical nature of our everyday worries. We live entrenched in stereotypes, burdened by countless perceived needs that, in truth, are often unnecessary. As Danya poignantly observed, humanity was not destined for this. We weren't meant to agonize over securing basic necessities or making ends meet. Our planet is abundant in space, housing, and food. Why don't we share these resources more equitably? Why have we constructed barriers and established social classes?

As cities came under fire, the need to shelter displaced relatives became a reality for many Ukrainian families. This situation was unforeseen by everyone involved. It's often easier to maintain positive family relationships from a distance, but living under the same roof is a different story. Old grievances resurface, and past frustrations amplify current tensions. Living together poses real challenges. Many of my acquaintances, friends, and clients from the charity platform have experienced fallouts with the relatives they've taken in. This situation is dual-sided; on one hand, there are the relatives who've lost their homes and endured the horrors of war, waiting to return to some semblance of normalcy. On the other are those providing shelter and sustenance. Each side holds its own perspective, yet conflicts are inevitable. Amid all these contradictions, under the shadow of fear, we didn't just face the war outside—we faced it at our own dinner tables.

During this time, Danya and I found ourselves calling our parents multiple times a day. We could hear explosions and gunfire over the phone—not directly where our parents were, but ominously close enough. It was a grim reminder that the conflict was spreading, bringing destruction and despair in its wake.

One evening, I held the phone tightly as I listened to my mother's familiar voice, trying to keep the conversation light, though tension weighed on every word. "Mama," I began softly, "How are things today? Are you and Dad staying safe?"

Her voice was calm but tinged with a weariness that betrayed her attempt to reassure us. "We're fine, don't worry," she replied, though the faint sound of an explosion in the background betrayed her words.

I shot Danya a worried look as I leaned in closer to the phone. "Mama, we can hear the bombs. It's not safe there anymore. You need to think about leaving."

There was a long pause. When she finally spoke, her voice was barely a whisper. "Leaving everything behind, our whole life . . . it's not easy. Your father and I, we still hope things will calm down."

Danya, unable to contain his frustration, grabbed the phone. "Mama, you don't understand how dangerous this is! Please, just listen to us for once."

There was another silence, then the sound of my father's voice in the background, steady and unyielding. "We're not going anywhere, kids.

Someone has to look after this place. It's our home, and we're not about to abandon it."

Danya's face tightened, and he struggled to respond. I took back the phone, feeling a pang of helplessness and desperation. "Please, just . . . promise you'll keep safe, okay?"

My mother's sigh was deep, filled with a sorrow I could feel through the line. "We promise. You both stay safe too."

Each call left us feeling more desperate, caught between the need to respect their choices and the fear of losing them. Bakhmut, my hometown, had always been a place of history and life—a place I was proud of. Located in the northern Donbas region, it was known for its rich history in salt mining, for having the largest sparkling wine factory in Eastern Europe, and even a unique underground concert hall in a salt mine. But now, despite its cultural and industrial significance, the war had turned it into a warzone, with explosions frequent and residential areas becoming targets. Important structures, like the railway station, military units, homes, supermarkets, factories, and even the prison, were bombed—all terrifyingly close to where my parents lived. We urged them to leave everything behind and evacuate, but the decision was not easy.

4

The Burden of Unspoken Pain

After two harrowing weeks, my mother couldn't bear it any longer and decided to return to us. This highlighted another challenge we faced: transportation. My mother doesn't drive, and my father was unable to accompany her. Eventually, after a painstaking search, we found volunteers who were transporting people from the most dangerous areas, and thankfully, they managed to bring her back safely.

Her return journey felt like a final goodbye, each moment weighed with the painful awareness that she might never see her hometown again. The devastation around her—homes and factories reduced to rubble, trees shattered, roads destroyed—marked her deeply. And yes, this time, my mother made the journey without the family cat.

Once she arrived and sat down beside me, I could see the weight of the journey etched on her face.

"I never thought I'd leave it like that," she murmured, her voice barely above a whisper.

"Mama . . ." I reached out, but words failed me.

"It's like a part of me stayed there, buried under all that rubble," she continued, her gaze distant, haunted by what she had seen.

We sat in silence, absorbing the enormity of all she had witnessed. But as heavily as it weighed on our hearts, life demanded we carry on, and we tried to settle back into our routines as best as we could. The battles showed no signs of abating; shelling continued, and with it, our constant worry for relatives and friends. Everyone had their unique wartime experiences.

There were peculiar aspects to this wartime life, such as the practice of taping windows with adhesive tape to prevent glass from shattering during explosions. There were various theories about the best method—some recommended taping in a cross pattern, while others suggested covering the entire glass. This not only increased the demand for tape but also significantly altered the appearance of buildings, turning windows from glimpses into private lives into stark reminders of the ongoing struggle.

There was also the strange rule of not turning on lights after dark to avoid attracting attention. Every evening, these safety rules and reminders underscored how exposed we were.

One night, I looked out the window to check on our car, a routine I performed several times a day and always before bedtime. To my alarm, the interior light was on. I initially feared the car was being stolen, but from the fourth floor, it was hard to see what was happening inside. Artur courageously went down to check. Fortunately, no one was there; the car was locked. It turned out that the interior light bulb was malfunctioning. Yet, during a time when lights were strictly forbidden, our car sporadically lighting up like a beacon was incredibly nerve-wracking and awkward.

The betrayal we felt in those days was hard to process. Knowing that others—especially those meant to protect us—were aware of the impending invasion but remained silent was deeply unsettling. Even the government, with precise knowledge of dates, chose silence, likely to avoid a mass exodus. In the weeks leading up to the invasion, rumors circulated—discussions on the news, whispers among friends and colleagues. International warnings, especially from the U.S. and European governments, signaled that an invasion was imminent. Yet, despite the rising alarms, the atmosphere in the country remained oddly calm at the time.

We had heard about the buildup of Russian troops near the border, and political analysts discussed the potential for escalation. Still, many of us, including myself, didn't want to believe that something so horrific could actually happen. When February arrived and the warnings grew louder, I still hoped it was just another moment of tension—something that would pass, as many other conflicts had in our history.

The government's decision not to issue widespread warnings left us with many questions: Why was there no preparation? Why weren't animals evacuated from zoos or vulnerable populations relocated? We saw reports of how other countries were advising their citizens to evacuate weeks before the invasion, yet our government chose to remain silent. This felt like yet another instance of being deceived by a government we had already learned not to expect much from. Their continued silence and lack of transparency left us feeling betrayed, especially as we scrambled to prepare ourselves at the last moment, when it was almost too late.

Furthermore, we could not understand why the aggressor, struggling with significant internal issues, chose to invade another country. Beyond a few major cities, their society seems trapped in the past, with many villages lacking basic amenities like electricity or sewage systems, rampant unemployment, and a generally low standard of living. They don't even need to build sets for historical films; their reality reflects those times. What could they possibly want from us? How can 140 million people not restrain one delusional leader dragging them into chaos?

To avoid getting swallowed by resentment and sorrow, we turned to a familiar escape. Danya and I spent our nights playing Heroes of Might and Magic. We connected the laptop to the TV, playing on the big screen, taking turns with each move, but we kept the sound off so as not to disturb the children, Masha and Dasha, who were sleeping nearby in the same room. Sometimes, Artur would join us. He didn't always play himself, but he'd sit nearby, watching us with quiet encouragement, occasionally suggesting moves and strategies.

As we played, Danya nudged me, grinning, "You should move there. It'll give you the advantage."

"Not bad," I admitted, moving my character.

Artur chuckled from his chair. "Both of you are underestimating the long game. Go for resources, not just quick wins."

"Alright, Mr. Strategy Master," my brother teased, smiling. "But remember, it's all about survival, not luxury."

Artur shook his head, amused. "In war and in games, a little planning never hurt anyone."

Danya and I were always amazed by his intelligence, so much so that we started calling him "Wikipedia." He just seemed to have answers to everything—wise, insightful, with a depth of understanding that often took me years to fully appreciate.

Those nights brought a rare sense of stability. Throughout it all, my husband's calm presence was an anchor, a reminder of the life we had built together. I love him deeply; he is the man with whom I want to spend my entire life. The strategy game absorbed us completely, giving us a brief reprieve. And yet, despite our immersion, the distant sounds of explosions would inevitably creep in, snapping us back to the grim reality outside, filling us with sadness and a sense of helplessness.

The children, knowing we were playing to distract ourselves, accepted our nightly ritual as part of our new reality. They had been sent on an extended break from school while the authorities tried to figure out how to proceed with education despite the chaos.

Even though life had become anything but normal, these quiet moments of distraction helped us cope with the overwhelming fear and uncertainty that surrounded us. Still, amid the new routines and constant adjustments, unexpected encounters and relationships began to take on a new significance. Life brings many encounters; some people fade from memory entirely, but others leave a lasting impact. Such was my relationship with a neighbor who lived a few floors above. She had a delightful dog, and while I took my children to the playground, she walked the dog in the courtyard. Our conversations were a highlight of my days.

One day, she mentioned she was moving temporarily to live with her daughter and planned to rent out her apartment. The timing was serendipitous, as life with my mother was becoming increasingly strained. When our neighbor offered her apartment at a reasonable rate, it was a perfect solution. My mother and Danya moved in, allowing my husband and me some much-needed space.

The separation brought a much-needed breath of fresh air. The space between us seemed to ease tensions and allow each of us to reclaim a bit of peace. Our relationships, though strained by proximity, found a sense of calm. Unfortunately, compelling circumstances cut this arrangement short, and after just two weeks, our neighbor returned and we resumed our previous living arrangement.

Our calls to my father continued daily amid the chaos. Explosions were so close that they once knocked him off his bed. The relentless bombardment was a constant presence, destroying my hometown by the second. He relayed the unfolding horrors—stores were closed, and only brave volunteers dared to deliver food and water to the hotspots. The city seemed abandoned, yet many stayed, clinging to their properties despite the danger. It's astonishing how we hold onto our possessions, even in the face of death. People spend their lives building and decorating their homes, creating comfort that, in the end, seems more valuable than their safety. Meanwhile, looters took advantage of the situation, pillaging freely in the deserted city.

As another month closed, we had settled into a routine, not out of comfort but necessity. The fear remained, yet we continued our daily activities almost mechanically, accepting the presence of air raid sirens and the fact of empty store shelves. We knew the drill during bombardments, and while the kids rode their scooters in the park, I maintained our home—cleaning, cooking, doing laundry. These small routines kept us connected to fragments of our old lives, as if holding on to them could somehow bring us closer to victory.

Watching my children adjust to these strange new habits, I couldn't help but wonder what they would remember of this time. When I think back to my own childhood, it feels like a different world entirely . . . I can't help but draw comparisons to the cramped conditions we now live in, squeezed into four hundred square feet with seven people and two feuding cats. One might think that growing up in poverty and in a tiny apartment, just 120 square feet, known as a "small family" unit, would have made this new reality easier to bear. Back then, I slept on a chair that unfolded into a bed, and we had so little that a quarter loaf of bread felt like a victory. My childhood was marked by simplicity and scarcity; meals consisted mostly of apples and jam, my grandmother's compensation from her orchard job. Those apples and jars of jam—once symbols of survival—are still difficult for me to face.

My childhood, set against the backdrop of the Soviet Union, was one without phones, computers, or internet. When I tell Masha about those days, she stares at me in disbelief, as if I were describing life in the Stone Age. I joke that we had to battle dinosaurs for food, and she laughs, but there's truth behind the humor. That world is as foreign to her as it is nostalgic to me.

As distant as those memories feel, they seem to echo in the present. The resilience learned back then has carried through to times like when my father joined us, bringing only a few essentials with him, clinging to the hope that one day he would return to his apartment. I'll never forget the relief and joy of seeing him safely arrive, having evaded stray bullets and dangerous checkpoints. We were grateful to be together, yet the weight of our situation settled in, testing our patience, resilience, and the strength of family bonds forged in times of both peace and profound struggle.

Here we were again, cramped together. This time, however, the circumstances felt different—worse, perhaps, for their familiarity and the added tensions of adulthood. The space that seemed barely adequate for a child now felt overwhelming to me as an adult with my own family. Six of us—Artur, Masha, Dasha, my parents and I—shared a single room, while Danya occupied a small nook originally meant for Masha. My parents slept on a fold-out sofa, Artur and the kids on the big bed, while I rested on an old fold-out chair. Every morning, I awoke to an aching back, feeling the strain of the day ahead.

The daily cycle of cooking, cleaning, and finding a bit of personal space wore me down quickly. Food vanished as soon as it was prepared, and chores piled up endlessly. My nerves frayed as every aspect of my life—parenting, household management, even the way I spoke—came under scrutiny from my mother. I understood that my parents were trying to adapt, but under our roof, old patterns and generational tensions resurfaced.

During a session, my trusted psychologist had advised me to distribute the household chores—a suggestion I ignored. I was accustomed to doing everything myself, finding it difficult to delegate, especially since no one seemed eager to help. This only added to my frustration, which was compounded by years of built-up grievances.

One evening, with only enough money left for two more days of groceries and payday still far off, tensions reached a breaking point. We had found my parents a beautiful apartment with a fresh, modern renovation, and Artur and I had offered to cover the rent. They had agreed, and we'd been waiting for the renovations to finish so they could move in. The next morning, they were supposed to move, and everything was set.

It felt like the end of something fragile we had managed to hold onto. After weeks of organizing and hoping for a little relief, my father approached me unexpectedly.

"Cancel the apartment," he said suddenly, avoiding my gaze. "Get the deposit and the realtor's fee back. It's too expensive for us."

A cold wave of disbelief washed over me. "But we agreed," I replied, barely able to keep my voice steady. "You waited until now to say this? I organized everything, and now you want me to just . . . cancel it? The realtor earned his fee fairly; he did his job."

He sighed. "It's just . . . we can't do it. We can't rely on you like this."

Frustration slipped into my voice. "And why didn't you say this earlier? I asked you to come with me to see the place, to help choose it. You didn't even go, and now—at the last minute—you want me to back out. It's embarrassing."

I stared at him in disbelief, feeling a mix of anger and helplessness. The frustration and disappointment I'd been holding in came pouring out. I had spent weeks organizing this move, making sure everything was perfect for them, and now, just hours before the move, they were backing out.

That night, amid the ongoing war and on the eve of my birthday, the argument left us all shaken.

This outburst, though regrettable, was a culmination of the intense pressures we were under. It highlighted the critical need for communication and boundaries even in the most trying times.

In a moment of overwhelming pain and revelation, everything I had suppressed came rushing out. Tears streamed down my face as I unleashed a lifetime of pent-up emotions and grievances. For years, I had been the quiet one, the girl who endured in silence. But that night, I couldn't hold it back any longer. My voice echoed through the room as I confronted my parents with everything that had been weighing on me. My father listened in silence; his only response was understanding and a quiet acknowledgment that they would leave.

The intensity of the confrontation left my children terrified. In the midst of our family crisis, the horrors outside seemed momentarily forgotten. My youngest daughter, Dasha, cried, confused and scared by the sudden uproar, while my eldest, Masha, could only stand frozen in the next room. This wasn't how any of us had envisioned the end of our time together.

Despite the late hour and the curfew that made it dangerous to leave, my parents were resolute about departing immediately.

The next morning was supposed to be my brother Danya's online graduation exam from technical school. I pleaded with him, hoping he'd change his mind. "Are you sure?" I asked. "You have your exam. You don't have to go with them. It's better for you to stay here and take it with a stable connection."

He looked torn, then sighed, giving me a reproachful look. "You're going too far," he said quietly. "They need me right now. I can't just leave them."

"And I don't?" I whispered, feeling the weight of Danya's choice press down on me.

His words stung, and it hurt deeply that he chose to side with our parents. Our relationship was something I cherished profoundly; I loved him more than perhaps I should. From childhood, I had longed for a sibling, someone with whom to share the burdens of a difficult upbringing. His birth had been a blessing, filling a void in my life and providing me with a connection I had always craved.

His decision to leave felt like a betrayal. It was as painful as if a child, still young and dependent, had decided to leave home. He had witnessed everything—the daily tensions, the breakdown of our family dynamic—yet he chose to stand with my parents. In that moment, I felt the ground give way beneath me. The loss of his support in the midst of our family's crisis was a blow that I struggled to comprehend.

I continued to cry as I helped them pack, the hysteria of the moment refusing to subside. Silently, they moved their belongings to the car and left, taking with them a part of my heart.

In an instant, the threads binding us seemed irreparably frayed. Alone, I sat on the sofa, my heart torn between the relief of having finally voiced my truth and the sorrow of what it might have cost. My husband, sensing the need for space, took the kids and quietly retreated, leaving me to my thoughts.

I was torn between shame for my outburst and a sense of relief that I had finally voiced my feelings. Yet, there was also a deep fear for their safety—where would they go in the middle of the night, especially with no money? The empty room seemed to echo with memories, shadows from moments now lost. I stared blankly at the television, the flickering light casting a pale glow over the silence around me, while inside, my emotions churned like a storm too powerful to quiet.

5

Picking Up the Pieces

Left in the wake of a tumultuous family conflict, a heavy mix of emotions pressed down on me. The night had been draining, and the burden of responsibility for my family, along with their departure under the cover of darkness, left me feeling both guilty and, in an unsettling way, relieved. I wished I had kept my composure, managed to hold myself together, but the pressure had simply been too much.

My husband's support during this time was like an anchor. Artur took over the household duties, allowing the children and me the space we needed. He offered quiet reassurance, reminding me that perhaps this was for the best—that it was a necessary step to protect the well-being of our family. As the silence of my parents' and brother's absence settled over me, I found myself sitting numbly, replaying the events, lost in thought, until the first light of morning arrived almost without notice.

After spending the day in shock, lost in thought, I met the dawn of the following day with an odd sense of detachment. It was my thirty-fourth birthday, though it hardly felt like a day for celebration. Yet, sensing the lingering tension, my husband gently suggested we embrace a moment of joy, to choose something uplifting amid the sorrow.

Artur suggested a small outing—a visit to a sauna with a pool—to let us momentarily escape the weight of recent events. Once we arrived, he went straight to the steam room, while I stayed by the pool with the girls. Masha and Dasha eagerly jumped into the water, their laughter and cheerful splashes filling the space, as if clearing away some of the tension in the air. But deep down, I couldn't relax.

I watched them play, laughing and splashing, trying to let myself enjoy the moment, but my thoughts kept returning to my family. I couldn't stop thinking about my parents, about my brother, and the painful distance left by our last conversation. The worry and unresolved pain hung over me like a shadow, and I could tell that Masha and Dasha noticed. Their joy would occasionally give way to cautious glances in my direction.

I tried to gather myself, to smile, to be present, pushing the heavy thoughts away as best I could. After all, the girls shouldn't have to feel my pain and worry. I wanted them to enjoy this rare moment of fun, to feel some peace, even if I had to work hard to give it to them.

Determined to shield the girls from the constant weight of war and uncertainty, I resolved to give them moments filled with life and joy, knowing that any experience could be fleeting. We visited a planetarium, which initially frightened my youngest, Dasha—she thought we were actually launching into space. After calming her down, we found solace at a country club known as "Berry Land," where Masha and Dasha could enjoy simple, carefree activities away from the ever-present shadow of conflict. This place became a cherished retreat for us, especially since access to the sea had been blocked by the occupation. Yet, each laugh and smile reminded us of the shadow of war that lingered nearby, like a ghost that refused to let us forget our harsh reality.

Punctuated by these brief escapes, the weight of our everyday lives pressed on, filled with both small moments of happiness and lingering tension. As I tried to keep our household going, to preserve some sense of normalcy, even simple daily routines brought fleeting moments of comfort.

Yet life, with all its complex layers, continued to unfold. One afternoon, as I was folding laundry, my older daughter Masha quietly approached me, a thoughtful look on her face.

"Mama," she began hesitantly, "I think . . . I might like someone."

I looked up, surprised yet warmed by this glimpse of normalcy. "Oh?" I smiled, folding a shirt. "Is it someone I know?"

She blushed, playing with the hem of her shirt. "Maybe. He's in the neighborhood . . . we see him sometimes when we're outside."

Trying to keep my tone casual, I asked, "What's he like?"

Masha's eyes brightened, and she smiled shyly. "He's . . . really nice. And funny. He always makes everyone laugh."

I nodded, feeling a surge of tenderness as I watched her face light up. Yet deep down, I knew that such simple joys could become rare in our world, full of uncertainty and fear. "Sounds like he's special to you," I said gently. "First feelings like this can be pretty exciting, can't they?"

She nodded, her cheeks still pink. "Is it normal to feel so . . . nervous around him?"

I chuckled softly. "Very normal," I assured her. "Those butterflies? They're part of the fun. Just enjoy it, sweetheart, and remember—take things at your own pace."

She looked relieved, as if my words had lifted a small weight off her. "Thanks, Mama," she said, reaching out for a hug. "I just wanted to tell someone."

I hugged her tightly, grateful for this moment, for her trust, and for the gift of this ordinary, wonderful experience. Moments like these felt precious, grounding us in the simple joys of life.

War has a way of making you reassess your priorities. Suddenly, the urgency of homework or the appropriateness of hair color seemed trivial. Masha, only ten, asked to dye her hair—an idea I would have opposed in peacetime. But now, I just wanted to give her moments of joy. We went to a salon where they bleached her hair and dyed the front strands pink. It looked enchanting, a small but significant gesture that brightened her spirits. I also let Masha and Dasha experiment with nail polish.

These concessions were about more than just altering appearances; they were about giving my children the freedom to express themselves during an impossibly hard time. As a mother, I understood that every act of support and joy mattered. So, when my daughters chose activities that brought them joy and a sense of normalcy, I knew how essential it was to support them.

One of the first activities Masha and Dasha chose was dance. The instructors were remarkable—young yet filled with professionalism and contagious enthusiasm. Watching them move so freely, expressing themselves despite the chaos outside, was one of the few moments that made me feel truly alive. It felt like a ray of light in a dark world, a reminder that life goes on even in the bleakest times. Even during blackouts, we would light the room with flashlights, and the children would continue to dance. It was a testament to their resilience and creativity—a reminder that the spirit is indomitable.

Sewing became a cherished activity, and soon they were creating beautiful handmade toys—a purple heart-shaped pillow and a purple axolotl. These were more than just toys; they became symbols of resilience, providing a sense of comfort and strength amid adversity.

On lighter days, we shared moments with neighbors at the playground. One day, the girls and other children gathered around with colorful chalk, drawing symbols of Ukraine—its flag, national emblem, and the trident—as a way to express their hopes for peace. Watching them, with such innocent dreams for an end to violence, brought tears to my eyes, a stark reminder that no child should have to endure these harsh realities.

As the days went on, the quiet moments began to weigh heavily. We tried to ease back into some semblance of normalcy, but a silence lingered in the air, filling the spaces where my mother's voice would usually be. It felt strange not to call her in the evenings, and my heart grew heavy with the realization that an apology or even a simple acknowledgment of the hurt from them might never come.

This mirrored Artur's longing to hear words of pride from his own parents, a desire similarly unmet. His parents lived under occupation in the city of Svitlodarsk, just sixteen miles from my hometown of Bakhmut, but under Russian control. We had no way of contacting them, and the uncertainty of their safety weighed heavily on Artur. A few times, his father managed to send Artur brief messages, letting him know they were safe, which brought temporary relief but never a lasting peace. In this shared experience of unfulfilled familial expectations and the agony of separation, we found an unspoken understanding between us.

As if the constant backdrop of war wasn't enough, daily concerns continued to pile up. Financially, we were stretched thin; Artur's salary had become irregular, and with our funds nearly exhausted, we awaited his next paycheck with no savings to fall back on. Even in our own home, the effects of war crept in.

The societal impact was impossible to ignore. Increased poverty brought a rise in crime, while gasoline shortages, worsened by bombings on oil refineries, led to theft. Thieves would puncture fuel tanks under the cover of curfew, draining gasoline and filling us with a continuous fear for our possessions. Cars in our area were not only siphoned for fuel but also broken into or even vandalized with acid—a painful reminder of how deeply the war affected our daily lives.

Amid these challenges, I tried to channel my energy into something positive, finding purpose in volunteer work. I had developed relationships with several regular clients, dreaming of the day I could meet each of them in person once the war ended. I envisioned driving across the country with Artur and our daughters to visit them, to sit and talk, to celebrate our collective resilience and victory, and eventually, to write a book about these experiences. My clients, diverse in their needs and locations, often just needed someone to check in on them, to provide a sense of connection in a time of widespread disconnection.

Among them, one young girl stood out. She needed more than psychological support; she needed a friend. Initially, she resisted any formal therapeutic interventions, making it clear that what she truly required was someone to talk to. Despite the complexity of her situation and my initial hesitations about my capacity to help her, I committed to being that friend. We spoke often, sometimes daily, about mundane and serious topics alike. It was a relationship that blurred the lines between professional help and genuine friendship, challenging but deeply rewarding.

This girl, whose spirit seemed dimmed by the burdens she carried, had been rejected by other psychologists due to the complexity of her case. Each rejection deepened her sense of isolation, and I could sense her longing for connection—a friend who could see beyond her struggles and truly understand her. She suffered from two incurable diseases and had endured a series of deep emotional traumas. She faced constant challenges in her relationships with parents, friends, and relatives, struggled with isolation, and was unable to build a personal life. On top of that, she had come to terms with the devastating reality that she could never have children. There seemed to be no end to the burdens she carried. But I couldn't bring myself to turn her away, as others had. I promised to be there for her.

Our conversations became a staple of her support system, a lifeline in her isolated world. It was a unique connection, one that exemplified the power of human contact and the profound impact of simply being there for someone else. Even though our interactions occasionally bordered on conflict when I tried to introduce more structured therapy, the essence of our relationship was based on trust and companionship—elements just as healing as any therapy. This commitment not only helped her cope but also enriched my understanding of the effects of empathy and support during times of immense personal and societal crisis.

Navigating the complexities of relationships during stressful times can truly test one's resilience and understanding. My experience with this client, to whom I had grown close, unfortunately turned sour over a misunderstanding about accepting a gift. She had offered me a small token of gratitude—a handmade bouquet of seven candies she had crafted during our sessions. While I appreciated the gesture, I gently declined, not because I didn't value her kindness but because I knew the challenges she faced with her mother.

Her mother was severely ill and strongly opposed to her daughter's involvement with psychologists. The girl couldn't send the gift on her own and would have had to ask her mother for help. If her mother found out who the gift was for, it would have caused serious problems for my client, something I deeply wanted to avoid. I declined the gift out of concern for her well-being, but she took my refusal as a personal rejection.

Shortly after I declined her gift, the first message came through: "I thought you understood me better than this. Apparently, I was wrong." I frowned, feeling a sharp sting of hurt but responded as calmly as I could, explaining why I couldn't accept it. "It's not that I don't appreciate it—I do. But professional ethics prevent me from accepting gifts. How about you enjoy the candy bouquet yourself and just send me a photo? That way, there's no trouble with your mother, and I still get to see your thoughtful gesture."

Her reply came immediately, each word sharp and unfiltered: "You clearly don't understand professional ethics." I reread her words, each sentence striking harder than the last. She wasn't holding back.

Trying to maintain professionalism, I replied, "I'm only trying to prevent any unnecessary conflict for you at home. It's really about protecting you from complications."

Her response was instant and searing: "Go study some more—you're not such a good psychologist after all."

Her words echoed painfully, tearing down the trust we'd built over time. Despite knowing my actions were meant to protect her, her accusations left me questioning everything, each sentence a painful reminder that my intentions hadn't been understood at all.

This incident coincided with a challenging period in my familial relationships, particularly with Danya. After our argument over the decisions made during the family crisis, there was a prolonged period of silence between us. When Danya finally reached out, it reopened a dialogue that was necessary, albeit painful. I expressed my feelings of betrayal, which he responded to by emphasizing his perspective: He had chosen to support our parents, viewing them as needing more help and perceiving me as stronger and more capable of handling the situation.

Our conversations highlighted the stark differences in our childhood experiences, despite sharing the same parents. His memories of a nurturing environment contrasted sharply with my recollections of hardship and struggle. These differing perspectives influenced our understanding of each other and our responses to family conflicts.

Rebuilding our relationship wasn't straightforward. There were more arguments, more expressions of pain and misunderstanding. Each conversation was a step towards reconciliation, but also a reminder of the deep-seated issues that had long been overlooked. My husband, ever supportive, had reservations about my renewed contact with Danya, reflecting his protective instinct and his own displeasure with the family dynamics. Despite his initial reservations, he stood by me, showing that support sometimes means backing a loved one's decisions, even if one doesn't fully agree with them.

At that point, Artur and I had been married for eleven years. We met at university, though we didn't immediately notice each other—well, he noticed me, but I didn't notice him at first. We were part of the same group of friends, and over the years, we grew closer as friends. Is there anything better than living with your best friend? Eventually, he confessed his love for me, but only when he was certain that our feelings were mutual. One winter, while he was away on a work trip, he called me unexpectedly and asked, "Will you marry me?" There was no ring, no elaborate gesture—just a simple, heartfelt question. I agreed without hesitation. Later, there was a more formal proposal, but in that moment, it was the sincerity and love in his voice that won my heart.

Just as my relationship with Artur was built on friendship, trust, and honesty, my relationship with my brother needed the same foundations to heal. Gradually, Danya and I began to find common ground again. It required honest conversations, admitting vulnerabilities, and a willingness to accept each other's perspectives. It wasn't just about finding a way back to how things were but about building something stronger from what had been broken. We needed to acknowledge our different experiences, respect our unique vulnerabilities, and commit to understanding each other better.

In the end, repairing and maintaining relationships is indeed hard work. It's about more than just making up after disagreements; it involves ongoing efforts to communicate, understand, and support each other through life's challenges. This ordeal reminded me of the essential truth that relationships are foundational to our well-being and require continual nurturing and commitment.

The emotional journey to reconnect with Danya was as heart-wrenching as it was healing. Artur's support during these difficult times gave me strength, and I often reflected on how important family connections are, even when they are strained. As we sat in a café, meeting for the first time since the falling out, tears flowed freely down my cheeks—a mixture of relief and unresolved pain. While I was relieved that Danya came alone, part of me had hoped our parents would join, perhaps offering apologies and reconciliation. However, his solitary presence allowed us a private space to navigate our strained relationship.

The conversation was fraught with tension and awkward pauses. I could feel my heart pounding as I struggled to find the right words.

"Why didn't you support me at that moment?" I asked him, feeling hurt.

"We have to stay on their side, no matter what our parents are like," he replied, but I felt frustrated.

"But we grew up in the same house and ended up with completely different childhoods." I snapped. " You don't understand!"

He looked at me with a mixture of surprise and defensiveness. "I thought they needed more attention. You were stronger in that moment; you shouldn't have acted that way."

I took a deep breath, trying to keep my emotions in check. "I just want you to know, I never meant to hurt anyone. I had to stand up for myself." Deep down, I was yearning for some kind of validation from him—that he would tell me I wasn't a bad daughter or sister, just someone who had reached her breaking point. But the words I hoped for never came. Instead, he sighed, looked away, and simply said, "We've all been through a lot."

The meeting was difficult, and although I didn't hear the words I had longed for, it was a step toward reconciliation—even if on fragile ground. As we said goodbye, there was a flicker of something in his gaze—an unspoken understanding. I didn't know if we could fully restore what had been lost, but I realized that, for both of us, this reconciliation meant more than any words could.

I left that meeting with a sense of change—stronger, but aware of yet another small crack in my heart. I was reminded that healing takes time and effort, and sometimes, embracing our vulnerabilities is necessary to move forward. I knew I would carry this ache with me, a reminder of the complexities of family bonds and the challenges we faced in a world reshaped by war. Perhaps, in time, it would heal, or I would learn to live with it, as I had with so many other scars left by the war.

6

The Gift of Respite

In an effort to find some respite and to show our children the beauty of their country, we planned a trip to the Carpathian Mountains, a region of Ukraine known for its stunning natural beauty and relative safety during the conflict. Despite the risks and the presence of military checkpoints at which men could potentially be conscripted, we were armed with an official document that safeguarded my husband due to his essential work at the largest private bank in Ukraine. His role in maintaining critical financial operations during the war allowed him to avoid conscription. This document became our shield during the journey, and although it provided some relief, the tension at each checkpoint was palpable, reminding us that even the smallest misstep could change everything.

The journey was eye-opening. We traveled one thousand miles, discovering that the standard of living in the western part of Ukraine was noticeably higher than in our hometown. This realization was bittersweet, highlighting disparities within our own country. For example, the roads were well-maintained, the buildings looked newer and better cared for, and there were more well-stocked stores and cafes, unlike the scarcity we had grown accustomed to in our region. Even the public spaces, such as parks and playgrounds, seemed better equipped and cleaner. However, the trip itself was a much-needed escape. For the first time, we traveled as a family—Masha, Dasha, Artur, and I—on a journey across our homeland, momentarily distancing ourselves from the war.

Staying at a hotel where we did not have to worry about cooking or cleaning was a delightful luxury. It allowed us to just be—a family on a vacation, experiencing the joy of exploration and the simple pleasure of being served. The trip reinforced the beauty of life amid hardship, the joy of discovery, and the importance of creating lasting memories with loved ones in the face of uncertainty. It was a poignant reminder of the resilience of the human spirit and the enduring beauty of Ukraine, a country rich in culture and nature, deserving of peace and prosperity.

In the morning, we embarked on a journey that would soon reveal its extraordinary charm. As we approached the forest and mountains, I was struck by their ethereal beauty. The forest enchanted me in ways I had never imagined possible, and the mountains loomed like towering sentinels around us. As we drove along the narrow path, the sky-piercing pines stood majestically. The air was fresh, the ambiance serene—nature at its most breathtaking. Ukraine's beauty captivated me, a beauty unmatched by any other place I've since visited. It remains a sanctuary I yearn to return to.

Upon arrival at our reserved cabin, we were greeted by a stunning sight: a two-story wooden house nestled amid the mountains, insulated from the war's shadows. There was no need for an air raid alert system here. To sleep for five nights without the fear of missile strikes was the respite we desperately needed.

A zoo was situated near our cabin, offering daily solace with its array of animals. The entrance fee was minimal, and we visited every day, purchasing dozens of food packets to feed the animals. It proved to be a therapeutic escape for both my daughters and me. While Artur worked remotely, the kids and I explored.

Each morning, Masha and Dasha ran eagerly to the zoo, their eyes wide with anticipation. The girls would race ahead, giggling, as they clutched their packets of food for the animals. Masha carefully extended her hand to feed a curious deer, her face lighting up with delight as it gently nibbled from her palm. Dasha, meanwhile, shrieked with laughter every time a goat playfully tugged at her coat, her cheeks flushed with excitement.

Watching them, I felt a deep sense of peace. In this small haven, my daughters could momentarily escape the shadow of war and experience the pure joy of being children. These moments felt sacred, a stark contrast to the tense reality we faced back home.

The simplicity and tranquility were rejuvenating, allowing us to unwind from not just the war but the stresses of life. Everything was affordable; we didn't have to worry about expenses. Surrounded by pure air and peaceful landscapes, it felt as though the war was a distant nightmare from which we had awakened in nature's embrace. That trip became the most profound of our lives, where the value of silence and peace became strikingly clear. The enveloping darkness at night was unique. The realization of our remote location on a map, surrounded by vast wilderness, brought a sense of isolation from civilization.

Masha clutched my arm tightly, her wide, fearful eyes looking up at me every time the bombings were mentioned. "Mama, please . . . let's stay here. I don't want to go back," she whispered, her voice barely audible, trembling with fear. "I don't want to hear those explosions again. Can't we just leave? Please, Mama . . ." Her whole body tensed at even the smallest mention of home, and I could see the terror etched deeply into her young face. The words of a child, begging for peace, cut into me more painfully than any threat of war. However, faced as we were with financial commitments like a mortgage, relocating seemed an insurmountable challenge. I feel a profound guilt for not considering broader possibilities amid the crisis, but how could I tear us away from everything we had built?

The thought of leaving the country, potentially separating from Artur, was something I couldn't even entertain. This is a heart-wrenching dilemma for many Ukrainians. The idea of living in safety while my husband remained in danger was unthinkable. How could I live with myself if something happened to him while we were far away? We needed to stay united as a family, despite the fears of Masha and the uncertainties that weighed heavily on all of us.

People argue that children should always be protected, even if it means leaving behind a spouse. Men, obligated to serve, cannot leave a country at war. Each perspective holds its truth, presenting a moral dilemma with no easy answers. It's a choice each person must make based on their values, but the guilt of potentially not doing enough for my children's safety weighs heavily on me. I was so focused on our financial obligations that I couldn't see any other possibilities.

Witnessing the emotional burden that conflict imposes on a family, especially on children like Masha and Dasha, who seek comfort and security from their parents, is devastating. The profound distress and helplessness you feel as your older daughter implores you to escape the danger encapsulate the severe challenges many encounter in war zones. Families are torn between safeguarding their loved ones and the complex realities constraining them.

Returning from the serene mountains to a home scarred by conflict was jarring. The contrast between nature's tranquility and the grim reality of war highlighted the emotional toll we carried. Yet in that peaceful space, we found not just physical refuge but also mental relief—a brief return to normalcy. We tried to hold on to that sense of stability through Masha's online schooling, walks, and simple routines. Even as the war loomed in the background, those moments became small anchors—sources of resilience, cherished memories, and reminders of the healing power of nature and family.

Those cherished moments in nature, where we felt a rare sense of peace and simple happiness, left a lasting impression on me. Experiencing this calm together reminded me of the resilience and strength we draw from each other, even in the face of hardship. It underscored how important it is to savor small joys that bring warmth and ease our minds from heavy thoughts. As Artur's birthday approached, I reflected on how each year I tried to make his day memorable. This year, despite the war, I resolved to bring him a gift that would add a touch of warmth and comfort to our lives.

As the war continued into its seventh month, I started thinking of a unique gift, something special, as I always did. One year, I'd collected video greetings from friends, a heartfelt compilation that deeply touched him. This time, however, the idea came to me unexpectedly when close friends, Lena and Artem, asked for help retrieving a kitten from a breeder who had to evacuate from the front lines. The suffering of the animals during the conflict was heartbreaking—as I've already mentioned, many breeders, especially those near the war zone, had been forced to leave behind their beloved pets.

At the train station, helping my friend Lena collect her new pet, I found myself thinking about adopting a kitten for us, especially given Artur's fondness for Maine Coons. Although all the available kittens were reserved, my friend's happy reunion with her pet made me more determined. Despite the chaos around us, I wanted to bring a sense of normalcy and joy into our home, so I decided to buy him a Maine Coon for his birthday—a gesture of love and resilience amid chaos.

I contacted the kennel that had evacuated, and they offered me a kitten with a small imperfection: a twisted paw. The flaw didn't diminish his beauty in my eyes, and I embraced it as I made the decision to bring him home.

I had been waiting for a couple of weeks for the kitten to be sent by bus from another city—Kharkiv, which was under constant, terrifying bombardment. It's a major city, almost on the border with Russia, and considered the cultural capital of Ukraine. After weeks of anticipation, the kitten was finally on its way. A couple of hours before its arrival, I casually told Artur, "We're going to the station to meet your best friend," piquing his curiosity.

"A friend?" he asked, raising an eyebrow. "Who is this mysterious friend?" I just smiled, keeping the secret to myself a little longer.

We stood at the station, watching as passengers began to disembark from the bus. Artur glanced around, still trying to guess who we were there to meet. He looked at me questioningly, but I only shrugged.

Finally, I approached the bus driver, showed him the necessary documents, and he came back with a pet carrier. As soon as I took it, Artur peeked inside and saw the kitten looking up at him. His expression shifted from confusion to surprise.

"A kitten? During wartime?" he exclaimed, half-laughing, half-annoyed. "Who buys a cat in the middle of a war?"

I couldn't help but grin. "It's a great deal for such a prestigious breed," I explained, knowing it would ease his concerns. Despite his initial reservations, I could already see his affection for the kitten growing.

Thus, despite the tumultuous times, we welcomed a delightful new member into our family.

Masha and Dasha were thrilled. The kitten, lively and playful, brought a burst of joy and carefreeness into our home. However, the air raids terrified him. During these times, he would tremble and needed extended comforting. It was a stark reminder of how sensitive animals are to the stresses of war, remaining on edge long after the danger has passed. Our other cat exhibited similar distress, seeking refuge and requiring constant reassurance.

Caring for pets in such conditions adds a layer of emotional complexity, but also provides immense comfort and joy. They are a poignant reminder of the simple joys and connections that sustain us, even in the darkest times.

As October rolled in, so did Halloween—a relatively new but growing tradition here. Typically, our Halloween involved face painting, photo sessions, and festive decorations. However, this year brought a unique twist when my neighbor, a mother of three with whom we have a friendly rapport, reached out one late evening by phone. She mentioned she was out of potatoes for her soup and asked if I had any. I didn't, but then she casually asked for a carrot, which puzzled me, yet I was ready to help.

As I was preparing the carrot, the doorbell rang. When I opened it, expecting my neighbor for the carrot, I was instead greeted by her, her husband, and their three costumed children, their faces painted for Halloween. "Trick or treat?" they called out with big smiles. It was clear that the request for vegetables had just been an excuse to come by and surprise us with a festive visit.

I was glad to have candy on hand, which I happily shared, along with some money. Masha and Dasha joined me at the door, their laughter filling the room as they admired the costumes. The visit, though brief, filled our home with warmth and laughter, turning an ordinary evening into something memorable. The joy of shared experiences and the comfort of friendships, however small, became a source of resilience and warmth, helping us feel grounded and connected amid life's challenges.

7

A Heartbeat Away

Amid the light-heartedness of Halloween, our close friends, Lena and Artem, were facing a devastating reality. Their teenage son had been diagnosed with a severe genetic heart condition, and the only hope was an expensive surgery in the capital. The news was heartbreaking for all of us. My husband, who worked with Artem, immediately got involved when their workplace organized a fundraiser to help cover the costs of the surgery. We contributed a large portion of our savings, knowing that saving their son was the most important thing.

Before their trip, we visited Lena and Artem at their home. The air was thick with tension, fear, and uncertainty. I could see the exhaustion in their eyes, the overwhelming weight of worry pressing down on them. We sat around the table, trying to offer comfort, but we were all painfully aware of the unknown that lay ahead.

"I just don't know how we'll get through this," Artem admitted, his voice shaky. "The surgery, the hospital . . . everything feels like too much."

"You're stronger than you think," my husband said, his voice steady. "And you're not going through this alone. We're with you every step of the way."

Lena, visibly tired but holding on, managed a faint smile. "It's just terrifying. We know it has to be done, but we can't help thinking—what if something goes wrong?"

"It won't," I said softly, though I shared their fears. "You're doing everything right. The doctors know what they're doing, and you have us here with you."

Despite the fear we all felt, we tried to focus on being there for them, offering as much support as we could. But it wasn't easy. The truth was, we were scared too—scared for their son, scared of what lay ahead for them, and scared of the helplessness we all felt in the face of such a serious situation.

Before they left for the capital, we hugged them tightly. "We'll come to Kyiv too," my husband said. "We won't leave you to face this alone."

"You've already done so much," Artem said, his voice thick with emotion. "You don't have to . . ."

"We want to," I interjected. "It's not about what we've done; it's about being there. You need support, and we'll be there for you."

Their eyes filled with gratitude, though the fear was still evident. "Thank you," Lena whispered. "It means more than you know."

As Lena and Artem left for Kyiv, the weight of the situation didn't ease. Our journey, when we followed them sometime later, felt like the beginning of a shared trial, a path we'd travel together, carrying each other's hopes and fears.

I had never been to the capital, despite its reputation as a cozy, inviting city. But knowing that Lena and Artem were there, facing the most terrifying days of their lives, I felt a deep need to support them in person. By the time we set out, the surgery had already been scheduled. It was supposed to last nine hours—a grueling wait on its own—but ended up stretching into twelve agonizing hours.

Their family was separated due to pandemic restrictions: Lena was by their son's side in the hospital, while Artem was forced to stay in a nearby hotel, isolated and powerless to be with them in those critical hours. We were constantly on the phone, trying to provide them with any semblance of comfort, but in truth, we were all on edge, counting the minutes as they turned into hours.

"How is he doing?" we would ask, time and time again, desperate for updates.

"We don't know yet," Artem would respond, his voice strained, echoing his helplessness. "They're still working on him. I just don't know what's taking so long."

Each passing hour seemed like an eternity. We could feel the tension in every message, every phone call—our own hearts ached with fear for them.

I remember sitting in our small apartment, staring at the phone, trying to keep my mind from racing to the worst scenarios. "It's taking too long," I whispered to my husband, anxiety bubbling up inside me. "Why is it taking so long?"

He squeezed my hand, though I could see the same fear in his eyes. "Maybe it's a good thing," he said, trying to reassure both of us. "If they're still working, it means they're doing everything they can. We just have to believe in that."

We tried to distract ourselves, but the gravity of the situation was overwhelming. Our thoughts were constantly with them. I would check my phone every few minutes, wondering if there would be any news, any sign of hope.

Finally, after twelve excruciating hours, we got the call. "He's out," Artem said, his voice trembling with a mixture of exhaustion and relief. "The surgery went well, but . . . it was longer and more complicated than they thought."

The wave of relief was immediate, but it was tempered with the knowledge that there was still a long road ahead for their son. "He's stable for now, but we're not out of the woods yet," Artem added quietly. "We'll just have to wait and see how he recovers."

Knowing there were still challenges ahead, we decided to travel to the capital to support our friends, believing we could be more helpful in person.

We were driving to Kyiv; the road was smooth and quite long, and I had picked up some speed. Off to the right, there was a large truck with a trailer parked on the shoulder. I noticed it immediately, but as we drove past, the truck suddenly started moving and began changing lanes, coming further and further left, straight toward us. The truck driver must not have seen us because just as we were almost parallel with him, he shifted into the final lane, leaving us with nowhere to go. In that moment, I realized we were about to crash. It was terrifying, absolutely horrifying. I slammed on the brakes, gripping the steering wheel, and realized we were pinned — the trailer was just inches from my car's hood, far too close to breathe.

At that moment, I truly understood the fear one might feel in the final seconds before a catastrophe, as I was convinced it was the end for us. My car was carrying the most precious parts of my life—my two children and my husband. It was an intensely terrifying experience. After I managed to pull the car to the side of the road, I stepped out, shaking so much that even holding a water bottle was a struggle.

Despite the fear, there was an overwhelming sense of relief that we were all unharmed; Masha and Dasha, not fully comprehending the danger, were okay, and my husband was by my side, visibly shaken as well. It felt miraculous that we had stopped in time, aided perhaps by the dry roads, good weather, or our vehicle's well-maintained brakes and tires.

That close call served as a reminder of life's fragility and intensified our purpose for coming to Kyiv—to stand with our friends, sharing in their hopes and fears. I was deeply thankful that we had escaped unscathed, giving us another chance at life. This incident was a stark reminder that life's fragility isn't confined to the perils of war. I recognized my responsibility in the risk—we were speeding, on an empty, inviting road, and I had unjustifiably endangered my family's lives. That day reshaped my approach to driving; I never exceeded speed limits again. It was a lesson I would carry for life.

We eventually arrived in Kyiv, and despite the earlier scare, the mood lightened as my daughter excitedly anticipated exploring the city, even mistaking open fields for the city's beauty. The capital itself was a delightful surprise, bustling and vibrant.

Artem had arranged for us to stay in the same hotel as him. Our reunion was joyous. He spent most days alone, visiting Lena briefly due to hospital restrictions. The complexity of their child's surgery added to the emotional weight of our visit. We aimed to provide quiet companionship, a presence to perhaps ease Artem's solitude.

We managed to explore the city a bit, visiting the aquarium, which delighted the children. Masha and Dasha were thrilled by their first glimpse of a real shark, and my younger daughter was captivated by the axolotls. These small adventures brought lightness to our heavy hearts.

However, our stay was punctuated by the harsh reality of the ongoing conflict, as we were jolted awake one night by explosions. Such experiences cemented our resilience and our collective resolve to never forget or forgive the atrocities of war.

The days we spent in Kyiv were filled with tension, but one day, things took a truly frightening turn. Lena and Artem's son's condition suddenly worsened—he grew pale, his breathing labored, and it became clear that something was terribly wrong. The doctors rushed in and, after what felt like an eternity of waiting, we learned that his heart had filled with a dangerous amount of fluid. It was a complication that none of us had anticipated, and the fear that gripped us in that moment was unbearable.

The doctors acted swiftly, draining the excess fluid, and thankfully, his condition improved soon after. But the emotional toll of those hours, filled with uncertainty and dread, was profound. I saw how the fear and stress weighed on Lena and Artem, visibly aging them, as though the weight of the world had settled on their shoulders. It's the kind of anxiety that leaves deep marks on the soul, the kind no one should ever have to endure, not even in the midst of war. Yet, despite everything, there was a small glimmer of relief—he had been saved, and we all held on to that fragile thread of hope.

Eventually, we prepared to return home, hopeful for Lena and Artem's return, knowing they had survived such a harrowing ordeal. Our journey back wasn't just about the miles we had traveled but about the emotional depth we had gained. The bond we shared with them had deepened through those intense days of fear, hope, and mutual support.

I remember the night before we were set to leave. My husband, our children, and I were sitting with Artem. The room was quiet, the weight of everything we had experienced together hanging in the air. He looked at all of us, his voice filled with emotion, and said, "Thank you. You have no idea how much it meant to have you all here. You helped me stay grounded, distracted me when I needed it, and helped me get through this."

It was a simple expression of gratitude, but it spoke volumes. We had been there to help Artem carry the emotional burden, to make the impossible a little more bearable. Sitting together in that moment, we felt the strength of our connection, knowing that sometimes, just being there for each other is the greatest gift we can offer.

8

Light in the Dark

Moments of Resilience

At home, we were greeted by a new set of difficulties. Our enemies had targeted the power grid, leading to frequent disruptions in our electricity and water supply. As winter approached, the days shortened, and the lack of power left us cold and in darkness. Initially, our home maintained power while others did not, causing friction with neighbors who couldn't understand why we were spared. Though we invited them over to charge their devices, their frustration was palpable. Eventually, our power too was cut off, as we learned our home was connected to the same line that supplied a hospital, giving us a brief reprieve before we joined the rest in darkness.

The schedule became a cycle of four hours with electricity followed by four hours without. Managing without power was an ordeal, particularly as the cold set in and the nights grew longer. We had to invent games to keep the children entertained—shadow puppet shows using flashlight beams, drawing contests by candlelight, and even storytelling marathons where we each took turns adding to the tale. Stocking up on candles and flashlights became part of our routine, as we tried to maintain some normalcy in our dimly lit home. The lack of basic utilities meant that daily tasks like showering or cooking became monumental challenges, and we had to adapt to this new reality, making the best of what little we had.

One evening, when we were once again without electricity, I tried to prepare dinner by the dim light of a few candles. But their faint glow wasn't enough to really see what I was doing. I turned on the flashlight on my phone and placed it on top of the cabinet, hoping it would provide enough light to make cooking a bit easier. It felt like I was cooking in near darkness, struggling to navigate even the simplest tasks.

For a moment, I forgot about the phone. When I reached up to open the cabinet to grab a pot, the phone slipped and crashed to the floor with a dull thud. It felt like my world shattered along with it. I stood there, staring at the broken pieces, tears welling up in my eyes. I sank to the floor, completely overwhelmed. I wasn't crying because of the phone—I was crying because of this life. A life without light, without water, always shrouded in darkness and cold. Every day felt like a new challenge, and the phone breaking was just the final straw. In that moment, I was flooded with emotions—exhaustion, helplessness, and despair. It seemed like even the simplest things had become impossible in this never-ending cycle of hardship.

The intermittent water supply forced us to store water in the bathtub for flushing the toilet or washing dishes, but then we faced dilemmas whenever the water returned unexpectedly. Should we drain the tub to bathe properly, unsure of when we'd have water again? Food preservation became a serious issue as well, with items spoiling in the powerless refrigerator, exacerbating the stress of already scarce food supplies.

Amid the hardships, there was a small stroke of luck that brought some relief: I won a power bank in an online giveaway. It came as a total surprise. Our internet provider held a social media contest, giving away a few power banks. All you had to do was be a customer and like their post. I didn't think I'd win, but to my amazement, I did! Having that power bank made things so much easier. When the electricity was out and our phones ran out of charge, I could turn on cartoons for the kids or use the flashlight when needed. It was such a small thing, but in those moments, it felt incredibly valuable.

In the absence of water, electricity, and any sense of normalcy, maintaining my usual appearance became nearly impossible. My hair had grown past my waist—a personal achievement I had long wanted to reach. But with the war, the constant need to wash and care for it became an unbearable burden. There's a phenomenon I noticed during the war: women often cut their hair very short. I'm not sure why—perhaps it's a subconscious desire to feel stronger, more resilient, or maybe it's just the practicality of it. After all, in war, nobody has the energy to worry about hairstyles or appearances. On top of that, war ages everyone by at least ten years. People around me seemed to age overnight, and I felt it too.

My long hair began to irritate me, to the point where I became obsessed with the idea of cutting it off. I thought about it day and night, desperate to be rid of the weight, both literal and figurative. So, I went to my favorite stylist. But when I asked her to cut it, she refused. She said she couldn't bring herself to chop off such thick, beautiful hair.

I went home, still fixated on the idea, and asked Artur for help. Together, we took the clippers and shaved my head nearly bald. The relief was immediate and profound. Looking in the mirror, I barely recognized myself, but it felt like I had shed a heavy burden. I wasn't concerned with beauty at that moment—what I felt was freedom. Washing my head took only a couple of minutes now, and even with the water shortages, I only needed a small cup to feel clean. I might not have looked beautiful, but I felt liberated, and that feeling was priceless.

In November, my husband received a call from a friend who had been fighting on the front lines since the very beginning of the war. He was overjoyed to finally get through and share everything he had endured, but the conversation was emotionally difficult. On one hand, we were relieved to hear his voice and know he was alive. On the other, we couldn't shake the heavy weight of guilt. My husband's exemption from mobilization didn't erase the feeling of responsibility we felt toward those who were out there, risking their lives. It's a guilt that lingers, not just for the men who aren't fighting, but for the women as well. Why are others sacrificing everything while we sit at home? How do you reconcile the fact that while some are dying, you are taking a moment to breathe, to find a little peace? It's a constant battle with your own conscience, a guilt that never fully leaves you.

But despite these overwhelming emotions, we were grateful—grateful to know our friend was alive, grateful to hear his voice. One evening, he called, his voice steady but tired. "I'm still here," he said simply.

"We know," my husband, Artur, replied, his voice filled with a mixture of relief and pain. "Every call from you . . . it's like a gift."

A small pause. "I can't promise anything," our friend continued, "but I'll keep calling as long as I can."

"That's all we need to hear," I replied, feeling a lump in my throat. "Just knowing you're there keeps us going."

Each call was a reassurance that he was still with us, still holding on. Even now, every time the phone rings and it's him, it's a powerful reminder that amid the chaos, there is still hope.

There was another moment I remember. When I drove to the store alone, on the way back, I could see my neighborhood—high-rise buildings and the main avenue. What should have been a comforting view of home filled me with terror. That view chilled my heart. Every time I drove alone, I was gripped by a constant, gnawing fear: the fear of seeing a missile strike near my home. And there, in that home, were my family—my children, my husband, and our pets. I was terrified that something could happen to them while I wasn't there, and the thought of living without them was unbearable. Each drive was filled with a haunting dread, knowing that if disaster struck, I wouldn't be able to live with the loss.

This fear echoed something my father once said about flying, even though he had never flown himself. "If you must fly," he said, "fly together. Don't leave anyone behind. If disaster strikes, let it take us all at once." His words stayed with me, especially during these dark times. In wartime, the desire to be with your loved ones at every moment, even in moments of disaster, becomes a painful reality. There's an instinctual need to stay together—to be there for each other, no matter the outcome.

In normal life, such thoughts wouldn't even cross your mind. But in war, death is no longer a distant concept. It moves in with you, quietly, from the first explosion, and becomes an unwelcome yet constant presence in your everyday life. That looming shadow changes you. It reshapes your fears, your desires, and how you live each day. The desire to stay with your loved ones at all costs, even in the face of death, becomes a horrifying but very real part of life.

War teaches you to adapt to the unimaginable. As the saying goes, when shit happens, you turn it into fertilizer. Sometimes, though, the strength to transform adversity into opportunity eludes you. But the necessity remains: to get your hands dirty, to delve into the muck, and from it, cultivate something valuable for life's garden.

As autumn waned, the first snowfall, which usually brought me joy, felt different. Instead of marveling at its brightening effect on the night, I thought of our soldiers, freezing in the trenches, a stark reminder of the brutal realities of war. The landscape, once a canvas of beauty, now underscored a grim narrative of suffering.

Winter brought with it a kaleidoscope of events—both bad and good. But let's focus on the good. At the dance club my children attended, the New Year celebration had arrived. In our country, the New Year is one of the most important and widely celebrated holidays, often marked with more festivity than Christmas because, according to our calendar, Christmas falls a week later, on January 7. New Year is a national holiday that unites families and friends, bringing hope and joy, especially during difficult times.

My children performed at the New Year festival in the dance club, and I felt an overwhelming sense of pride. Masha did an outstanding job. She danced with her group, and it was truly energetic, exciting, and beautiful. Even though she was only ten years old, she was performing with older, almost adult dancers, and she stood out among them with her height and confidence. I was so proud of her, so proud of my children.

The challenge was even greater for Dasha, who at just four years old, had to perform all by herself. She stood alone on the stage, such a tiny figure in front of a packed auditorium filled with parents, children, and participants. My heart was racing with worry for her. I couldn't even imagine what my little girl must have been feeling, standing there in front of so many people. Just before she went onstage, she looked up at me, her little hand squeezing mine tightly.

"Mama," she whispered, her voice barely audible, "what if I forget the dance?"

I knelt down beside her, brushing a stray hair from her face and giving her hand a gentle squeeze. "Just look at me, Dasha," I said softly. "I'll be right here, watching you. And no matter what happens, you're already the bravest girl I know."

She nodded, taking a shaky breath but managing a small smile. "Okay, Mama."

I was terrified for her, but also so proud. Even if she had frozen, gotten scared, and walked off the stage, I was ready to run up, hug her, and tell her it was okay.

But then the music started, and Dasha lit up the stage. The entire hall applauded for her. She danced so well, moving to the fun, rhythmic music, and she absolutely nailed it. I was bursting with pride. In moments like that, you realize as a parent that all the hard work is worth it. Seeing your child conquer their fears, standing on stage and giving it their all, touches a mother's heart in a way that brings tears to your eyes. I couldn't hold back—I ran to Dasha, scooped her up, and cried tears of joy. She had done it. She conquered her fear, and in that moment, she helped me conquer mine.

That performance gave me a renewed sense of hope. If my little girl could be so brave, then we, too, could overcome anything. It was a deeply emotional experience, and I'm so grateful to the club for organizing such a beautiful event for the children, despite everything going on. At the end, all the participants even received sweet gifts, which added to the joy of the day.

Despite all the chaos around us, we were determined to keep our New Year tradition alive. As always, we invited entertainers dressed as Santa Claus and the Snow Maiden to come to our home. For the children, it was a magical event—gifts, songs, and the feeling of wonder. But for me, it wasn't just a festive celebration. It was a way to hold on to a sense of normalcy, a reaffirmation that the joys of family traditions could still bring light into our lives.

This month, we had another important family celebration—Masha's birthday. My husband and I always tried to celebrate it with friends, organizing parties at children's entertainment centers with animators, gifts, food, and cake. This year, we had planned something special: a joint birthday celebration with the daughter of our neighbor, who had come to our house for Halloween. It was she who suggested combining the parties, as our girls shared the same birthday. We gladly agreed, and everything was planned: a café, the entertainment center, animators, gifts, a cake, and a piñata.

But just as we were about to leave, we received a call from the café with bad news. Their power had been cut, and their generator had broken down. The party was canceled. The children, Masha and Dasha, were dressed up and excited for the celebration, but suddenly we had no place to host it. After a frantic search, we managed to find another venue with a working generator. They could only offer a limited menu—salads and fries—but it was better than nothing.

Despite all these last-minute changes, the animators came, and Masha and Dasha played, danced, and laughed, and in the end, the birthday party was a success. It wasn't what we had originally planned, but the joy on the children's faces showed that the spirit of celebration can overcome any obstacles.

But in times of war, joy and sorrow walk hand in hand. Every moment of happiness was a reminder of how close loss always was, hiding in every shadow. That month brought a profound personal tragedy. One of my dear classmates, Roma, a close friend, was killed in combat. We had kept in touch throughout the war, and I had tried to offer him psychological support through our messages, always sending encouragement and trying to lift his spirits. He would always respond with humor, making light of the situation, though I knew the heavy burdens he carried. He had a wife and a young daughter who had evacuated to another country for safety. Now, his little girl would grow up without her father, and his wife would have to bear the unimaginable weight of this loss. The thought of that tiny child facing life without her dad was devastating. Nothing can ever replace a father for a child, and the pain she would endure seemed unbearable.

I will never forget the moment I found out. I was driving when a message from Danya appeared above the GPS on my car's dashboard screen. As I glanced at it, the world seemed to stop. I read the words over and over, not wanting to believe what they were telling me. At first, it felt unreal, as though I had misread or misunderstood. But there it was, clear and unmistakable—Roma was gone. I kept hoping that somehow it was a mistake, that Danya had the wrong information. But deep down, I knew it was true.

The grief hit me suddenly and intensely. My vision blurred as tears welled up, and I had to pull over to the side of the road. The pain was overwhelming, and I couldn't stop the tears from streaming down my face. I sat there, gripping the steering wheel, shaking as I tried to process the enormity of what I had just learned. My heart ached not only for the loss of my friend Roma but for the family he left behind. It was a moment of profound sorrow, one I could never have prepared for.

Reflecting on our time together, from high school through our weekly university commutes, I remembered how comforting it was to have him by my side during those early morning walks to the train station. After we graduated from school, we attended the same university in a neighboring city. Every week, we would travel there together—early on Monday mornings and back home on Friday evenings. He was a good guy—simple, kind, and a true friend. I always felt safer walking to the station at 5 a.m. in the dark because I knew I wouldn't be alone.

His presence made those cold, quiet mornings feel less intimidating, and I appreciated having him with me. Now, the thought that we will never be able to sit together at the same table with our families again is deeply painful. His daughter, who is still so young, will have to grow up without her father. She was far too little to lose him. It breaks my heart to think of the void his absence will leave in her life, and I can't stop thinking about her.

9

In the Grip of War

A Household of Dread

There's a strange psychological mechanism—a sort of shield that many of us build to survive. The horrors of war seem distant as long as they don't touch you directly. I found myself thinking, "Well, nothing's hit our home yet. As long as the bombs fall somewhere else, we're safe." This illusion of safety brings a strange kind of calm but also a sense of shame. It's as if you're justifying staying in the line of fire, convincing yourself that as long as the war isn't right at your door, everything will be fine. But deep down, you know it's only a matter of time.

January 14, 2023, began as a quiet Saturday. Despite the distant sounds of shelling, we took Masha and Dasha to dance practice, hoping for a normal day. Dasha finished first, while Masha had a second class to attend. We went to a nearby café to wait for her—a brief escape from the tension that always seemed to follow us.

As we sat there, Lena called, her voice tight with urgency, explaining that her son had suddenly felt dizzy. We had planned for them to come over to our house for a relaxing afternoon together, but given the circumstances, I suggested canceling the visit to avoid putting extra strain on them, especially since their son had recently undergone heart surgery. However, Lena insisted we come to their house instead, assuring us that everything would be fine. Shortly after, Artem called my husband, echoing her plea with a sense of urgency that we couldn't ignore. Though we initially hesitated, their insistence led us to change our plans and visit them at their home that afternoon.

Masha, already anxious about the ongoing airstrikes, was reluctant to visit their high-rise apartment, fearing its vulnerability. I reassured her, promising this would be our last visit to such a precarious height and planning for safer future gatherings.

Adding to my personal challenges, I have a significant fear of elevators stemming from a harrowing experience when Dasha was just a baby. Trapped in a plummeting elevator, I was consumed by terror, fearing for her safety and the uncertainty of who would care for my eldest if something happened to me. Thankfully, the elevator eventually stabilized, but the ordeal left a lasting impact, making me opt for stairs whenever possible.

That day, as we gathered in the apartment of our dear friends, joy and laughter filled the air, reminding us of the power of deep, meaningful connections. It was one of those rare moments when the war seemed distant, overshadowed by the warmth of friendship and shared history. I vividly remember the day we first met Lena and Artem, never imagining then how crucial they would become in our lives.

From their balcony, the proximity of our homes allowed us to see the roofs of our building. But that peaceful afternoon on January 14, 2023, was shattered in an instant. While Artur and Artem stepped out onto the balcony to smoke, the rest of us stayed indoors, enjoying a quiet moment together. Suddenly, a deafening explosion tore through the air, shaking the entire building.

Everything froze. I saw my husband on the balcony, a column of smoke rising behind him. The thought struck me: This is it—our home is under attack. Panic surged. My daughters, wide-eyed and trembling, clung to me as the building swayed, nearly knocking me off the sofa. Lena and Artem's son ran in, terror mirrored in his mother's eyes. We all had the same thought—What if the building collapses?

On the balcony, Artur and Artem looked back at us through the door. My husband's face was blank with shock—he had been deafened by the blast, his movements slow and disoriented. When he came back inside, he explained what had happened: While they were talking, Artem had been gesturing with his hand, showing Artur the possible trajectory of a missile. And at the exact moment Artem lowered his hand, the explosion hit. Later, Artur tried to lighten the mood with a joke: "Maybe you shouldn't demonstrate missile trajectories anymore—seems like you have too much influence." We all managed a shaky laugh, but deep down, the terror was still raw.

We huddled together, holding each other tightly, waiting for what felt like an eternity. We feared another missile would come, and the thought of falling from the tenth floor haunted us. Every second felt like a countdown, and I couldn't shake the fear that we might be next.

At that moment, I was convinced the missile had struck our home. From the balcony, we couldn't see our yard—only the roofs—so I had no way of knowing if our house had been hit. My mind raced. The uncertainty was unbearable, but Artur held me back, saying it was too dangerous to leave just yet, especially with smoke everywhere and no clear sense of what had been hit.

The immediate aftermath was pure chaos. Communication lines were down, leaving us cut off from the outside world. My first thoughts were of our pets—material possessions didn't even cross my mind. Phones were dead, and the internet was gone. We were trapped in the unknown, unable to check on our home, our animals, or anything.

As the hours dragged on, we learned the truth. A massive anti-ship missile had struck the nine-story building right next to our home, obliterating two entire sections from the ninth floor down to the first. Almost a hundred apartments were gone, reduced to rubble. The scale of the devastation was unimaginable. I couldn't stop thinking about how we had once considered buying a home in that very building, in the section that was now destroyed. It could have been us.

As we returned, the streets were packed with people fleeing while we drove into darkness and destruction. Only headlights pierced the thick blackness, sirens wailing around us, amplifying the dread with each passing moment.

I was terrified of what we might find when we got home. Was our building still standing? Were our pets okay? The fear gripped me with every turn, but we kept going. We held onto each other, clinging to the small thread of hope that had kept us going. We had survived—but barely. And in the aftermath of the destruction, we knew that nothing would ever be the same.

When we finally reached our building, the sight of it mostly intact provided a small relief, but the closer inspection revealed the true impact. The damaged windows, the remnants of our shaken home, and the overwhelming smell of burnt flesh mixed with rocket fuel hit me profoundly. It was a visceral reminder of the disaster's proximity—an odor that represented loss, terror, and unanswered questions.

Inside our apartment, the scene was chaotic. The ceiling had partially collapsed, windows were shattered, and everything was covered in glass. The emergency services outside struggled to control the flames fueled by the rocket's remnants, casting an eerie glow through our damaged windows. Artur and I managed to secure the windows with plastic wrap and leaned the frames back in place, doing what we could to keep the cold and any animals out.

Shocked, I reached out to friends and neighbors, desperate for news of their safety. Each call was fraught with anxiety, but thankfully, most of my neighbors were okay—some had been outside at the time, others were at home or away. The relief of hearing their voices brought a measure of peace amid the chaos.

However, the lack of concern from my parents was a piercing disappointment. In times of such dire crisis, I had hoped for a sign of care or worry from them. The silence from their end was deeply hurtful. While I had disagreements with them, I believed that such extreme circumstances would bring us together, reminding us of the essential bonds of family. Danya was the only family member who reached out, confirming that he hadn't heard any concern from our parents either. His call, while comforting, also underscored the isolation fueled by our parents' indifference.

That night, the thought of staying in our compromised apartment was unbearable for Masha, and understandably so. The fear and instability were too much for her, and for all of us, really. Sleep was an impossibility; the night stretched before us, filled with the sound of our own anxieties and the distant efforts to extinguish the fire.

As we faced the reality of our situation, the need to support each other and find a way forward was clear. The devastation outside our windows was a stark reminder of how quickly life could change, and how the remnants of a normal day could turn into a landscape of survival and recovery. The experience bonded us in our vulnerability and resilience, reminding us of the preciousness of safety and the unpredictable nature of life in a time of war.

The aftermath of the missile strike was a stark illustration of the harsh realities of war—random, brutal, and without mercy. The missile, intended for a nearby power station, veered off course, resulting in a devastating impact on a residential building filled with ordinary people living their lives. The contrast between their everyday normalcy and the sudden, catastrophic intrusion of war couldn't be more jarring.

The community's response was immediate and heroic, with neighbors and emergency services working tirelessly to assist the injured and clear the debris amid the flames that refused to die down. Yet, not everyone was able to contribute physically to these efforts. My own response was paralysis; overwhelmed by the shock and horror, I found myself unable to join the rescue efforts. As a psychologist, I understood the trauma and the urgent need for emotional support, yet in that moment, I was the one in desperate need of psychological help. The guilt of merely observing from a distance, unable to muster the strength to act, was crushing.

That evening was a sleepless vigil. My younger daughter, somehow oblivious to the gravity of the situation, managed to find sleep, while Masha was understandably terrified—her sense of security shattered. No child should have to endure such a nightmarish reality. Thankfully, our pets were unharmed, small mercies in an otherwise grim scenario. It highlighted the randomness of survival; a random decision to visit friends likely spared us from being direct casualties of the strike.

The night was filled with the eerie glow of fires fueled by rocket fuel, the air thick with the acrid smell of destruction. Rescuers worked frantically to reach those trapped, including a young girl on the eighth floor, standing precariously in the remnants of her room, a stark symbol of the fragile line between life and death.

When communications were restored, the full extent of the tragedy began to unfold online. Stories of loss, of families torn apart, of lives cut short in senseless violence flooded social media. The narrative of each victim added layers of sorrow and outrage. My reaction was to donate nearly all our money to help the victims, driven by a deep sense of community and shared suffering. Despite my professional training in wartime psychology, the immediate shock left me feeling helpless, contributing in the only way I felt capable at the moment—financially.

This event underscored the cruel randomness of war, where a single misguided missile can obliterate lives and dreams in an instant. It also highlighted the complex tapestry of human responses—heroism, despair, paralysis, and resilience. As the community rallied to rebuild and support each other, the struggle to find meaning and justice in the face of such indiscriminate destruction continued. Each of us, in our own way, grappled with the impact, trying to contribute to the healing process while dealing with our own deep wounds.

Among the most heart-wrenching news from that day was the loss of two incredible women, taken by the tragedy in the blink of an eye. They were walking to the gym, just passing by the building that was struck. These weren't just any women; they were remarkable souls—kind, intelligent, and full of life. Both were accomplished dentists and surgeons, and I knew them personally. One was my dentist, Ira, and the other, Olya, treated my husband. Their loss hit me hard, not only because they were so close to us but because of the bright futures and full lives they should have had.

These women were shining examples of strength and beauty in every sense. Each had a loving family, with young children and supportive husbands. My dentist, Ira, in particular, was someone I admired deeply. She was the epitome of success—beautiful, fit, intelligent, always impeccably dressed, and, above all, kind. She balanced her demanding career as a dentist and surgeon with a rich family life, bringing joy and ease into every conversation we had. She was a role model to me, a woman I aspired to be like. We connected on many levels, often sharing stories about our children, our lives, and our fears.

During one visit, she told me a story about her eldest son bringing home an axolotl. "Can you believe it?" she laughed. "He just showed up with this . . . lizard-fish thing, like it was a puppy! I had no clue what to do with it, but he was so thrilled I couldn't say no." At my next appointment, I asked how the axolotl was doing. She chuckled, "Oh, it's doing great . . . well, it was until it died." Her voice softened a little. "No one told me it needed special water, and of course, my son was heartbroken. It was a whole ordeal." I admitted I knew all about the axolotl phase—my own daughter was begging for one. We ended up talking at length about the joys and surprises of motherhood, connecting over our children's quirks and their endless fascination with unusual pets.

Ira was also a source of comfort during my second pregnancy. I was nervous, knowing what I'd have to go through again, but she reassured me by sharing her own recent experiences. She joked about how hard it is to carry a baby for the second time, saying that by the end, every mom just hopes to give birth a few days early because it's exhausting. I could relate, and her humor lightened my fears. She even comforted me about my fear of flying. She shared how she, too, was scared of flying but often traveled with her husband. She had a little ritual—drinking a glass of champagne at the airport to calm her nerves.

Her death, along with Olya's, was more than just a loss—it was a profound injustice. These women were young; they had so much more life ahead of them. They should have been able to watch their children grow, to experience all the joys of family and life. It felt deeply unfair, and the weight of it was crushing. I remember one particular video that Olya had sent for my husband's birthday—a lighthearted message where she joked about his smile, saying, "Don't worry, we'll fix it if you need." Watching that video a year later, after everything, brought me to tears. It was unbearable to think that such vibrant, kind-hearted women were gone, leaving behind children who would now have to grow up without their mothers.

The hardest part was thinking about their children. How could they possibly move forward without their moms? I couldn't get their faces out of my mind, imagining the pain they were going through, the emptiness that would follow them for the rest of their lives. No child should have to lose a parent this way. No family should have to endure this kind of grief. I wanted to do something, anything, to help, so I donated nearly all of our remaining funds to support Ira's family. It was a small gesture in the face of such an immense tragedy, and I knew no amount of money could ever replace the love and presence of a mother.

This was my personal tragedy. The pain was too deep, too overwhelming. I couldn't stop crying, overwhelmed by the thought that nothing could ever bring them back. It was a pain that spread far beyond one person, touching so many lives, so many hearts. All from the single push of a button, one missile launch.

As I moved forward, I knew that this loss would remain within me, an open wound that would never fully heal. It was not a moment that would fade with time but a scar that would stay, a reminder of how fragile and precious life is, and of the lives that were taken too soon. In the end, I carry this pain as a testament to them, a silent promise to remember what was lost.

10

Shattered Roots

Escaping the Shadows of Home

In the shadow of such a catastrophic event, the decision to leave our apartment became inevitable. The realization that we were living beside an ongoing disaster site, with the rescue operation unfolding just outside our windows, made it impossible to stay. The emotional and psychological toll of being so close to the devastation was overwhelming, and the constant reminder of danger was too much to bear.

The practical implications hit hard—if our apartment were to be destroyed, the mortgage wouldn't simply vanish. The thought of navigating endless bureaucracy to prove the damage, all while continuing to pay, weighed heavily, adding urgency to our decision to sell.

Surprisingly, Artur agreed with my suggestion to sell the apartment, despite the bleak prospect of finding a buyer. As we stood there, an unspoken understanding passed between us that this was not just a sale; it was a severing of ties to the life we once knew.

"We both know this is the right choice," I said, my voice barely above a whisper.

"I just can't shake off the feeling that it won't sell," Artur replied, running his hand through his hair.

"I know it's hard to leave, but we can't stay here," I replied, looking him straight in the eyes. "This isn't a home anymore. It's a place of destruction and fear."

Artur paused, gazing around the room. "But we put so much effort and love into this place. It feels like I'm betraying it by leaving."

"You're not betraying it; we're just saving ourselves and the kids. Home isn't these walls; it's what we build together, wherever we are."

I took his hand, looking into his eyes, and said, "That's why we have to try. Even if it takes six months or a year for the apartment to sell, we need to move on. We can't keep living here, and paying the mortgage makes no sense. We have to let it go and trust that it will sell eventually."

We were both acutely aware of the dire situation and the unlikely chance of selling given the recent tragedy. The decision was made, and we needed to act quickly. Selling felt like a form of escape, but the weight of what lay ahead quickly surfaced. Now we had to decide which pieces of our life would come with us. Immersed in preparations, we couldn't help but think about those who had been part of our lives here for so many years, including our daughters, Masha and Dasha.

"What do we even take with us?" Artur asked, looking around at the clutter that had once felt like home.

"I think we should take the photos and the children's toys," I suggested, my heart heavy with nostalgia.

Much to our surprise, after contacting a realtor recommended by my husband's colleague, we discovered quick interest in our property. We had braced ourselves for a long, arduous wait, fully expecting the empty feeling of despair that accompanies a home left unsold. But as soon as the phone rang with interest, a flicker of hope ignited within us. The realtor, who himself had suffered in the tragedy, was eager to help and moved quickly to list the apartment.

After listing it for sale at a price 30 percent below market value, we were astonished when a buyer emerged within just an hour. Outside our windows, rescue crews continued their relentless work, clearing rubble and searching for survivors, a stark contrast to the swift interest in our property. This juxtaposition served as a sobering reminder that even in the aftermath of tragedy, life moves forward in unexpected ways.

We planned to rent another apartment; in Ukraine, it's common for rentals to come furnished. Finding an unfurnished place was nearly impossible, so we had no need for most of our furniture. But the children had accumulated so many toys, and, in general, we just had too many belongings. Ideally, everything for the move needed to fit into one car trunk.

I took a few toys but had to give away or leave the rest. As I sorted through our things, I tried to distribute them thoughtfully.

While parting with the apartment itself felt manageable, letting go of the belongings that held our memories proved far more challenging. As I came to terms with our decision to sell, I realized that it was the tangible pieces of our lives—the photos, toys, and little keepsakes—that truly anchored us to our home. Each item weighed heavily with meaning, evoking countless memories, and I found myself grappling with the question of what to take and what to leave behind.

Our possessions became symbols of our past, embodying the laughter and love that had filled our days. Piece by piece, I pondered who among our neighbors might appreciate the items we couldn't bear to simply discard. Each decision felt like a small farewell to the life we had known. As I approached one of my neighbors with a cherished toy in hand, she looked at me with concern.

"Are you really leaving everything behind? This toy meant so much to Masha and Dasha," she asked, her eyes wide.

"I know, but I want it to go to someone who will cherish it," I replied, my voice trembling.

"I promise to take good care of it," she assured me, reaching for the toy.

"Thank you, it means a lot to me," I said, feeling a lump in my throat. "This toy was always their favorite."

The neighbor smiled, clutching the toy. "I know this isn't easy, but it's the right decision for them."

"Yes, they deserve something better than constant fear," I replied, wiping away a tear. With a few more items in hand, I passed them on to the top-floor neighbor. She and her two kids were truly wonderful, kind people. I entrusted her with not only toys but many other personal items I couldn't bear to leave behind. As I handed them over, I felt a quiet farewell to fragments of our previous life.

I had so many precious things—a beautiful Christmas tree, exquisite decorations, fine bedding, a fluffy white carpet, and an electronic piano gifted by my father. There were countless personal items that meant the world to me: my plate, my fork, my sheet, my towel.

We thought it might be a good idea to search for a rental in a different part of the city, somewhere away from power stations, though in these uncertain times, nothing was guaranteed. That night, we checked into a hotel. However, we had three cats, and by the evening, after I had already informed our neighbors that we were selling our apartment and relocating, one of the kind neighbors offered to take one of the cats. Close friends adopted our Maine Coon, leaving us with just one—the cat Masha had bonded deeply with, having chosen it from a shelter as her dearest companion.

Parting with the pets was tough, but we clung to the hope that it was only temporary, just until we could secure new housing and reunite with them. Every corner of the hotel room reminded us of what we had left behind, and the environment felt like a stark contrast to the warmth of our home, amplifying the sense of loss. Finally, for the first time in a while, we managed to sleep soundly. Our minds and bodies desperately needed just to lie down and rest.

Since our apartment was under a mortgage, we needed documents from the bank that, for some reason, were stored across the country. It took over two weeks to obtain these documents, causing daily anxiety for us and the buyer. The sale was fraught with issues, but eventually, we managed to close the deal. However, during the transaction, we realized we had been significantly deceived about the final payment.

We had agreed on one set of terms, but when the payment came, it was 25 percent less than expected. The buyer had manipulated us, taking advantage of our trust. My stomach twisted in anger and disbelief as I scanned the paperwork, realizing too late where they'd slipped in hidden fees. My throat went dry, and my fingers, gripping the papers, trembled slightly. Could it be that they had truly tricked us? For us, contracts had always been straightforward—a handshake meant trust. But here, in our moment of vulnerability, they'd used our trust against us. This assumption of good faith led us to sign the documents before realizing that the payment was much lower than what we had agreed upon. Moreover, all associated transaction fees were deducted from our payment, despite the verbal agreement that the buyers would cover those costs. By the time we noticed, it was too late to dispute; we had already signed.

We realized the truth right after the transaction was completed. In our presence, the dealer and buyer began discussing how many apartments they had managed to acquire in our neighborhood during the panic and how many more deals were underway. It was then we understood they were working together—one as the realtor, the others as buyers. They exploited people's trust and inexperience to buy properties at low prices, acting like vultures.

I remember Artur stepping away from the deal, feeling frustrated and disillusioned. He hadn't expected such betrayal. Though I fully supported him, I also felt an immense sense of relief. Frankly, I was incredibly glad that we had finally freed ourselves from this apartment and the burden of the substantial mortgage debt tied to it.

We had only bought this apartment a year and a half before the war, after renting it for some time. Moving from renting to buying, and then to selling it again in such a short span felt overwhelming, like being pulled into a relentless cycle of beginnings and endings. Letting go of this financial burden offered some relief, but the experience still haunts Artur; he hasn't yet managed to put it behind him.

Now we were essentially free, living out of a hotel, though with no clear sense of what lay ahead. The betrayal in the sale stayed with us, a bitter reminder of how fragile trust becomes in desperate times. In this delicate state, every decision felt magnified; we had to fiercely guard whatever remained ours. With the final money from the sale, Artur made the choice to pay off our car loan. It left us nearly broke, yet debt-free, a small weight lifted in a sea of uncertainties. Oddly, owning the car outright brought a sliver of relief.

The hotel was our shelter, but every day reminded us of how much we'd left behind. In the end, my children, Masha and Dasha, were left with very little. They deeply missed their home, especially Dasha, who longed for her toys and the childhood stability she had known. Masha, though nostalgic, was afraid of our old apartment and had no desire to return. Artur's job was remote, and the kids' school and kindergarten were online. I continued volunteering online.

Life was somewhat easier for my children in the hotel, though not being at home was tough. We lacked amenities like a washing machine, and the kitchen wasn't fully equipped. Living out of suitcases and facing constant uncertainty was challenging. Our lives felt as if they were balancing on the edge of a precipice, with no clear path forward. Each day felt like a guessing game, where every decision might lead us further into the unknown.

We still didn't know where to go next or what to do. Then it occurred to me: Now that we were free birds, unattached to any place, why settle for an apartment on the other side of the city, in an area that could be targeted next? Why not escape to the mountains in the western part of the country? It was relatively safe there, and the serene environment would be soothing.

Artur and I began considering a move. We began searching for a place in the mountains, planning to relocate there. I had even packed some items to send ahead by mail, since not everything could fit in my car.

That same evening, another intense shelling occurred. We were at a loss about where to run for shelter in the hotel. The rooms were wooden and in two-story structures, with ours on the second floor. The noise was deafening, the situation terrifying. The children were petrified. Our cat was especially distressed, clearly terrified by the shelling. Amid this chaos, Masha begged us again to move away from all this horror, as she could no longer bear it.

Contrary to our initial plans, Masha asked not to go to the mountains, feeling intimidated by the formidable wilderness. The pine walls and pitch darkness at night felt oppressive to her.

Instead, she pleaded with us to move abroad. Terrified by every noise, she was convinced that only another country could offer her safety. Unfortunately, that wasn't an option at the time, and we had to deny her request again—a painful decision. As a parent, it's heart-wrenching to see your child so fearful for their life, begging for safety, while you're unable to provide it.

So, we decided to head to a city near the border of a neighboring country, hoping to find some semblance of peace and figure out our next steps from there. One thing was certain: We had to get away from the ongoing terror.

Artur and I decided to stay a couple of days longer to say goodbye to all our friends and wrap up our affairs. Masha pleaded with me not to delay, to leave as soon as possible. She was very scared. But we needed this time; I couldn't leave without saying goodbye.

We arranged to meet with friends and I also planned to see Danya. We informed everyone that we would be moving to the other end of the country, and that this gathering would be our farewell. Everyone was deeply upset, seeing our departure as a grim sign—if we were leaving, things must be truly dire. I called a friend from the neighborhood where we had sold our apartment to tell her about our plans. She said it would be wonderful if we managed to relocate. Many wanted to do the same but were too frightened to even step outside. There were numerous checkpoints to pass to reach a new home, and men risked being drafted on the spot without even a check of their documents, so many stayed indoors to avoid inadvertently getting caught in combat.

We met with some friends who were very sad about our departure, but we had to go. The heaviness of their sorrow mirrored our own, as we struggled to find the right words to say goodbye. I had to save my children and my husband at any cost.

On the penultimate day, I met with Danya. My children were with me, and I found myself overwhelmed with emotion, tears flowing freely throughout our meeting. Danya, ever the pillar of support, was genuinely happy for us. Since the war began, he had been steadfast in his belief that we needed to leave to protect the children. They didn't deserve this life, filled with danger and horrors that no child should ever witness.

Saying goodbye to him felt like an unbearable weight pressing down on my heart. When you part with someone, fearing it might be for the last time, the reality is terrifying—especially when that someone is so close to you. In that moment, I promised myself we would meet again, and perhaps even live near each other someday.

After a lengthy and heartfelt conversation, the moment to part ways arrived all too soon. As we stood facing each other, the reality of our impending separation settled like a heavy fog, a suffocating silence enveloping us as we both realized the weight of what lay ahead.

"Promise me you'll take care of them," Danya said, his eyes searching mine for reassurance.

"I promise. We'll find a way to be safe," I replied, my voice trembling.

"And remember, you're not alone. We're family," he added, his tone firm yet filled with warmth.

I nodded, feeling his words sink deeply. "You've always been there for me, even from afar. I won't forget that."

Danya hugged me tightly, his voice wavering slightly. "Take care of them, and I'll be waiting for the day we meet again," he said.

I struggled to hold back tears, whispering, "I'll do everything to make that happen."

Danya met my eyes and added, "You're my rock."

"I know, and that means everything to me," I whispered, feeling the gravity of his words.

I hugged my brother tightly, tears streaming down my face. "Take care of yourself," I said softly, the emotion catching in my throat.

"You too," he replied quietly, holding me just as tightly. His words resonated with a shared, unspoken understanding—this might truly be our last goodbye. Those embraces held so much weight. On one hand, I felt like a complete traitor for leaving my brother, friends, and relatives amid the war while I sought safety for myself and my children. On the other hand, I had to prioritize their well-being.

It's a painful dilemma many Ukrainians face, forced to choose between options where no right or wrong answer exists. If I had the means, I would have gladly taken everyone to safety—my brother, friends, parents, everyone I loved. Unfortunately, that wasn't possible. As we got into the car, I couldn't shake the thought that if something happened to him, I would never forgive myself. With my daughters by my side, we headed back to the hotel, the weight of our goodbyes heavy in the air.

The next day, it was time to say farewell to our closest friends, Lena and Artem. My daughter begged me not to return to their tenth-floor apartment. I could see the fear etched on her face, and it tore at my heart to witness the turmoil of a child caught in a world of uncertainty. Yet, they couldn't come to us, so we had to visit them one last time. My daughter tearfully resisted; her love for our friends clashed with her terror of the possibility of another missile strike. I gently urged her to face this one last time.

We visited them, sharing laughter and warmth, but the looming farewell cast a shadow over our time together.

Sitting in Lena and Artem's kitchen, surrounded by the familiar scents of tea and fresh pastries, I felt every corner of their home was infused with memories. Lena handed me a cup, as she had done countless times before, but now, it was a gesture of goodbye.

Their apartment, always so cozy, felt like an oasis of calm in the midst of chaos. Masha hugged Lena, and I could see a mixture of fear and attachment in her eyes, blended into one.

When the moment came to say goodbye, tears flowed freely, each of us mourning the parting of such significant relationships.

"I can't believe you're leaving. It feels like a nightmare," Lena said, her voice trembling with emotion.

"I know. But we have to think about the girls," I replied, struggling to keep my composure.

"You'll always have a place to come back to, no matter what," Artem assured us, his tone steady yet filled with sadness.

"Thank you. That means more than you know," I said, feeling a surge of gratitude mixed with the heartache.

As I looked into their tear-filled eyes, I felt a deep ache in my heart. It was incredibly hard to leave them; they had been such an integral part of our lives. I cried openly, hoping it wasn't truly our last time together—that we would meet again, share joyful moments, and create new memories.

That evening, we had to return to the hotel because the next morning a new adventure awaited us. We packed our belongings, but when loading the car, only a small portion of our things fit. I had to part with many belongings, including toys handcrafted by the children—which felt heart-wrenching. I felt like a terrible mother, ashamed that my children had to part with things they created themselves.

As we packed, I watched Dasha clutching her favorite toy, tears welling in her eyes. "Mommy, do we have to leave this behind? I love this toy!" she cried, her small voice trembling.

I knelt beside her, trying to comfort her. "I know, sweetie. It's hard to say goodbye, but we need to take only what fits in the car. We'll find new toys and make new memories, I promise."

Masha, who had been silent, looked at us with determination. "But I want to leave right now! I want to go to a safe place where we can be happy again. I don't care about the toys!"

Dasha shook her head, still holding her toy tightly. "But they're special to me! I made them! I don't want to leave anything behind!"

Masha sighed, frustration creeping into her voice. "Dasha, think about it! If we stay here, we might get hurt. We have to go!"

I hugged them both tightly, feeling the weight of their emotions. "I know this is hard, but we'll be together, and that's what matters. Let's focus on getting to safety first, and we can always find new things later."

Reluctantly, Dasha wiped her tears and nodded. We took our cat and drove to another city, each of us holding onto our hopes for a brighter future.

As we drove away, I watched the place I once called home fade from view. My tears had dried, but the bitterness of leaving remained. Perhaps I'd never forgive myself for this departure, but I knew one thing: I was doing this for my children's future, for the chance, however slim, to give them a life without constant fear and pain. And perhaps, someday, we would see everyone we had to leave behind once more.

11

A Last Embrace

On the Edge of Escape

The journey was long, but we managed to pass military checkpoints and book a hotel room. Our route took us through Mykolaiv, a city in southern Ukraine that had endured severe shelling and lay perilously close to active conflict zones. At that time, Russian forces were advancing from the south, threatening to capture the city. The sight of bullet-riddled buildings and the eerie silence of empty streets underscored the devastation. Crossing Mykolaiv felt like stepping through a war zone, amplifying our fears yet bringing us closer to our destination.

Leaving the city in the distance, I felt a profound sense of relief, though uncertainty still lingered. I found myself reflecting on the journey that had brought us here and what lay ahead. We arrived in a new city across the country—afraid, unsure, and with no clear idea of the future. We hoped Odessa would offer solace, but as we drove closer, its beauty mingled with our lingering anxiety. It felt like a fragile promise—a beautiful facade that concealed the turmoil of our hearts.

It was our first visit to Odessa, the city on Ukraine's southern coast along the Black Sea. I had always dreamed of visiting but had never been there before. It was a beautiful city—so interesting and magnificent. I felt a mix of awe and fear as we drove through the streets. The beauty of the architecture contrasted sharply with the turmoil in my heart. I couldn't help but wonder if we would truly find safety here. I hadn't realized how wonderful our country was. It's a marvelous place to live, to be born. The fields, the cities, the vast landscapes—it's incredible.

As we settled into this new city, our lives took on a different rhythm, marked by both the excitement of exploration and the ongoing challenges of war. We stayed in a hotel, but that turned out not to be the best idea because it was quite expensive. So, we looked for housing, found a small, cozy house right in the city center, and moved there. In Odessa, it was dangerous for men to go outside. Artur stayed indoors for a month, avoiding the streets where enlistment officers roamed. The chances for a man to step outside and not be sent to war were extremely slim. It was a tense and frightening time. Artur continued his remote work at the bank, confined indoors. One night, about four weeks in, I suggested he at least step into the backyard to breathe some fresh air.

I often found myself walking alone with the children, and every day after Masha's online school sessions, we would go out. We visited a local amusement park that had a skating rink. Masha, eager to revisit her previous figure skating experiences, enjoyed the rink tremendously. We also went to a dolphinarium, which delighted us immensely. The view of the sea was magical. We walked along the shore, careful not to get too close because the area was mined. There was a special pier, though, from which you could safely watch the sea, feed the seagulls, and watch the waves crash. It was truly magnificent and so calming. Although the city was still somewhat dangerous due to less frequent but ongoing shelling, it seemed a bit easier for my eldest daughter to cope there, despite some nights when we had to hide in what seemed like the safest part of the house. It was all very unsettling.

That month, amid the shadows of uncertainty and the distant echoes of conflict, we celebrated Dasha's fifth birthday, determined to create a moment of joy despite our fears. We decided to make the day special, starting with a small celebration at home with Artur. Later, the girls and I went to a children's entertainment center with trampolines and mazes and asked for their help in organizing the party. They responded quickly, and soon we were celebrating Dasha's birthday.

Everything was top-notch, from the food and cake to the piñata, gifts, and entertainment. For a few precious hours, the laughter of the girls echoed around us, and I managed to forget about the war. The atmosphere was magical, marking an unforgettable day. I felt a slight sense of pride that, despite a year of full-scale war, we had managed to move away from the epicenter and still have a great time. At one point, I even felt that the girls seemed a bit calmer and happier, savoring every moment.

Since we didn't know how long we would stay in Odessa, we initially booked the little house for a week and then extended for another week. Eventually, someone else booked it, and we had to find another place to stay. I found an apartment nearby in a very old building, but it was terrible. I realized I didn't want to stay there, nor did the children. So, I searched again and found a house in a small town about twenty minutes away.

The next day, we moved to the new house close to the sea, which was typically rented out to tourists during the resort season, now nonexistent for the second year. Because it was off-season, the house was available at a very reasonable price. It wasn't fully prepared since the owners hadn't planned to rent it out before summer, but we liked it there. We tidied up and enjoyed our own little yard. Artur could go outside, there was a barbecue, and we could cook delicious food over the fire. My husband recalls it as one of the most wonderful places and times we had ever spent as a family. We were happy, secluded, and alone. There was a parking space for our car within a fenced area. It was a remarkable time. Masha continued her online studies, and Artur worked remotely. The children and I would drive into town for groceries and to visit the playground.

We asked the homeowners if we could walk down to the sea since it was within walking distance. They assured us it was safe, without mines, and we could go there. We ventured to the sea one day, enjoyed a wonderful, cool, and windy walk with no one around. The descent to the sea was quite steep and long. We collected pebbles and shells, ran around, and had a healthy time before heading home.

A few days later, we decided to revisit that spot. As we started our descent, we heard gunfire. Terrified and unsure of the source, we felt a sense of panic: It seemed to come from everywhere, a barrage of echoes. Artur and I shielded the children with our bodies and laid them on the ground. We tried to assess the situation, then moved toward our home, bent over with the children, until we were far enough to start running. It was terrifying, absolutely horrifying. I understood that every sound outside could be the last. I couldn't allow myself to lose them because they embodied my entire life, all my love. Masha and Dasha are not just children; they are my hope for a better tomorrow that we must protect, no matter what.

Later, when we inquired with the homeowners, they explained that the area was sometimes used for military exercises, and we had stumbled upon one. It was a nightmarish experience that shattered the illusion of safety we had clung to during our time at the beach. In a place that should have been an escape, we were reminded once again of the looming dangers surrounding us. My children were trembling and terribly frightened, and I was scared for them. It was unsafe, and we never went to the sea again, despite living nearby.

A couple of days later, the exercises continued, making life under constant gunfire unbearable. We informed the homeowners we were leaving and returned to the city, settling in a hotel with an excellent restaurant. That night, another attack occurred, damaging a monastery and residential buildings. Our nerves were frayed.

As we sat together in our hotel room, Masha looked up at me with wide eyes. "Mom, did you hear about the monastery in Odessa? Why did they target it?"

I sighed, feeling the weight of her innocence. "I did hear, Masha. Sometimes, they attack places that should be safe. It's hard to understand why."

"But it's a monastery! It's where people pray and find peace," she insisted, her voice trembling.

"I know, sweetheart. It should be a safe place," I replied softly, trying to comfort her. "We have to remember that not everything makes sense right now. People are hurting, and that's why they do these terrible things."

Masha furrowed her brow, her concern evident. "Is there a safe place in our country? Or anywhere on the planet?"

Her question struck me hard, and I paused for a moment, searching for the right words. "I wish I could say yes, Masha. It feels like there are fewer safe places, but we must hold on to hope and comfort each other."

She leaned against me, her small frame trembling. "Will they ever stop? I want to go back to when everything was normal."

I wrapped my arms around her, holding her close. "I want that too, Masha. We just have to stay strong and hope for better days ahead."

The next day, I realized I couldn't stay within those four walls any longer; I felt I was going mad. The pressure was too much. I gathered my daughters, Masha and Dasha, and suggested we leave the hotel to clear our minds. Masha, in tears and deeply affected by the shelling, agreed. The girls needed a distraction too. We drove to an entertainment center, enjoyed the attractions and the skating rink. It was a great day, particularly for Dasha, because Masha and I found it hard to fully distract ourselves. But we needed to fill that day with activity. It was essential, as the anxiety seeped through our attempts to stay composed and pray for better times. After we had our fill of fun, walked on the pier, and fed the seagulls, we headed back to the hotel.

We called a taxi that day because I was too anxious to drive. On the way to the hotel, Masha burst into tears. She was exhausted from the constant fear and longed for peace. It broke my heart to see her, so young, enduring such terror.

When we arrived at the hotel, I suggested we walk a bit before returning to our room. We strolled, admiring the city's architecture, and soon stumbled upon a wax museum just around the corner. Having never visited one before, I thought it might be a good distraction for the girls. We were the only visitors there. We paid the entrance fee and began exploring the eerie, dimly lit, semi-basement space filled with lifelike figures. The atmosphere was so spooky that it felt like the figures might move at any moment. We hurried through the maze of rooms and quickly made our way back outside, momentarily distracted from our worries.

As we emerged, we saw an electric carriage offering city tours. I inquired about the cost and found it reasonably priced, so we decided to take a ride and learn about the city's history. The tour was fascinating. The elderly guide drove us around, passionately sharing stories about Odessa's past and present. He showed us the heart of the city, including the famous Potemkin Stairs, a monumental staircase descending toward the sea, where countless historical events have unfolded. We passed by the Odessa Opera and Ballet Theater, one of the oldest and most beautiful in Ukraine, its architecture echoing stories of resilience and grandeur.

The guide then took us to the Odessa Passage, an architectural masterpiece from the early 1900s. Built by talented architects who combined Baroque and Art Nouveau elements, the Passage was once a hub of commerce and culture. Its elaborate sculptures and stained glass told stories of a thriving port city that welcomed traders and travelers from around the world. Even now, the intricate designs and grand arches continue to reflect Odessa's rich heritage and artistic spirit.

As we traveled through these historical sites, we discussed the ongoing shelling and war, and I felt deeply for the guide; it's heartbreaking that elderly people must witness war. No one on this planet should have to see war. Why do we fight? We're all human, living on the same planet. We should be united, helping each other prosper. It's like living in an apartment where one tenant decides to destroy a room. How do you continue living there? We should be supporting each other, sharing resources. We are not animals, and even animals behave more humanely than we do at times.

During the tour, the guide asked why we hadn't left the country for the safety of our daughters. I explained that my husband was at the hotel and we couldn't just leave him. The guide insisted that no one needed to be left behind; we should just go. He mentioned that there were no official travel bans and that the restrictions on men of conscription age were more about intimidation. He even named a border crossing that his acquaintances had recently used to leave the country safely. This information was both shocking and intriguing, dominating my thoughts for the rest of the tour.

Back at the hotel, we had dinner and then went up to our room to watch cartoons. As the girls settled in, Artur and I sat on the edge of the bed, deep in discussion about whether we were ready to take such a bold and risky step.

"I don't know, maybe we should stay a little longer," Artur said, running a hand through his hair. "What if they take me at the border and send me to fight?"

I felt a knot tighten in my stomach at his words. "But what if we stay here, and something happens? We can't predict what will happen next."

He sighed, clearly struggling with the weight of our situation. "And what if we trust the tour guide? What if it all turns out to be a mistake? What if we leave and can't come back?"

I looked at him, torn between fear and hope. "But we can't live like this forever, Artur. The constant stress, the uncertainty . . . it's unbearable."

He nodded, his expression pained. "I just keep thinking about the girls. What if we make the wrong choice and put them in danger?"

The minutes dragged into hours, feeling like time had stopped and the world had frozen. We were lost in our thoughts, grappling with the dilemma of whether to risk everything for the chance of safety.

Then, suddenly, another round of shelling began in the city. The sounds echoed ominously through the walls, and our hearts raced. In that moment, the decision became clear.

That was an incredibly difficult time, a truly heavy moment, because I'm the type of person who can't be alone. Artur needs to be by my side. I could never be the wife of a police officer or a firefighter; I simply couldn't handle the waiting, the not knowing. It's too hard for me—I get too anxious and struggle with the loneliness. My admiration is immense for the women who support those in such dangerous professions. They do incredible work.

The evening before we took the bold step to risk leaving the country was mentally agonizing, as it felt like it could be our final evening together. Anything could happen on the road; he could be taken and sent to the front. I remember that evening. He was sitting on the edge of the bed. I hugged him, held his hand, and tried to memorize every detail of his hand, as if I were an artist trying to capture a beautiful image in a painting. The fear of losing him was overwhelming. I felt I couldn't survive if I lost him. He was the only person on this planet who loved me, who supported me, who was truly there for me. He was the only man I ever wanted to be with. He has been and remains everything to me—more than a husband, more than a friend, more than a support.

I never thought I could love someone this deeply. Yes, I love my daughters, Masha and Dasha, immensely, and that's a different kind of unconditional love. But with Artur, our relationship has only improved with age and over the years together. True, deep, everlasting love isn't easy; it's something you work hard to build. If one doesn't meet halfway, nothing will work out. I'm so grateful that Artur has always been open to meeting me halfway. He is an incredible man, reliable, strong, loving, kind, always there for me.

Given that my husband and I have never been apart—he worked from home, and we were always together—it was unbearable even to think of spending a night without him in the house, let alone taking such a drastic risk. But we had to do it. We had to save our children. I had to save my husband. I couldn't live without him.

No politics, no state structure—nothing in this world, on this planet, in this universe—has the right to take people's lives. In our country, those who flee abroad to save their lives are seen as traitors by those who stay. Both sides have their reasons. At that moment, it didn't matter to me how we were viewed by the country, by friends, by family. My primary goal was to save my family by any means necessary. I felt guilty enough for putting them in danger. I wouldn't wish on anyone the pain of potentially saying goodbye to their loved one for the last time, especially to a beloved partner.

It's terrifying. I was so scared, so hurt. I wanted to scream. Why us? Why did we have to go through this? Why? It was overwhelming. I wanted to cry, but I was afraid to do so in front of Artur. I wanted to support him, knowing he was scared too, that he felt the weight of our decision as much as I did. He understood all the risks involved. He didn't show it, but I wanted to be there for him, to support him through those agonizing hours. Let all loved ones be together. Let all children be with their parents. And let no one on this planet ever know the horrors of war.

Part 2

THE ROAD TO SAFETY

Europe

Each step toward safety is a step away
from what was once called home.

12

A Fragile Peace

First Steps in Foreign Lands

The next morning was set for our journey to another country. I had never been abroad, let alone driven internationally. I was incredibly nervous. I hardly slept, but I knew I needed at least a little rest for the long drive ahead. We packed our belongings and tried to relax, though it was hard to fall asleep. However, we managed a bit of rest just before dawn and were ready to embark on our journey with the girls early in the morning.

As we loaded the last bags into the car, I turned to my husband and said, "Artur, I'm with you, no matter what."

He looked at me, his expression softening. "Thank you. That means so much . . . but honestly, it's terrifying. Are you sure about this?"

I took a deep breath, trying to keep my voice steady, and replied, "More than ever." Inside, I was trembling with fear, but I knew we had to move forward for our family's safety.

Before sunrise, we got into the car and set off.

We drove to the border, where there wasn't a typical customs office, just military personnel who checked our car, noted how many people were inside, and handed us a paper confirming the number of passengers. With that, we proceeded. The experience was incredibly nerve-wracking, but as we drove on, the tension seemed to fade with each passing mile. I could feel my heart start to lift, the hope of safety replacing the fear that had held me tight just moments before. The emotions were complicated: I was fearful because I had never driven so far before, and I was also scared that my husband might be taken at the Ukrainian border.

As we neared the Moldovan border, our radio started picking up stations from across the frontier, broadcasting in a language other than Ukrainian. Masha exclaimed in surprise, finding it fascinating that we were listening to a foreign station. It was an exciting and inspiring moment, especially knowing where we were headed. I was driving toward safety in Moldova, prepared to travel any distance necessary. I was confident that we would make it.

It was the end of March. Following the GPS, I came to a small fork in the road but continued straight as directed. It was only after passing the fork that I realized I had missed the customs station. Panic surged through me as I realized my mistake. How could I be so careless at such a critical moment? It appeared I had inadvertently entered Moldova without going through the proper checkpoint.

We turned around and headed back to customs. I was right; that was indeed the customs area, but it was surprisingly easy to bypass. We waited in an incredibly long queue, which moved slowly, adding to my anxiety. I was also worried about the cat and whether all our documents were in order. The fear of having missed something and potentially having to turn back to complete documents was overwhelming.

When it was finally our turn at customs, the military and customs officials took our documents, and after what felt like an eternity, returned them with an entry stamp for the country. We proceeded on our journey.

I could hardly believe we had made it. The weight of uncertainty that had burdened me for so long began to lift, replaced by a profound sense of gratitude. Then it hit me—we had done it! I turned to my family, my voice shaking with emotion.

"We did it!" I exclaimed, almost laughing and crying at the same time. "We actually made it!"

Artur looked over at me, his face still pale but with a hint of a smile breaking through. "I still can't believe it," he said, exhaling. "I don't think I've ever been this nervous in my entire life. It's just . . . unbelievable."

Masha, sitting in the backseat, leaned forward, her eyes wide and filled with a mixture of disbelief and hope. "Really? Did we actually leave? This isn't a dream, is it, Mom?" She grabbed my hand, as if making sure it was real.

"Yes, Masha, it's real," I said, squeezing her hand. "We're free. We're safe now."

Dasha, our little light, not fully understanding the seriousness of everything, hugged her favorite toy and asked softly, "Mama, are we going home now?"

"Yes, Dasha, we're going to a new home. A safe place where we don't have to be afraid," I explained, feeling tears well up in my eyes.

Artur lowered his head, sighing with relief. "I've waited for this moment for so long . . . Every day felt like a test, and honestly, I still can't believe it's all behind us."

Masha looked at us again, a slow smile spreading across her face. "So . . . we can sleep peacefully? We don't have to be afraid of waking up to a siren?"

"Yes, sweetheart," Artur said, turning to her. "Now we can sleep peacefully. This is our new life."

We drove on, hardly believing that this was actually happening. It felt like a heavy weight had been lifted from our shoulders, making room for hope, for joy, and for a new chapter we were beginning together. Embracing each other, we knew there would still be challenges ahead, but we felt stronger than ever, ready to face them together.

I called Danya first. I asked him to guess where I was, and while he didn't guess the country correctly, he guessed the direction right. He was very happy for us. He had wanted us to get out, to ensure his nieces were safe. After calling Danya, I reached out to Lena and Artem. They had been our pillars of support through everything, and hearing their joy for us was incredibly uplifting. They shared our relief, and knowing we had their encouragement meant the world. We were very fortunate with our friends, and I felt especially blessed to have such a caring brother and such dear friends in Lena and Artem.

During our drive, a sudden loud scream from the girls startled us. "Mama, Papa, a rocket, a rocket!" they yelled, covering their heads in the back of the car. Artur and I were terrified, confused at first. They continued screaming about a rocket, but when I looked up, I saw it was just a passenger plane. That moment highlighted just how deeply the war had affected my children.

As I looked at Masha and Dasha, their innocent excitement, it was heartbreaking to realize that their world had been altered so drastically.

My heart ached for them, knowing that the shadows of conflict lingered in their minds, turning a simple airplane into a source of terror. I wanted to shield them from these fears, to let them know they were safe, but the war had woven itself into the fabric of their childhood. It was heartbreaking.

We pulled over, and I hugged them, trying to reassure them that we were now safe. I told them they could sleep peacefully, look up and see only the beautiful blue sky, airplanes flying with hope, and birds fluttering freely. Our girls were safe now, and it was time for them to start adjusting to a new life, a safe and peaceful life with their parents.

We continued our journey and reached Chișinău, the capital of Moldova, by night. We checked into a hotel and had dinner. The feeling of finally being safe was fantastic. Yet, beneath that relief lay a thread of anxiety as we faced the unknown. In the midst of these conflicting feelings, we craved a small escape from reality. This was a new chapter, yes, but one filled with uncertainty, navigating a world where we had yet to establish roots. An incredible life awaited us. At the same time, being in a foreign country was intimidating. We didn't know the language, had no idea where to go next, and hadn't even planned which country we would end up in. Artur was still working remotely.

From the outside, it might seem romantic to just drive off into the unknown, perceived as a wonderful opportunity. In reality, all your possessions are crammed into a car's trunk, which hardly fits anything substantial. There you are, with your children and a cat, almost randomly pointing to a place on the globe to choose your new home. But there's nothing beautiful about it because you're responsible for your children. Resources are scarce. You can't just fly somewhere you desire, rent a place, buy a car, and so on. Our options were severely limited. We were utterly clueless about what to do next.

The following day, we went to McDonald's, and it was a real celebration for us. Due to the war, chains like McDonald's and KFC, as well as stores like H&M and Zara, had closed in Ukraine because they didn't want to risk their employees' lives. Masha and Dasha were incredibly happy to be safe and were delighted by McDonald's. How easily visiting McDonald's can blend into the routine, something people hardly notice amid their everyday lives. But for us, it was so much more—a symbol of life itself, a reminder of normalcy, peace, and the simple joys we had missed.

As we sat down with our meals, I looked at Artur, unable to hold back my emotions. "I still can't believe we made it out. I'm so happy . . . but I feel like I need time to process everything."

Artur reached over, giving my hand a comforting squeeze. "You did it. You got us all here. Take all the time you need. We're safe now."

Masha took a big bite of her burger, her eyes lighting up. "Mama, this is the best thing I've ever tasted! I missed this so much." She and Dasha giggled, examining the little toys from their Happy Meals, delight shining in their faces.

Masha looked up at me, her face full of excitement and relief. "Mama, I'm so happy we left. I'm not scared anymore. Thank you for listening to me, for getting us out of there."

I felt a rush of emotions, looking at the joy in her eyes. "Oh, my sweet girl, I'm so glad to see you happy again."

That was wonderful. I was so happy just being with Artur. In moments like these, you realize how trivial domestic squabbles are. Whether a cup isn't washed or socks are scattered around—it all becomes meaningless. We waste so much of our lives worrying about petty things that don't deserve our attention. We can simply negotiate the small stuff, no need for arguments or disputes. Just a conversation is often enough. It's wonderful to have a loving partner by your side, to have a family, to be safe. How beautiful the world is when you don't have to fear a bomb falling on you at any moment, to know this for certain, to feel secure—the world becomes a beautiful place. At that moment, I felt like the happiest woman in the world. I was with the man I loved. We were safe. We had made it. We hadn't planned it. We didn't even expect that we would end up outside our country. But we did it. We succeeded. Yet, much lay ahead.

Leaving Moldova behind, we ventured through Romania, Hungary, and Slovakia in just two days—a whirlwind journey through new countries and uncharted territory. Each border crossed felt like a step further from the dangers we'd left, but our final destination still remained uncertain.

We planned to stay in Poland for a few weeks, hoping to take some time to process everything we had been through. Ever since crossing the Ukrainian border, we had been driving relentlessly, stopping only for brief overnights. Arriving in Poland felt like a natural step; we were close, having spent our last night in Slovakia, Poland's neighboring country. This pause would allow us to finally catch our breath and reflect on the journey, a much-needed break after days of constant movement.

But our thoughts drifted further west—to Portugal. There was something deeply comforting about the idea of this country on the edge of Europe. Known for its peaceful ambiance and coastal beauty, Portugal felt like a haven, a place as distant as we could imagine from the chaos we'd left behind. Its location, bordered by the vast Atlantic, seemed to create a natural barrier, and that sense of security was a powerful draw for us.

Portugal's stance during World War II, when it remained neutral and untouched, resonated with us as a symbol of peace and resilience. Deep down, we feared the possibility of another global conflict, and the idea of building a new life in a country with a legacy of stability gave us hope.

As we journeyed toward this dream, the countries we crossed left an unexpected mark on us. Traveling through Romania, the scenic roads and towering mountains felt like an extension of the familiar, yet brimming with newness. The kindness of strangers added warmth to the journey. At a small eatery, a woman taught us to say "Mulțumesc frumos, a fost delicios"—a heartfelt "thank you, it was delicious" in Romanian. Each gesture reminded us of the strength in shared humanity. When language failed, Google Translate became our bridge to the world around us, allowing us to order food and navigate through unfamiliar terrain. Romania's beauty and the hospitality we encountered left a lasting impression.

Crossing Hungary in a single day, we finally arrived in Slovakia, a country as breathtaking as it was unfamiliar. Passing through a tunnel cut directly through a massive mountain, we marveled at the stunning landscapes—a captivating sight for Masha and Dasha, who were filled with excitement as each turn revealed another snowy peak or valley. While these new views were beautiful, the uncertainty of what lay ahead weighed on us. We wondered how we would rebuild a life with only what we could carry.

To my eldest daughter, Masha, the journey was like a dream come true. She had always yearned to travel, inspired by her classmates' tales of far-off adventures. Now she had her own, yet these adventures came with a bittersweet edge. Our cat, distressed from the long car rides, cried and fell ill at times, adding tension to the trip and mirroring the stress we all felt. The kids' occasional squabbles only amplified the strain, but we pressed on.

One surprising moment was when we crossed from one EU country to another without a single checkpoint. Alarmed, I worried we'd bypassed a customs office. I pulled over to explain the situation to a nearby police officer, who kindly reassured me, "In the EU, you're free to cross without border checks." His casual smile was a small comfort, a glimpse of the freedom and unity Europe could offer us in this time of upheaval.

Eventually, we reached Poland and settled in the western part. I'm not sure why we didn't continue to Portugal. Maybe we just needed to pause and process everything after all the constant moving. We needed a place to rest and gather ourselves, as the constant drive was exhausting.

The day after arriving, we tried to find housing but encountered several challenges. First, I didn't know the language and had to rely on Google Translate for basic phrases to communicate that I couldn't speak Polish and that we needed an apartment. Many people didn't even want to speak with me. Although Polish and Ukrainian share some similarities, and I could intuitively understand a few words, my attempts were largely in vain. Either people refused us because we were Ukrainians, or they had preconceived notions. When the war started, it was primarily the less fortunate families who left first, often with government assistance. This created an initial impression of our country that didn't represent us at all, and we faced rejections simply because we came from Ukraine.

Determined not to waste any time, Artur and I decided to head to Warsaw, where he had a schoolmate who had lived there for many years. Despite the friend's invitation to stay with him, we opted for a hotel and continued our search for a place to live. We encountered sideways glances even from those who agreed to meet with us, and more than a week passed without success. People seemed to view us as if we were impoverished or unable to pay rent, despite showing proof of my husband's stable and substantial online income.

Finally, Artur reminded me of my lifelong dream to live by the sea. While the Baltic Sea in Poland is cold, it is still the sea. We decided to explore coastal living options and found a large resort town where we rented a hotel for the night. The very next day, I called about an apartment advertisement and it turned out to be perfect—a three-bedroom on the first floor, ideal since I didn't want to bother anyone with the noise from Masha and Dasha running, jumping, and dancing.

The apartment was wonderful, the people were incredibly kind, and the place had a secure courtyard on the outskirts of town, which I liked immediately. Most importantly, the owners agreed to rent to us. We spoke in English, and that same evening, we decided to move into our rental. The next morning, we bought the essentials—blankets, pillows, linens. The apartment was furnished but lacked bedding, towels, and some kitchenware, requiring us to spend a significant amount to make it livable. And so, we began our new life.

Of course, I was thrilled that we were just forty minutes from the sea. As soon as possible, we took the kids to the beach. It was sheer happiness. I don't know why, but the sea is my place of power. I feel energized by the shore, loving to swim but never going too far out. I could sit by the sea forever, watching the powerful nature unfold. It was happiness—simple, accessible, the kind we had almost forgotten. This was pure, human happiness—safety, family, all alive and healthy. It was a magical moment, one I'll never forget. The feeling of lightness, freedom, security, and the sense of accomplishment of finally bringing my children to safety after more than a year of war was truly magical.

In our new rental apartment, we had a dishwasher, which was a marvel to me since I had never owned one before. Initially, I was hesitant to use it, accustomed as I was to washing dishes by hand. Eventually, I decided to start using it deliberately, gradually getting accustomed to its convenience. The dishwasher seemed almost magical, washing dishes on its own and freeing up so much time that I could spend with my children.

Masha was also thrilled because she finally had her own room, and she felt safe enough to try sleeping there by herself. In the backyard, there was a small playground with a trampoline that belonged to a neighbor's girl. My kids were eager to jump on it, so I suggested that when the girl was out playing, we could ask for permission to use it. One day, we saw the girl who owned the trampoline. She looked about my daughter's age, so I encouraged my older daughter to go over and introduce herself. It was a perfect moment for her to step out of her comfort zone, conquer her fears, and perhaps make a new friend.

Despite their language differences, the girls used technology to communicate, and soon they were jumping together on the trampoline. Dasha joined in, and they all had a wonderful time together. I was so proud of Masha for overcoming her shyness and making a new friend. These small steps, typical in ordinary life but significant for us, symbolically distanced us from the war. We still followed the news relentlessly, supported our loved ones back home, and did everything we could for our country's victory.

My motivation for Masha to meet the new girl was partly because she seemed lonely, often jumping alone on the trampoline after school. It turned out she didn't have many friends and was delighted to make one in Masha. It was incredible to watch my kids from our window playing on the trampoline right below. After school, the girls would bring toys and snacks to the trampoline, where they'd watch cartoons, jump, and play. I was overjoyed that my daughter had made a new friend, as most of her friends from our home country were only in touch through messages. It's so crucial to form new connections in a new country.

Every evening, Masha would teach me new Polish words she had learned, eager to communicate without a translator. However, our happiness was short-lived. One day, the girl's mother came home early from work and saw her daughter playing with Masha and Dasha. She began yelling from the balcony, and though I couldn't understand everything since it was in a different language, it was clear she was forbidding her daughter from playing with us because we were from Ukraine.

It was tough to explain to Masha that it wasn't her fault, that the world just works that way sometimes, and that it didn't reflect on her personally. Masha was deeply hurt and confused about why they couldn't be friends when they got along so well. This incident was painful for both of us. I wanted to protect my daughter, but there was little I could do.

Later that night, as I tucked her into bed, I could see the sadness still lingering in her eyes. She looked up at me and whispered, "Mama, why is her mother against our friendship? Did I do something wrong?"

I stroked her hair, trying to find the right words. "Oh, my sweet girl, you didn't do anything wrong. Sometimes people act in ways we can't understand, but that doesn't mean there's anything wrong with you. You're a wonderful friend."

"But we were so happy playing together," Masha murmured, her voice barely above a whisper. "It feels so unfair."

I nodded, feeling the ache in my own heart. "I know, darling. It isn't fair. Life can be that way sometimes, and it hurts. But you are brave, and one day you will find friends who will always be by your side."

Masha hugged me tightly, and I held her close, wishing I could shield her from these hard truths. "Thank you, Mama," she said quietly. "I feel a little better now."

The pain lingered, though, for both of us. The next day, the girl's father approached us, clearly embarrassed, and offered an apology. He explained how sorry he was about the situation, how he wished things were different. But that didn't take away the hurt Masha felt.

After he left, I looked at Masha, who was watching him walk away with a sad expression. All I could do was be there for her, helping her find the strength to move forward, even when friendship proved complicated and unfair.

As the days passed, I watched my daughter's quiet sadness linger. Despite small joys—a new dress from H&M, a special treat at McDonald's, or laughter over fries at KFC—her spirit felt dimmed, touched by the ache of lost friendship. She would gaze out the window sometimes, watching her former friend sitting alone on the trampoline, their distance now a silent reminder of the world's unpredictability.

I wished I could mend her heart, erase the unfairness, and return her to the innocence of friendships unburdened by adult fears and judgments. Yet, even as my daughter grappled with this painful truth, I sensed a new strength forming within her—a quiet resilience, an understanding of the world that, though bittersweet, would make her braver and wiser.

As I held her close one evening, I whispered, "Life can be difficult, but we're stronger together. Love and kindness will always find their way back to you, my dear." She nodded, resting her head against my shoulder, and I felt hope spark again within both of us.

And so, in this new place, with all its uncertainties, we continued our journey, discovering a fragile peace—together, side by side.

13

The Atlantic Awaits

Letting Go and Looking Forward

On April 21, 2022, the United States announced the "Uniting for Ukraine" program, which offered Ukrainians fleeing the full-scale invasion a chance to temporarily stay in the United States for a two-year period under humanitarian parole. I had never even dreamed of moving to the U.S. It seemed so far-fetched, almost as if it existed only in Hollywood movies. I had always imagined living out my life in my hometown and never anticipated relocating from one city to another, across different countries.

During my volunteer work, I had spoken with hundreds of Ukrainians and heard about their experiences in various countries, forming my own, perhaps misconceived, opinions about each. A friend who had moved several times with her family told me about their plans to try for the U.S., which sounded as distant as moving to Mars. Ukrainians needed to find an American sponsor—either an individual, an organization, or a family—to help with documentation. The process involved the U.S. government approving the sponsor's application before the Ukrainian family could apply. If approved, they received travel authorization. The sponsor was expected to support them initially, without any state benefits. The program was limited to two years.

My friend explained that finding a sponsor could be challenging, with an official website offering limited registration slots and Facebook groups where people posted their stories hoping to attract a sponsor's attention. She had been searching for a sponsor for nine months, a testament to the waning interest over time as many who wanted to help had already done so. I listened to her story but didn't consider looking for a sponsor because even moving to a neighboring country had been a huge leap for me, let alone thinking about the U.S.

We continued our lives, trying to figure out what to do next as further travel through Europe wasn't financially feasible. We needed to earn more to move on, so staying where we were seemed the only option. This uncertainty was exhausting. I longed for a home to return to, not a perpetual limbo with our belongings packed in a car trunk, accompanied by two children and a cat.

One evening, I pondered the idea of applying for the "Uniting for Ukraine" program. I figured that since it seemed like a long shot, at least I wouldn't be disappointed if no one responded. I knew the registration times for the website and set a reminder on my phone. When the moment arrived a few weeks later, I refreshed my browser every second until the registration form opened. I managed to fill out the form and successfully registered on my first attempt. There were many people from different states on the site willing to help, and while it was intimidating, I didn't truly believe it would lead to anything. I sent a few applications at random, expecting no response.

Artur chuckled at the effort, shaking his head as he imagined the distance between us and America.

"You're really something," Artur said with a doubtful smile. "America? That's nearly impossible . . . I doubt anything will come of it." He shook his head and added, "We should be more realistic and focus on what to do next. Just live as we are and look for somewhere to settle."

I gave him a hesitant smile, despite the worry tugging at me. "Maybe . . . but, you know, sometimes it's worth trying something impossible. What if it works out?"

He sighed, somewhat relenting, and looked at me warmly. "Just don't get your hopes up that someone will respond, so you won't be disappointed," he said. "You know yourself that it seems almost impossible."

We smiled at each other, and his words somehow gave me confidence. Yet, I still didn't expect anything to come of it. But just a couple of days later, to my surprise, I received a notification on my phone: A family had replied to my request and wanted to meet us over a video call. I was shocked and a bit nervous; I was about to talk to real Americans.

We set up the call. It was incredibly daunting. I prepared hypothetical answers on ten sheets of paper, using Google Translate to convert my thoughts from my native language to English. I was terrified of speaking English, afraid of making mistakes and appearing foolish.

The video call wasn't a guarantee of anything, and I couldn't imagine it leading to a positive outcome. When the time came, my family gathered around the computer. I nervously shuffled my notes, and Artur tried to calm me. We connected, but the American man did not turn on his camera; it was 5 a.m. there, and he was likely not ready to be on video. Nevertheless, we talked. He asked about us, our lives, Ukraine, and everything in between. It felt awkward due to the language barrier, and I often peeked at my notes.

At the end of the conversation, his voice softened. "Well, I'd be happy to sponsor you. I'll start the paperwork on my end."

I was stunned, barely able to process his words. "Really? You'd . . . you'd do that for us?" I stammered, feeling both excitement and disbelief.

"Of course," he replied. "I can't imagine what you've been through, but we're glad to help however we can. This isn't final yet; my wife would like to join on a future call to get to know you all better, if that's alright."

"Yes, absolutely," I said, trying to keep my voice steady. "Thank you so much. It means more than we can say."

He responded warmly, though I couldn't see him on camera. "We're looking forward to it. And don't worry—we'll be in touch every step of the way."

After we hung up, I sat there, shaking, overwhelmed by the reality of what had just happened. Artur looked at me in amazement and asked, "Are we really considering moving to America?" I replied, half joking, "It seems so."

Artur was concerned about the costs, like airfare, and the practicalities of such a move. I was frightened too. What if it was a trap? What if this person was not who he seemed? But then, I found his professional profile online. He was a professor, and his photo matched the one on the sponsorship site. His wife wasn't in the picture yet, but we agreed that if we could see both of them on video next time, it would confirm their legitimacy.

We discussed how incredible it was that someone from across the globe was willing to help strangers. It was a profound reminder of human kindness, contrasting sharply with the horrors of war we were trying to escape. This experience rekindled a belief in humanity at a time when we needed it most, offering a stark contrast to the devastation back home and a glimmer of hope for a new beginning.

On one of those evenings after our meeting with the American sponsor, as I was cleaning the apartment, it finally hit me. If you want something, you just need to act on it. It's a simple truth, but it's one thing to know it and another to truly understand it. As someone great once said, to live as you never have, you must do what you've never done. This realization brought both excitement and fear. We had never even been on an airplane, and the thought terrified me. There were so many questions and no answers.

Soon, we had our second video call. They turned on their camera, and it was indeed the people I had researched. This calmed my nerves. My cheeks were red, my hands were shaking, and I was sweating from nervousness, embarrassed about my English. But the meeting went wonderfully. We got to know each other better, and they were amazing, kind people. It was thrilling—I was just Natasha, and here I was, talking to real Americans. My excitement knew no bounds.

After several meetings, we sent the necessary documents to apply. It turned out we were the second family these wonderful people were sponsoring. They submitted our applications, and the average response time was about a month. We began to wait, occasionally calling them to catch up. It was always a pleasure to talk to them, and we eagerly anticipated each video meeting. They had also won over my children. We discussed relocation logistics, and they promised to help with plane tickets. We felt awkward about this and agreed to repay them once we settled and found jobs.

Still, there were countless unanswered questions. They planned to create a GoFundMe page for us, hoping for support from their friends and family. I understood the necessity of this, and I appreciated the tremendous help it would offer everyone involved. Yet, it felt uncomfortable. It's hard to go from having enough, just having bought a flat and a car, to being on a fundraising page for assistance.

Among the unresolved issues was our cat. Traveling with her was expensive, and our sponsor's wife was allergic to cats, yet they had planned for us to stay with them initially. I couldn't bear to separate Masha from the cat, the only remaining link to her previous life. She had lost nearly everything—her toys, books, room, and friends had all turned into online shadows. She couldn't just go out and swing carefree with a friend anymore. Nearly all her wardrobe was gone. Taking away her beloved pet was unthinkable.

I was incredibly grateful to our sponsor's son, who found friends willing to temporarily house our cat until we could find our own place. This gesture meant the world to us.

We also needed to figure out what to do with our car. It had become more than just transportation—it was a lifeline, a symbol of hope and survival, carrying us through the hardest moments. Leaving it behind felt impossible, as if we were being asked to let go of a piece of our past that we had fought so hard to hold onto.

For Artur, it represented hard-won accomplishments, a tangible piece of the life we had built and lost. After leaving behind our apartment and possessions, it was the last valuable item we could cling to in a life suddenly stripped of stability. It wasn't just a car; it was our refuge, carrying us to safety when bombs fell, braving miles of uncertainty alongside us. Selling it felt like giving up the last remnant of our previous life, a promise to ourselves to keep moving forward no matter what.

Artur discovered that there was a company that helps with transporting cars from Europe to America, provided that the car meets American standards. Luckily, our car did. It was originally an American model, bought damaged at a U.S. auction, shipped to Ukraine, repaired, and then bought by us. So, in a way, the car was an American returning home. We began planning its "homecoming."

Honestly, we had no idea what we would do upon arriving in the U.S., how we would find jobs, or settle in. The time difference with our country was seven hours, and how to continue working, pay taxes, and adapt to new work cultures—there were countless questions. As we solved some, others appeared. We dove headfirst into this adventure, learning to swim along the way.

While waiting for the U.S. government to approve our application, our sponsor arranged several job interviews for Artur through a friend who owned an IT company. The process was lengthy and nerve-wracking, with no final decisions until we arrived in the United States. This slow pace was typical for America but unusual and stressful for us.

After three-and-a-half weeks, I received a joyful notification on my phone: Our sponsor had been approved. That moment was incredibly uplifting. I had joined a Telegram group founded by another Ukrainian awaiting sponsor approval. This group, which had grown to over ten thousand members, was a valuable source of information and support. We were all united by hope and plans for the future.

Once approved, we filled out the necessary documents for travel authorization. I was terrified of making any mistakes, as the smallest error could lead to denied approval or issues at the airport. Many people learned at the airport that their travel permission had been revoked by the U.S. government without any explanation, adding to the anxiety.

I filled out the necessary documents for travel authorization, knowing that the response could come within an hour—or take several months. One day, while out shopping, I received the notification that Dasha had been granted permission to fly. Half an hour later, Artur received his approval, then me, and finally, an hour after that, Masha. Within a couple of hours, our entire family had received permission to fly to America. I was ecstatic. I jumped and screamed with joy. It was a surreal moment—something unimaginable was actually happening.

When I shared the news with everyone, Masha's eyes went wide with excitement and disbelief. "Wait . . . do you really think we're actually going to live in America?" she asked, her tone both excited and hesitant, as if afraid this was just a dream.

I smiled, my heart full of joy. "Yes, Masha. This is real. We're going to America."

Her face lit up, and she looked at me, her eyes shining. "Mama, am I really going to go to a real American school? Like in the movies?" she asked, barely able to contain her excitement. "Will I even get my own locker? And will I ride to school on a yellow bus?"

I laughed, nodding, as her happiness radiated. "Yes, Masha, just like in the movies! You'll have all of that."

Dasha's face brightened too, and she looked up at me, her eyes filled with curiosity. "Mama, what kind of toys do they sell there? And . . . is there a war in America?"

I knelt down and hugged her tightly. "No, sweet girl, there's no war there. And as for the toys," I smiled, "there will be so many new ones to discover. You'll see."

Artur joined in, smiling down at both of them. "It will be different, Dasha. There are new things to see, and new places to explore, but some things are the same. We'll be together, and that's what matters most."

Masha took a deep breath, processing it all, and then asked, "But . . . what will our life be like there? Will we have a house, a school . . . friends?"

I wrapped my arm around her shoulders, squeezing her gently. "I don't know exactly what it will be like, but we'll build a new life together. It may be different, maybe even challenging sometimes, but we'll figure it out as a family."

Artur chimed in, his voice steady and comforting. "Yes, it's a new adventure, Masha. And we're going to make so many new memories there. Imagine all the places we'll visit and the stories we'll have to tell."

Dasha's eyes sparkled as she asked, "Will there be parks, like here? And maybe a beach?"

I laughed and nodded, brushing her hair back. "Oh, yes, America has parks and beaches, and so much more. You'll see things you've only seen in pictures, like big cities and mountains. It's a big country."

They both beamed with excitement and wonder, and I felt an overwhelming sense of gratitude that this dream was finally coming true for us all. Artur looked at me, his gaze filled with pride and warmth. "Can you believe it?" he said softly, almost as if he were talking to himself.

I nodded, feeling a rush of gratitude. "No, it still feels like a dream. But it's a dream that's coming true."

We informed our sponsors, who were thrilled and said it was time to start buying plane tickets. They preferred that we arrive at the end of June. I was slightly disappointed because I had hoped we would fly sooner and didn't expect to wait another two months. However, the news was joyous, and we were deeply grateful. We eagerly awaited the end of June, ready to start our new chapter in America.

While we waited, Artur and I realized we had only a few thousand dollars, clearly not enough for our initial expenses in the U.S. Despite my deep attachment, Artur insisted we had to sell the car. In our country, it was valued at $10,000, but in Poland, we could only get $6,000 for it. This meant I would have to drive back to Ukraine, sell the car, and then return—a daunting journey by bus or train since there were no flights.

This initiated a personal crisis for me. The car wasn't just a vehicle; it was part of me. My father had been a bus driver and often took me on trips, especially during the summers of my childhood. These are warm memories for me. Vehicles, from cars to buses, have always been more than just transportation; they represented a fascinating world that opened up countless opportunities for our lives.

One of my acquaintances in Ukraine had been dreaming of buying a car and had even considered mine because she wanted something similar. I reached out to her to see if she had made a purchase yet. She hadn't, struggling to find a good car. I told her I was selling mine, which was in perfect condition. We agreed on a price of $9,000—a compromise that seemed fair. We just hadn't set a date for me to return to Ukraine and make the sale, but planned for it to happen within a week.

If the thought of selling the car was incredibly painful, the idea of returning to Ukraine was terrifying due to ongoing bombings. I dreaded the long solo drive and was overwhelmed by my emotional attachment to the car. Every time I drove, I would stop and cry, particularly moved by Miley Cyrus's song "Nothing Breaks Like a Heart." I felt like a traitor, abandoning a part of myself. It took me weeks to come to terms with the inevitability of letting go, and just when I had nearly accepted it, during another video call with our sponsors, the conversation turned to the car.

I explained that I had found a buyer and planned to return to Ukraine to sell it. The sponsors were concerned about the safety of returning and suggested that it was a bad deal. They pointed out that the car would sell for much more in the U.S. and that even with the costs of shipping from Europe, it would be cheaper than buying a similar quality car there. They urged us not to go back to Ukraine and to bring the car with us to America.

It felt like a miracle. For the first time, I didn't feel like a traitor. Their willingness to help navigate the shipping was incredible. We were almost out of money after arranging for the car's transport, and they asked how much we needed to complete the process. We considered arranging the shipment from a port in Poland ourselves to save costs, but after researching and contacting various companies and ports, I found that the prices were higher than using a firm in Germany.

Eventually, we decided to travel to Germany to ship the car to the U.S., and from there, fly to America. This resolution lifted a huge burden from my shoulders, transforming a period of intense stress and emotional struggle into one of relief and gratitude. Our sponsors' support and understanding in preserving a piece of our past as we prepared to embrace a new future was a profound gift, making this transition far more bearable.

Our sponsors also generously purchased plane tickets for us—and, as it happened, our departure date coincided with our twelfth wedding anniversary, giving added symbolism to our new chapter. Although the GoFundMe page they set up did not raise as much as hoped, they reassured us that the most important thing was our safe arrival in the U.S.

As we prepared for the flight, I grappled with the logistics of air travel, which was entirely new to us. We could only bring carry-on luggage due to our financial constraints, limiting us to essentially starting anew with very few possessions. We purchased essential clothing from H&M and packed minimal personal items, ensuring we had just enough to start over. The sponsors had arranged to lend us a vehicle upon arrival, alleviating my concerns about transportation, though I was wary of using someone else's car.

In a generous turn of events, when we informed our apartment landlords in Poland about our move, they released us from our contract without demanding the typical fees, touched by our story and the opportunity that awaited us in the U.S. Their kindness was a reminder of the goodwill that still exists in the world.

As we sat in their small, warmly decorated kitchen, our landlord shared a story that surprised us both. "You know," he began, looking down at his hands with a wistful smile, "I spent my whole life working as a sailor. I've seen a lot of the world from the deck of a ship. America . . . that was always the dream for my wife and me. For fifteen years, we tried everything we could to get there."

He paused, glancing over at his wife, who nodded gently in understanding. "We applied for visas more times than I can count, but each time, we were refused. We tried the green card lottery too, year after year, hoping for that one lucky chance. But . . . it just never happened for us."

I felt a pang of sadness at his words, knowing how deeply this dream had meant to them. His wife took his hand, and he looked back at us with a warm smile. "But hearing your story, knowing that you and your family will have this chance—it brings us joy, truly. I'm happy that someone else's dream of America will come true, even if it's not ours."

I was deeply moved by his kindness and sincerity. "Thank you so much," I said, my voice thick with emotion. "Your generosity means so much to us. We'll carry your story with us, and we'll remember your kindness."

He smiled, his eyes bright. "Go and make the most of it. You're carrying a little piece of our dream with you."

In the month leading up to our departure, I administered calming medication to our cat to prepare her for the flight. We decided to spend the remaining time in Poland before moving to Germany, close to the port from where we would ship our car. This serene setting was a stark contrast to the anxiety we felt about our future.

Our time by the sea was marred only once by a hurtful encounter with two men who mistook us for Russians and insulted us. This incident painfully highlighted the broader geopolitical tensions affecting personal identities and reminded us of the challenges we might face abroad due to our language and heritage.

As we prepared to embark on this significant journey, our emotions were a mix of excitement for the new opportunities and a natural anxiety about the unknowns of life in a new country. We also faced new challenges.

The transport company unexpectedly increased the shipping cost for our car, forcing us to reach out to our sponsors for help. Although it felt uncomfortable, they responded with understanding and support, which was a huge relief. We moved closer to the German border, settling into a modest motel, and continued preparing for the upcoming move. We faced many worries—from financial strains to the uncertainty of even being allowed across the border. Yet, despite all these fears, we were determined and believed we could face it together.

We sat together on the bed in the small motel near the German border. I looked out the window, where the endless dark horizon stretched beyond, like a symbol of the future—just as shadowed and uncertain.

Artur took my hand, looking into my eyes with a faint smile.

"What do you think awaits us across the ocean?" he asked quietly.

I took a deep breath, searching for the answer. "I don't really know. It'll be strange to live among strangers, to start life from scratch, but . . . maybe it's the chance we need. A new purpose, somehow."

Artur nodded, his gaze thoughtful as he looked at me. "You know, Natasha, I've realized just how much you mean to me. You've been by my side through everything, and without you . . . I don't think I'd have made it this far."

I smiled, a warmth settling over me.

We sat quietly, listening to the silence around us, without the sound of explosions or sirens. Just a calm, quiet night—like those waiting for us across the Atlantic.

14

Through European Crossroads

Balancing Hope and Fear

Driving through Germany was an intense experience. The autobahns were vast and fast, and I felt overwhelmed by the high-speed traffic. Upon reaching the small port city of Emden, we were struck by the uniformity of the red-brick houses, giving the impression that the wealthiest person in Germany must be a brick manufacturer. The city was quaint, and the apartment was beautifully appointed with everything we needed, offering a brief respite from our stresses.

Saying goodbye to the car was bittersweet. Even as we dealt with the formalities at the port, I pleaded with the inspector to allow us to leave a small heart-shaped pillow made by my daughter Masha in the trunk—a piece of our memories. After a careful inspection, she agreed, and we were grateful.

Before handing over the keys, I took a photo of the car, standing alone in the vast German port, surrounded by brand-new vehicles. Our "Bluebird," as we called it, had become so much more than just a car to us; it was a symbol of all the memories and dreams we had brought with us. I worried we might never see it again, afraid that if we weren't allowed into America, it would remain an ocean away, forever lost to us. Sending it off on a ship to cross half the world was a risk that filled me with anxiety. I couldn't help but wonder if we had made the right decision—trusting that it would reach us safely in a new world, waiting on the other side.

After handing over the keys, we took a taxi—allowed access inside the port—back to our apartment. As we drove in silence, the weight of our upcoming new life in the United States hung over us, mixed with a sense of hope and determination.

The two weeks leading up to our flight felt interminable. Each minute seemed to stretch as I counted down to our departure. Overwhelmed by fear, I sought solace in online information about flying and scheduled a session with my favorite psychologist, who skillfully bolstered my confidence and soothed my anxieties.

Packing our carry-ons, we realized that more than half of our belongings couldn't fit. We faced yet another round of parting with our material possessions. We ended up donating the PlayStation 4 to our apartment landlords, a gesture that felt heavy with the symbolism of letting go. Life without our car had been inconvenient and challenging, adding to the discomfort of our transition.

As we checked our belongings once again, Artur watched me with a gentle smile, seeing how anxious I was about my first flight.

"I can't believe you're this nervous," he said warmly. "You've overcome so much, and here you are, stressed about a plane ride."

I sighed, feeling he was right, but the fear refused to go away.

"It's different, Artur," I replied quietly. "It's not just a flight. It feels like a point of no return—we're flying so far, to a new continent, with so many changes. And I'm scared for all of us."

At that moment, Masha, who was packing her books and headphones into her backpack, looked up at me.

"Mom, did you know that schools in America are totally different?" she said, her eyes lighting up with excitement. "I watched some bloggers who moved to America, and they talked about days when kids actually go to school in pajamas! Can you imagine? Pajama Day! I'm so curious about what it's like to go to school in pajamas and not worry about uniforms."

I smiled, remembering how long Masha had waited for the chance to leave behind the strict school uniform.

"In Ukraine, we always had to wear uniforms, and only when President Zelensky came into power was it finally canceled," she added with relief, thinking of the recent change. "I was so happy!"

I smiled, watching her enthusiasm, and felt that somehow, our fears and her excitement about the new balanced each other out.

"You know, Masha, it might be hard at first, but you'll handle it. And later you'll be telling everyone how great it is," I tried to encourage her.

Just then, Dasha pulled on my hand, looking concerned.

"Mom, if we live in America now, will Santa Claus still come to me?" she asked anxiously, her eyes wide.

I smiled and stroked her head.

"Of course, Dasha, he comes to children all over the world," I assured her. "It doesn't matter where you are—the important thing is to believe in him and wait with excitement."

Yet, despite the warmth of the moment with the children, my thoughts kept returning to the family I was leaving behind. I couldn't shake the worry about Danya. No matter how calm and confident he tried to appear, I understood how fragile life was, especially with the war. Now, leaving for two years under the U.S. humanitarian program, I knew I wouldn't be able just to go back and see him or my parents if something happened. These two years we were to spend in the United States felt so long, and the thought of not seeing them all this time weighed heavily on me.

"I just hope Danya and my parents will be okay," I said softly to Artur. "I'm scared to leave them, knowing we can't come back on the program, even if something happens."

Artur took my hand, squeezing it gently, and said quietly, "They're strong; they'll be okay. And we're going to create a future for the kids. It's not easy, but you know we're doing the right thing."

I nodded, knowing Artur was right, but the quiet worry inside me still lingered. Every small challenge seemed to remind me of the distance we were putting between ourselves and everything familiar. Even here in Germany, the simplest tasks often became complicated, like when we discovered we couldn't exchange dollars for euros to pay for our apartment because local banks wouldn't serve non-customers. Used to a more straightforward process back home, we found these obstacles frustrating and draining, making our temporary stay feel like a constant navigation through small challenges of tourist life.

We headed to the railway station to purchase tickets to Frankfurt, our departure city. The process was complicated by the language barrier, but with the help of Google Translate, I managed to secure our tickets. I had heard tales of the capricious nature of German public transportation—stories of trains that simply decided not to complete their journeys—but I had dismissed these as exaggerations.

However, our train journey to Frankfurt proved these stories true. Midway through our trip, an announcement led to commotion among the passengers, which we couldn't understand. We sought help from the conductor, who informed us through my phone's translator that the train would not go any further and that we would need to disembark at the next station. The abrupt end to our journey was shocking. We were directed to another train, which was far less comfortable and overcrowded. Despite the discomfort, we managed to reach Frankfurt.

Upon arrival, we took a taxi from the station to our hotel. The city was bustling, more so because of a concert by Beyoncé the following day, an event that thrilled Masha. She was ecstatic about spending the night in the same city as the music icon.

Early the next morning, after a restless night, we headed to the airport. It was our first flight, and we had been advised to arrive three to four hours early. The taxi dropped us at the international terminal. Stepping into the airport, we were awestruck by its vastness—the enormous halls, trains running above us between terminals, and the close-up views of airplanes. It felt less like an airport and more like a fantastical world.

We asked an airport employee for directions and began the check-in process, which included weighing our cat and checking our documents. I double-checked our flight permissions early that morning, relieved to find everything was still in order. After check-in, we moved to the next floor where the duty-free shopping area began. We also had to pass through another security check conducted by a German officer who seemed in a bad mood. Unable to understand us, he called an English-speaking colleague. After a brief interaction, where we managed to address all questions, the officer reluctantly stamped our passports and gestured toward the duty-free area.

As we walked through the luxurious shopping area, the reality of our journey began to sink in. We were about to embark on a new life in a completely different world, filled with both incredible opportunities and daunting challenges. The mix of excitement and nervous anticipation coursed through us as we awaited our first flight, marking the beginning of a major transition in our lives.

We were incredibly anxious because we had heard stories about the strict Frankfurt airport and how many Ukrainians were not allowed to board by the German authorities. I knew our documents were in order, that we hadn't applied for any assistance in Germany, and that we had only been there a little over two weeks. However, there was no stamp in our passports indicating our date of entry into Germany—a common issue in the Schengen Zone. This was why the officer had interrogated us so thoroughly, wanting to know where we had stayed and for how long, and demanding proof. Thankfully, modern technology came to our aid. I showed him photos on my phone, which were time-stamped with the exact dates and times they were taken. It was an incredibly nerve-wracking experience, but afterward we managed to distract ourselves by browsing the duty-free shops.

We decided to grab a bite to eat since we had over three hours until our boarding began. Waiting was exhausting for both us and the kids. A mix of excitement, fear, anticipation, joy, and uncertainty overwhelmed us. Time seemed to stand still, but eventually, our hour came. We went through another security check where they checked our luggage, required us to take out our cat from its carrier, and even had us remove our shoes. We were directed to the boarding area, only to find out our flight was delayed. This was frustrating as we had a connecting flight in Atlanta with only two and a half hours to spare. Now, every minute counted as we faced a crucial meeting with an American officer who would decide whether to grant us humanitarian parole—a process that could be quite lengthy.

And then, yet another check began. Everyone waiting in the seating area near the boarding gate was asked to step out and go through an additional ticket check. When our turn came, we were not allowed to pass and were taken aside. An officer arrived and asked us to follow him. We were led into a room and instructed to go in one by one, although I was allowed to stay with the girls. In that room, we were asked to remove our shoes and outerwear, and our hand luggage was thoroughly searched. They inspected us from every angle. It was such an unpleasant, even humiliating, experience. We had already been checked multiple times, with our hand luggage, the cat carrier, and even the cat itself examined. Simply being asked to remove clothing like that was stressful enough. I felt sorry for the girls. I don't know why they treated us this way, but we went through it and finally headed to the gate. This time, our tickets were accepted.

As we walked down the corridor toward the plane, a wave of fear hit me. Through the window, I saw our massive airplane, and panic seized me. I wanted to turn around and flee. The thought of actually getting on the plane filled me with dread. I forced myself to keep moving, even as every fiber of my being screamed to go back. My heart pounded as we boarded. Our seats were at the very back, with two by the window and two in the middle. The girls unexpectedly asked to sit together by the window, eagerly anticipating the takeoff. They wanted to capture the flight with their phones. Artur and I sat in the adjacent row. We placed the cat under Masha's seat.

I had no idea how I would cope with a twelve-hour flight, fearing a panic attack might strike. Dasha was not right beside me but an arm's length away, separated by the aisle. I desperately wanted to hold their hands during the flight. The engines started loudly, and Artur joked that it wasn't even at full volume yet. It took a while before we finally moved to the runway. As the engines roared to life, the noise was deafening. I couldn't hear my family over the sound. I grabbed my husband's and daughter's hands as the plane sped up, and soon, I saw through the window that we were lifting off the ground. My children gazed out with delight, thoroughly enjoying the adventure. As we ascended and the ground shrank away, I was petrified. The takeoff caused intense sensations of free-falling, and I even yelped, which embarrassed me. But the children were thrilled, showing no fear at all. Artur held my hand tightly, knowing I needed his support to get through this.

Finally, we were airborne, and I looked out the window to see clouds floating by. The roar of the engines was loud, yet the sensation was like being on a bus, as if we were simply speeding along a highway. Our cat struggled terribly with the takeoff. She screamed so loudly that I couldn't believe such a sound could come from her. I felt incredibly sorry for her, but according to flight regulations, I wasn't allowed to hold her. I can't even imagine what she was feeling, especially since she gets carsick. As we ascended, passengers looked around trying to locate the source of the crying cat. I too put on a surprised face and asked, "Whose cat is crying?" I was embarrassed to cause discomfort to the other passengers. But I am very grateful that right after takeoff, she quieted down and remained silent until we landed.

The plane soared at a high altitude, traveling over 950 km/h. We flew above the clouds, heading toward a new world, toward life. Toward a new version of ourselves.

The height at which we traveled and the silent stillness among the clouds suddenly brought a sense of lightness to me. I felt that we, like this plane, were moving forward toward hope that was yet to be realized. Looking at the children, at Artur, and feeling the invisible, powerful support of the sky beneath us, I felt confidence for the first time in a long while. We were flying toward a place where a chance awaited us to start anew, in a new world ready to welcome us.

Part 3

THE AMERICAN DREAM, REIMAGINED

Dreams change, but the will to rebuild remains unshaken.

15

Arrival in the Land of Dreams

Crossing the Atlantic Ocean, I realized that many adverse events in our lives often lead to positive outcomes. My yearlong estrangement from my parents had paradoxically given me the freedom to leave the country. Otherwise, how could I have ever left them behind? It was the anger from our disagreement that fueled my courage to make such a move. My life is filled with such ironies.

As I drifted in my thoughts, contemplating the vicissitudes of life, the clinking of trays and faint, familiar aroma of airplane food pulled me back to the present. The journey wasn't just a mental escape but a tangible, sometimes uncomfortable reality. Sitting at the very back of the plane, we were left with the least appetizing food that other passengers had rejected. As a result, we were quite hungry, with only a few snacks to tide us over. Despite this, the children behaved wonderfully, and Dasha even managed to sleep. The cat remained calm; I offered her water and food, but she refused. Every hour, Masha would show me the time on her phone, which stayed the same due to changing time zones. It was an odd sensation, as if time had frozen amid the constant drone of the engines.

Over the twelve-hour flight, we flew over numerous countries, only able to imagine what they looked like from our high vantage point. We saw glaciers, vast stretches of white land, and patches of green interspersed with civilization. We couldn't take our eyes off the flight monitor embedded in the seatback in front of us, which showed our current location. We eagerly awaited the moment our plane would enter U.S. airspace. When it finally happened, Masha exclaimed that the clouds over America were incredible. Artur and I laughed and told her clouds are the same everywhere, but she insisted, "You don't understand, America's clouds are different and uniquely breathtaking."

As we began our descent, the plane slowed down, and we experienced a brief sensation of freefall again. But we were eager to land after such a long flight. The landing was a bit rough, but we were just happy to touch down on solid ground.

We peered out the window at the airport, hardly believing we were finally in the United States. After landing, a wave of relief mixed with tension hit me, knowing that one final challenge awaited us. We disembarked, weary but eager, and made our way to the immigration checkpoint—the place that would decide our future. It wasn't just a line; it was the threshold between hope and uncertainty. Failure meant returning to Europe without money and being unable to retrieve our car.

We moved through the control process, each step feeling heavier than the last. The flash of the camera felt stark, and the cold surface against our fingers as they took our prints left me feeling strangely vulnerable. When we were finally led to a small, secure room with its imposing walls and no direct exits, the reality sank in—our future hung in the balance here, within these silent walls. Officers were present, and the room was filled with chairs. We sat and waited to be called, surrounded by other people in similar situations. Finally, an officer called us, took our documents, and took our fingerprints again before sending us back to wait.

The waiting felt endless. Artur and I held hands, and I could see the anxiety in his eyes. I whispered to him, "No matter what happens, we're in this together. We can handle anything, right?"

He squeezed my hand tightly, a small smile playing on his lips. "Yes. Together," he replied, and I could feel his strength and resolve despite the tension.

After what seemed like an eternity, the officer called us again and stamped our passports with humanitarian parole valid for two years. For a moment, we simply looked at each other, stunned. Then, Artur's face lit up.

"We did it," he whispered, and this time, his voice was filled with joy and confidence.

I nodded, laughing softly. "Yes, we really did."

I turned to the girls, who were watching us with wide eyes. "Masha, Dasha," I said, my voice catching, "We're staying! We can really stay here."

Masha's face broke into a grin as she clutched Dasha's hand. "Does that mean we're Americans now?"

"Not quite yet," Artur said, chuckling, "but it means we can start building a life here. We're safe."

Dasha's eyes sparkled as she looked up at us. "Does that mean we can go to Disney World someday?"

Artur and I burst out laughing, and I ruffled her hair. "Yes, little one. One step at a time."

As we walked out of that intimidating room, I felt a weight lift from my shoulders. Artur pulled me into a quick hug. "We've got this," he said quietly. I nodded, holding onto that moment, our girls beside us, as we took our first steps into our new life.

We immediately called our sponsors to share our success. They were thrilled and informed us that they had changed our tickets for a domestic flight so we could reach them that same day. Due to the lengthy delay, we had to rush to catch this next flight, literally sprinting through the airport. Yet, amid the rush, we couldn't help but observe the people around us with fascination. We were in America, surrounded by people speaking an English we somewhat understood. The realization of being in this new country flooded us with emotions. Masha marveled at every person, brick, and word she heard, completely enchanted by it all.

We barely made it to our boarding time, and the thought of flying again filled us with dread. We were exhausted, having been traveling for over twenty-four hours. Just as we were about to board, the flight was delayed due to bad weather. A storm was raging outside, with terrible downpours, and plans to release any planes were put on hold. After we had stood tiredly for an hour near the gate, as there were no seats available, boarding was finally announced. We took our seats, and the wait for takeoff was prolonged. I felt so sorry for my exhausted cat. I suggested to Artur that we rent a car and drive across several states instead, but he insisted that this was the last stretch and that we needed to endure this flight. The pilot warned us about the bad weather and potential turbulence, trying to uplift the passengers' spirits.

As the plane began its ascent, we lurched forward, a sudden wave of turbulence rippling through the cabin. It felt as if the sky itself resisted, testing our resolve, and every bump reminded me of how far from home we'd flown. The girls clutched the armrests, their wide eyes mirroring my own momentary unease. The jolt was so strong that, had we not been strapped in, we might have been thrown from our seats. Artur sat across the aisle from where the girls and I were, gripping his armrests with a tense expression. Terrified, her eyes wide with panic, Dasha started crying.

"Mama!" she cried, her voice shaking. "Mama, what's happening? Why is it so bumpy?"

I tried to reach out, pulling her close despite the jerking plane. "It's okay, Dasha. I'm right here. We're all right. Just hold on tight," I whispered, though the rough shaking made even holding her difficult.

Behind us, I heard a young woman sobbing loudly. Two soldiers beside her were murmuring reassurances, one of them placing a hand on her shoulder, as she squeezed her eyes shut.

Just then, Masha turned to me, fear in her own eyes. She leaned in close, her voice almost a whisper. "Mama . . . are you sure planes don't crash from turbulence?" She tried to sound calm, but I could hear the tremor in her voice.

I took a breath, doing my best to steady my own nerves. "No, sweetie," I said firmly. "Turbulence can feel terrible, but planes are built to handle this. We'll be fine."

Masha nodded but looked away, her gaze fixed on the rattling seat in front of her. For a moment, I saw her grip tighten on the armrest, her knuckles white.

Dasha, though, was still sobbing, clutching my arm as tightly as she could. "Mama, I don't like it! Will the plane crash?"

Masha's face softened at the sight of her sister, and despite her own fear, she turned to Dasha and took her hand. "Hey, Dasha, you're going to be okay," she said, her voice steadying. "You know what? Planes are just really loud sometimes. It sounds worse than it is."

Dasha looked up at her sister through teary eyes. "But . . . but it feels like it's breaking . . ."

"No, it just feels that way," Masha said, squeezing Dasha's hand tighter. "I know it's scary. I was scared too. But I'm not anymore, because I'm here with you."

Dasha clung to me, burying her head in my arm, while Masha held her hand tightly, stroking it gently. "You're so brave, Dasha," she whispered, leaning close. "Just a little longer, okay? I'm right here."

Dasha looked up at her sister, her tear-streaked face trembling, but she nodded, her grip on Masha's hand not loosening. Masha kept her gaze steady, her own fear set aside as she focused on comforting Dasha.

"We're together, Dasha," I murmured softly, squeezing both their hands. "We'll get through this, all three of us."

Even as the plane shook, I felt the tension in Dasha's body slowly ease. Masha's calm presence beside her, whispering gentle reassurances, seemed to give her strength. Through every jolt, we held each other close, not letting go until finally, finally, the plane steadied above the clouds.

During wartime, some people develop an adrenaline addiction when living under constant threat and possibility of death, with adrenaline continually being released, becoming a habit, and then turning into a dependency. For example, before the war, I would have naturally avoided all possible stressful situations to protect myself and consciously not take risks. But now, during air raid alarms, part of me wanted something to explode somewhere—far from me, of course—just so I would get scared but nothing truly bad would happen, like a missile being intercepted in the air. Realizing this is terrifying. It makes you feel like an utterly abnormal person. If I didn't have my degree in psychology, I might think I was a mad and abnormal fool.

It's incredibly unpleasant to realize this, and on the plane, as we flew through the severe turbulence, I realized that I was not scared; I even liked it, and that was horrifying. I never thought I would feel this way. I'm not a skydiver, not a soldier; I'm not in a profession linked with constant adrenaline. Yet, people in such professions really develop such dependencies. For instance, soldiers often ask to be sent back on missions because they miss the threat of death and the adrenaline rush. It made me feel so disgusted with myself. It's like you're watching yourself from the outside, and you dislike what you see. You just look and think, who is this insane person before me? And realizing it's you is very hard, very tough.

As the plane managed to navigate through the storm, we ascended above the clouds. It was already dark. The flight normalized. We eagerly anticipated meeting our sponsors, who were waiting for us at the airport. Despite the storm during takeoff, the landing—and the takeoff itself—were much smoother and gentler, without significant air pockets or the sensation of falling in zero gravity. Perhaps it was the pilot's skill, but the landing was perfect. And so, we headed toward the airport exit, where our sponsors eagerly awaited us. From that moment, we considered it the beginning of a new chapter in our lives—a chapter incredibly interesting, rich, and beautiful.

Three people greeted us—a remarkable family holding a colorful sign that read "Welcome to the USA." The feeling was both pleasant and exciting, like stepping into a long-awaited dream. Masha's eyes lit up, and she rushed forward, wrapping them in a big hug, her joy spilling over.

"Oh, sweetheart," the woman said softly, hugging Masha tightly. "We've been waiting so long to finally meet you all."

Dasha peeked out shyly from behind me, clutching my hand. The man in the family knelt down, giving her a warm smile. "Hi there, Dasha. We're so happy you're here."

Dasha's eyes brightened, and she offered him a small, shy smile in return. "It feels like a dream," she whispered.

Artur extended his hand, but they pulled us all into a big group hug. "Only hugs allowed today," one of them chuckled, squeezing us tight.

"Thank you," I murmured, feeling a wave of emotion wash over me. "Thank you for being here."

The woman gave my arm a gentle squeeze. "You're here now, and you're home with us. Come on, let's get you settled. There's so much we want to show you."

Hand in hand, we walked to their car, feeling the warmth of family surrounding us in this new beginning.

Stepping outside the airport in Virginia, I was met with an incredible heat, despite it being night. I realized just how hot it was here, and it was so unfamiliar to me. All I could think about on the way to the car was how I would manage to live in such a humid and hot environment.

We got into the car and drove to their home, chatting about various topics along the way. We had just met, yet it felt like we could talk forever. We had so many questions, and everything was so fascinating and unusual. From the car window, I eagerly observed the state of Virginia, wanting to take in as much as I could on this short journey. I was intensely curious to see what America was really like from the inside. I greedily took in every house, every road, every passing car. I wanted to imprint it all in my memory. The sensations were utterly fantastic.

Their home was a large house by a lake in a very picturesque area, just like something out of a movie. The lawns were meticulously groomed, and we drove past beautiful large houses with several cars parked outside each. Despite the night and heat, the view was beautiful. We entered a cozy home and felt our exhaustion intensify. These twenty-four hours had felt much longer than a day. We chatted briefly and then went to sleep.

The first rays of morning light filtered through the curtains, gently stirring me awake. For a moment, I simply lay there, almost afraid to open my eyes, worried it might all vanish. But as I sat up, the warm, unmistakable scent of a foreign summer drifted in, and the realization washed over me—"I am in America." Excitement bubbled within, and I had to stifle a laugh, not wanting to wake anyone just yet. Surprisingly, I thought the flight and the significant time zone change would disrupt our schedules and that we would need time to adjust. However, we all woke up fresh, rested, and happy.

Unable to contain my excitement, I jumped out of bed and hurried to the window to make sure it wasn't all a dream. Outside, beautiful lawns and lovely houses bathed in bright sunshine confirmed it was summer, and life seemed to have fallen into place just because I was here. This was real; our new life had truly begun.

I turned to see Masha stirring in her bed, slowly opening her eyes. "Masha," I whispered, smiling, "Can you believe it? We're really in America!"

She blinked a few times, still waking up, then a smile spread across her face as she sat up. "Really, Mama? We didn't just dream it?"

"No dream this time," I said, reaching over to hug her. "It's all real. Our first morning in America."

Masha leaned into the hug, looking out the window with wide eyes. "It's even prettier than I imagined."

I laughed softly, brushing her hair back. "Just wait until we explore it all, my love. Our American adventure has only just begun."

In that moment, with Masha by my side and the bright morning sun streaming in, it felt like my turn had finally come to live the American dream.

The first few days were spent simply enjoying life and settling in. We were getting used to speaking English, which is quite different from learning it in school and actually using it with native speakers. Thankfully, our sponsors spoke slowly to ensure we understood everything, making it quite comfortable to communicate with them.

They showed us around the area, pointing out schools and shops. It felt like I was in a movie. Everything seemed unreal because I had only seen such neighborhoods and shops in American films. I also adore single-story buildings because I'm very afraid of elevators, so the prevalence of such architecture in America really appealed to me. I was also fascinated by the cars on the roads. When we had just gotten married and visited Artur's parents for a city festival, I saw a truck for the first time—a large red vehicle, which Artur mentioned he dreamed of owning someday. These trucks, so popular here, were not as common back home. I was also intrigued to see a Buick for the first time because I had only read about this brand in the detective novels of James Hadley Chase, and it was thrilling to see one in person.

As we walked through the stores, the prices, all in dollars, seemed unusual. The vast size of the shops and the large quantities of products people purchased at once were also new to us. Yet, we felt a profound happiness. Somehow, the mere fact of having moved to America seemed to guarantee a splendid future for my children.

I imagined myself as the grandmother my grandchildren would thank for giving them a life in America. It felt as if I had won the life lottery, never having imagined that I could simply move to the United States and live in this wonderful country.

16

Celebrating Freedom

A few days later, we traveled to the neighboring state of North Carolina, where our sponsors owned a house by the ocean. It was a fantastic place with a view where dolphins swam in the mornings, appearing almost magical. We attended a large concert and fair celebrating Independence Day, which we thoroughly enjoyed. The authenticity of the American music, live performances, military choirs, hot dogs, and burgers, along with the novelty of being surrounded by English conversation, was both surreal and fantastic. I watched people with keen interest, and we were fascinated by the surroundings and houses—it was like living in a fairy tale.

And there, I cried profoundly because, after years of running from death and war, I could finally stop, look back, and realize I was far from all that danger, finally able to relax. I was ecstatic, overwhelmed with joy that my children would no longer hear the sounds of explosions or face danger. They could sleep peacefully and dream sweet dreams in America.

Despite years of working on myself, I've always struggled with low self-esteem. I've often felt like I was not a good enough mother, wife, or daughter—that I was far from perfect, that I would fail—and often felt discouraged. But being in the USA felt like concrete proof that I had done well, that I had succeeded. It was an incredible feeling, and I wish everyone could experience such immense pride in themselves.

After the fair, we went back to the ocean, where neighbors organized a parade. Each household had a vehicle, mostly golf carts, and everyone dressed up and decorated their carts for a ride around the neighborhood. It wasn't just any parade; it was a celebration of unity and community spirit. I was filled with emotions as I saw families dressed in costumes, all vehicles decorated, showcasing incredible neighborly cohesion. It felt powerful and supportive. I smiled all evening, my cheeks aching from joy, and we were the only ones without costumes.

I was particularly inspired by an elderly couple dressed wonderfully—the woman as Wonder Woman and the man as Captain America, their cart decked out in a Justice League theme. It was fun, communal, and marvelous. Observing it all, I felt the warmth of this society and reveled in the joy of being part of it at that moment.

In the evening, a large neighborhood picnic awaited us where everyone brought some food. We were warmly welcomed and had a great time. I will always remember that small corner of happiness by the ocean, with wonderful, incredible people. We were so glad to be part of that celebration, to share the joy. It was wonderful how vividly they celebrated Independence Day.

As we settled near one of the tables, a charming middle-aged couple approached us, both smiling warmly.

"Welcome to the USA!" the woman said, lifting her glass slightly. "We're so happy you're here to celebrate with us."

I smiled, feeling their warmth and friendliness. "Thank you. It's wonderful to be here with all of you," I replied, glancing around at the lively gathering.

The woman leaned in, nodding toward the creamy cocktail in her hand. "This used to be my favorite drink—a White Russian," she said with a soft laugh, "but right after the war started, I couldn't call it that anymore. So, I renamed it to Zelensky, after your president of Ukraine. Figured it was more fitting," she added with a wink.

I felt a wave of gratitude at her gesture. "That's so thoughtful . . . and honestly, so touching. It's incredible to feel this support here."

Her husband nodded, raising his own glass. "You're one of us now. We all look out for each other here."

I looked at Artur, who shared the same emotion in his eyes. This moment, surrounded by people who welcomed us so openly, felt surreal yet comforting. In that small corner by the ocean, with such wonderful people, I felt at home, truly accepted as one of them.

That evening, as the fireworks began, our sponsors were particularly concerned about us and our children. The sounds of fireworks, faintly resembling the echoes of explosions, can be profoundly distressing for those who have survived war. When the fireworks started, Dasha was afraid. I tried to reassure her, attempting to bring her to the window to show her that these were just fireworks, a display of joy and safety, but she was too scared to even step forward. Masha ventured outside to watch, though she too was frightened.

Artur suggested I join her, and honestly, we both felt scared as well; we hadn't fully recovered from the war. We knew it was just fireworks, that we were in a safe place, but inside, I could feel adrenaline coursing through me, the sounds triggering intense reactions.

I stepped outside to stand next to Masha, and she immediately wrapped her arms around me tightly, burying her face in my shoulder. "Mama," she whispered, her voice trembling, "I'm so scared, but . . . I'm happy, too. I know these sounds aren't dangerous. I just . . . wish I didn't feel this way."

I stroked her hair gently. "I know, Masha," I murmured, my voice cracking. "It's hard, isn't it? We know we're safe, but our hearts are still remembering all that fear."

She looked up at me, her eyes wide and shining with tears. "Do you think," she asked quietly, "that one day I won't be afraid? That I can hear fireworks and just . . . enjoy them?"

My heart ached, and I hugged her even closer. "Yes, Masha," I whispered. "One day, these sounds will mean only joy and celebration. And I'll be right here with you until then."

She took a shaky breath, pressing her face against my shoulder. "Thank you, Mama. I feel safer when I'm with you."

We stood there, holding each other tightly as the fireworks continued to light up the sky, each burst of color a reminder that we were free and safe now. And as I held her, tears streaming down my face, I promised myself that, together, we would find peace in this new life.

The next day, we returned to Virginia, where there was also a fireworks display in the evening. While everyone else went to watch, I stayed inside with Dasha and our sponsors' dog, who is also terrified of fireworks. The dog trembles long after the fireworks have ended, and they usually give her a sedative, which only works marginally. So there we sat, under the sound of fireworks, Dasha on one side and the dog in my arms on the other, trying to comfort them both. It saddened me deeply, and I found myself wondering how the dog would manage in Ukraine, with its sensitive heart and profound fear. It was a relief to know that she lives in a peaceful country and only has to fear fireworks once a year.

Living in someone else's home was quite stressful. Firstly, because it was uncomfortable and awkward, and secondly, having two children, I was constantly worried they might break something. Unfortunately, that fear was realized when my younger daughter, playing and running through the hallway, knocked over a small table with charming candle holders, breaking one. We were upstairs, our sponsors downstairs. I had no choice but to take responsibility, picking up the broken candle holder, going downstairs, and confessing. I felt incredibly embarrassed and just wanted to disappear into the ground. I offered to replace it but was told that they were no longer sold. All I wanted then was to find our own place and leave this home with as little damage as possible, because no matter how hard you try, small children can be like a hurricane, especially in someone else's home.

And of course, as representatives of different nationalities and cultures, we encountered some peculiar habits. For instance, I couldn't understand how one could leave the house without ironing their clothes, which always amused our sponsors who couldn't see the need for my habitual ironing. And we couldn't grasp why they wore shoes inside the house, as we always take ours off.

Despite everything, I was deeply moved by how these people welcomed us, how meticulously they prepared for our arrival. An impressive amount of preparation had gone into it—there were even daily menus set up, possibly enough for an entire month. We arrived to find all sorts of personal care items provided for us. It felt like we had always lived with them, making us incredibly comfortable and at ease.

Their kindness and attention to detail touched me deeply, filling a place inside me that had long felt empty. Growing up, I had often wished for a sense of warmth and unconditional love, especially from my grandparents, but it was something I rarely, if ever, experienced.

My paternal grandparents were far from the warm and caring figures I had hoped for. My grandmother openly disliked me—she would give gifts to all the grandchildren except me. I remember one New Year's Eve when we celebrated at my aunt's house, where there was a rare abundance of real food. For me, it was pure joy, as such occasions of plenty were extremely rare. My grandfather, my father's father, was also there—a man who always made me uncomfortable. That night, as we lay down to sleep, he ended up next to me. I woke in horror to find his hands and mouth in places they should never have been. Frozen in fear, I fled to the adults, but I couldn't bring myself to explain what had happened. The shame and terror stayed with me for years, buried deep within.

My connection with my maternal grandparents was no easier. My mother's mother, my maternal grandmother, was an alcoholic, and I rarely saw her. I never knew my maternal grandfather—he abandoned my grandmother when she was pregnant with my mother. My mother grew up alone, without love or support, facing neglect and cruelty from a young age. Perhaps this is why I always felt an acute longing for the kind of grandparental love and support I saw other children receive. It seemed like there was no one who loved me simply for being me.

Later, when I met people who genuinely cared about me and my family, who included us in their lives with kindness, it was profoundly touching and healing. Their support wasn't just help in the present; it felt like a balm for the things I had missed in childhood. There is a psychological concept called transference, where people unconsciously project emotions and unmet needs from past relationships onto new ones. I found myself doing exactly that, seeing these caring individuals as the figures I had longed for. Their sincere kindness and warm support seemed to fill the emptiness left by old wounds.

Our sponsors were incredibly open and extraordinary. I honestly cannot fathom how they dared to live with strangers; it's such a significant step. Moreover, they occasionally left for their other home in North Carolina, sometimes for several days, trusting us to stay alone in their house—something that still amazes me. This showed a tremendous amount of trust, and we treated their home and possessions with the utmost respect. We were very careful about how we moved and interacted with everything around us. We cooked traditional Ukrainian dishes and welcomed them warmly when they returned.

After the celebrations, as we settled into this new life, a deep sense of responsibility weighed on us. It wasn't just a fresh start; it was a chance to build a safe, stable life for our children, far from everything we had endured. With that in mind, Artur was the first to act, calling his prospective workplace to inform them of our arrival and his readiness for an in-person interview.

Our sponsors helped prepare him for the interview, advising him that it was crucial to wear a suit, which seemed strange to us because, back home, wearing a suit to an interview for such a position is optional and depends on the job level. We bought a suit, and he went for the interview. I was very anxious, only imagining what salary they might offer, if any at all. Time seemed to drag on. I could hardly wait for Artur to return and share the results.

When he came back, he said there were no substantial updates yet; they would contact him. I was very disappointed. In our country, everything is much faster, including job placements. It's difficult for people accustomed to quick resolutions to understand, because if I am looking for a job, it likely means I need money immediately.

That evening, as we sat together, I couldn't hold back my frustration. "Artur," I began, frowning, "How could they not hire you on the spot? You have such an impressive resume! More than a decade of experience at one of the largest banks, and your English is excellent. What else could they possibly be looking for?"

He sighed, giving my hand a gentle squeeze. "I know," he said, a hint of resignation in his voice. "Back home, it would be so different. But here . . . things just work slower. They probably need time to go through their own process."

I shook my head, still unable to understand. "But they should see what an asset you are! It's not fair to keep us waiting, especially when we need this job so much."

He looked at me with a tired but calm expression. "I get it, believe me. It's frustrating, and I feel the same way. But we can't change how things work here. We just have to be patient."

I took a deep breath, trying to calm my emotions. "You're right," I admitted quietly. "It's just hard to accept that they don't see your value right away."

Artur smiled softly, his calmness grounding me. "We'll get there. I know it's difficult, but we'll manage. I'll keep doing what I can with the remote work for now, and eventually, something here will come through. Together, we'll make it work."

Though his words helped, the sense of injustice lingered. But I knew we had no choice but to wait, as hard as it was to accept.

As the days turned into weeks, we learned that waiting is part of the process here. Our sponsors mentioned that it's perfectly normal in America to spend six to eight months job searching. But how is one supposed to live during that time?

We were not used to waiting so long, and it felt torturous. After some time, there were a few calls, and they said they would send an offer. We eagerly awaited this document, but days passed without anything arriving, compounding our anxiety.

The day the offer finally arrived, we were very happy. However, the salary was not what we expected and did not match my husband's level of expertise. It was disappointing, a common grievance among many Ukrainians who move to the U.S., because work experience from Ukraine is often undervalued and irrelevant here. Everything must start from scratch. What's worse is that often, even the educational qualifications need to be reacquired because our education is not recognized here. It's one thing to arrive young and another to come at an older age and have to study again. Meanwhile, you still need to eat, live, and support a family. Artur was hired as a junior specialist, which was upsetting given that he was a top-level expert in Ukraine. The low salary meant that I needed to urgently find a job.

When Artur went to his new job to familiarize himself with the office and team, he was assigned to a project outside his expertise. He tried to explain his strengths lay elsewhere, where the company needed expertise, but they didn't seem to listen, placing him where he might be less effective. This saddened me deeply. I remember crying bitterly in the car with our sponsor, feeling immense sympathy for my husband.

Earlier that day, we had gone to look at nearby schools and churches with her, but on the way back, right as we reached her driveway, I couldn't hold back my frustration anymore. "I just don't understand!" I exclaimed, my voice breaking. "This is completely illogical. It's like forcing a top surgeon to retrain as a dentist! Why would they make him work on something far from his expertise when they clearly need someone with his skills?"

She sighed softly, her hand reaching over to rest on mine. "I know, dear. It doesn't make any sense. It's frustrating to see someone so qualified not being appreciated for what they can truly bring to the team."

"It's like they don't even see him," I murmured, tears filling my eyes. "He's worked so hard, and I know there's an open position in his exact specialty. I just don't understand why they'd put him anywhere else."

She nodded, giving my hand a gentle squeeze. "Sometimes, the process here is hard to understand. But I have no doubt that in time, they'll realize his value. Until then, we're here for you. You're not alone in this."

As I looked at her, I felt a small surge of relief, knowing we had her support through this difficult adjustment. It's tough to lose one's professional status, financial security, and societal position upon relocating. My husband handled it admirably, always prioritizing our family, which was both heartwrenching and difficult considering how illogically his company acted.

That evening, as I watched Artur, tired but unwavering, I felt a renewed sense of determination. No matter how many setbacks we faced, I knew we would find our way. He had already given so much for our family, and now it was my turn to stay strong. Together, we had crossed oceans, left behind everything familiar, and braved the unknown. And somehow, I was certain we would rise again.

This was just another beginning—one of many in this new land.

17

Between Gratitude and Growing Pains

Due to our eagerness to find our own place, our sponsors helped us look for housing. We saw several options from the outside but didn't schedule any viewings. We liked one house in particular, but unfortunately, we never got a response about viewing it. Time was passing, and it was crucial not to overstay our welcome. Eventually, our sponsors found us a townhouse. We visited and it was decent, but I didn't really like it. However, I felt awkward being picky since options were limited and our sponsors were covering the first month's rent.

The day I went to see the interior of the townhouse, it became clear it wasn't the dream home I had imagined—but it was a start. I preferred a detached house because the girls, Masha and Dasha, can be noisy, and I didn't want to cause or experience discomfort, especially in a foreign country. But we had no other options, so I agreed to take it. I tried to set my expectations aside, reminding myself that this was only temporary, but it was hard to shake the small feeling of disappointment. Finally, though, we had a place of our own to settle into and call "home." The first step felt like a relief—until I realized the next hurdle lay ahead. The house was completely unfurnished, and, to my surprise, that was the norm here. It was unexpected since rental homes in our country usually come with furniture. Here, moving involves not just personal belongings but also large furniture hauls. Now we had a house but no furniture.

Since our sponsors had prepared for our arrival and told their friends about us, some donated furniture. Someone gave us a dining table and chairs, another an old sofa, and another a bed. Accepting help from strangers, relying on donated items—these were foreign experiences for us, and I felt both grateful and humbled. Every small kindness felt like an immense gift, even if it came with moments of discomfort and adjustment. Gradually, our new home started to take shape, piece by piece, thanks to these gestures of support.

We still needed to find beds for the girls, desks, and other pieces. Our sponsor directed us to a website offering free furniture for pickup. We found some small necessary items, a bed, and mattresses. We had to drive around picking them up, which was uncomfortable because not all the furniture was in good condition; much of it was in terrible shape, even unusable. Yet, we had to express immense gratitude and thank people for their generosity.

Adjusting to life in America involved navigating a myriad of challenges, and it was particularly tough handling situations that dealt blows to our self-esteem. Picking up used furniture from strangers was one such challenge. Although incredibly grateful to those who helped furnish our home, it was a bittersweet experience. It's distressing to feel like you're begging for items, especially when they are in poor condition. This struggle was compounded by our cultural unfamiliarity with buying second-hand items, which seemed perfectly normal to our sponsors but was unacceptable to me. Despite arriving with practically nothing, I made it a point to buy new clothes for Masha and Dasha, wanting them to have something that no one else had worn.

Once we settled into a place, we were able to enroll the girls in a nearby school. They were excited because during the pandemic they had grown tired of online learning but had been forced to continue this way due to the war. They longed for live interactions, and Masha frequently cried in anticipation of meeting new friends and just being a regular girl again.

One evening Masha sat beside me, her eyes sparkling with a mixture of hope and nervous excitement.

"Mama," she began, "do you think . . . do you think I could have friends like Mei does in *Turning Red*? I just want friends like that so much."

I smiled, recognizing the familiar look on her face—she had watched that movie dozens of times, captivated by the close friendship of Mei with her best friends, Miriam, Priya, and Abby.

"I know you will, Masha," I reassured her, stroking her hair. "I can see you already imagining it, can't you?"

She nodded enthusiastically, her voice brimming with anticipation. "I picture it all the time, Mama. I imagine us sitting together in class, passing notes, sharing snacks during breaks, just like Mei and her friends. They always laugh together, even when things are hard. I really want friends who are just . . . always there, no matter what."

I hugged her gently. "You deserve friends like that, my love. And I'm sure there are people waiting to meet someone as wonderful as you."

She smiled, leaning against me. "I want to show them all the things I love, Mama. And maybe they'll like me for who I am."

In that moment, I felt her excitement and her dreams for a new beginning, a chance to find a group of friends who would become her own "sisterhood," just like in the movie. It made me realize how much she had missed out on, how deeply she craved connection.

As we focused on settling into our new life, another long-awaited piece of home finally reached us—our car had arrived in America and was waiting for us at the port in Baltimore. After days of navigating new rules, unfamiliar routines, and countless minor challenges, the arrival of our car felt like a light at the end of a long tunnel. It was a piece of our old life, a reminder of home that brought a sense of stability. And with the car came the chance to explore, to break free from these constant worries, even if just for a short drive to the coast.

A neighbor of our sponsors offered to help by driving me there to pick it up. The drive to Baltimore passed in a flash thanks to his company. He was an incredibly intelligent man with a rich history, making the journey enjoyable and the conversation fascinating. I found myself genuinely enjoying the time with him—he was remarkable, and his stories were captivating. Despite the long journey, I felt deeply grateful for his selfless help.

As we drove, he asked me about the war, his tone filled with genuine sympathy and sadness.

"I'm so sorry for what your country is going through," he said, shaking his head slightly. "The news here is heartbreaking. But do you think the way they report on Ukraine here is accurate?"

I nodded. "Yes, completely. What you see in the U.S. news aligns with what we know is happening. But Russia . . . well, they show their people a completely different story."

His eyes widened slightly. "Really? How different?"

I sighed, thinking about Artur's family, who were under occupation. "It's night and day. My husband's parents are with his grandmother under Russian control. She only has access to Russian television, and the things they broadcast are... insane. It's nothing like the truth. They twist everything."

He looked at me with genuine disbelief and sadness. "It's hard to imagine, being cut off from the truth like that. It must be so confusing for people."

"It is," I agreed, feeling a mix of frustration and sorrow. "Sometimes, it feels like they're living in a different world entirely. I just wish they knew what was really happening, but that's the control they have."

He nodded solemnly. "It's tragic, really. But remember, you have support here. There are people who stand with Ukraine."

Those words touched me deeply, a reminder of the compassion and understanding we had found here. This wasn't just a trip to retrieve our car—it was a reminder of the shared values and empathy that connect people, even across continents.

Reaching the port and finally seeing our car was a profound moment of joy and accomplishment. The process of retrieving it involved some bureaucracy, but eventually, I was handed the keys. Overwhelmed with happiness, I impulsively hugged the port worker. I felt like a child whose dream had just come true. I was somewhat embarrassed by my emotional display, as it was uncharacteristic of me. Starting the car was another relief; we had worried that the battery might be dead after such a long transit, but it started without issue, waiting faithfully for me under the Baltimore sun.

There's a screenshot I keep as a memento of Artur worrying about our car. When I sent him a photo of the car, his joy was immense. We headed home, me following our neighbor. However, my phone was nearly dead, and mysteriously, the charger was missing from the glove compartment. Moreover, the car's built-in navigation system only had European maps, so neither it nor I knew the way. It was just my nearly dead phone and me, trying to navigate our way back to our new life.

Lost amid the flow of traffic, I felt a wave of panic. My phone was barely clinging to life, and I worried about being stranded somewhere in the middle of America, unable to call our sponsors or Artur for help. The reality of driving alone in the U.S. was daunting; the road signs here differed from those in Europe. Despite having learned the new traffic rules, I was quite afraid.

I am grateful that my phone's battery lasted long enough to get me home. In hindsight, I realize I could have stopped at a gas station to buy a charger. Why didn't I think of that then? When we finally arrived, Artur and the children rushed out to greet me, and we took the car for a spin around town, relishing the freedom it brought us from relying on taxis just to get to the nearest store.

In addition to the joy of finally having our own car, it meant I could fulfill a lifelong dream: to see the ocean. Living only two and a half hours from the coast, I was thrilled. Standing there, feeling the waves lap around my ankles, I could finally breathe deeply. It was as if the vastness of the ocean washed away some of the stress and doubt that had been building inside me. For a few precious moments, everything felt manageable. The ocean's waves mesmerized me; the warm water made it a moment I wished could last forever.

We initially drove around with Ukrainian license plates, which surprisingly made us a bit of a local curiosity. People often took photos and asked us about our origins at traffic lights. Proudly, I didn't want to change them, but eventually, we had to comply with U.S. law. Registering the car took months, filled with challenges, but it was worth it.

Obtaining a U.S. driver's license seemed straightforward since I had spent much of my life driving. I mastered the road signs and rules in English, but passing the theory test took five attempts, which was frustratingly difficult. Each failure was heartbreaking, especially since I was determined to pass in English, despite the challenges. Finally, I opted to take the test in my native language and passed easily, including the driving test. Getting my driver's license was about more than legality; it symbolized my ability to adapt and thrive in America.

One of our sponsors' friends, remarkable and wonderful people we will always remember with special warmth and gratitude, gifted us a desk for my younger daughter, Dasha. This desk, though not in the best condition, held immense emotional value for them as it was handcrafted by the woman's father and passed down through generations in their family. Artur and I decided to repaint it pink.

When we sent a photo of the repainted desk to the woman who gave it to us, she sent back a heartfelt message. She expressed how happy her father would have been knowing the desk was still bringing immense value to children and had gained a new life. The refurbished desk looked fantastic and as good as new, a testament to the power of human sincerity and kindness.

Since we had repainted the desk, we also decided to freshen up the paint on our porch, which was peeling and clearly needed a touch-up. We thought we had matched the paint color perfectly, but a few days later, we received a stern letter from our property management company. They informed us that we had illegally repainted the porch, threatened legal action, and demanded we return it to its original color. This was shocking to us because, in our home country, tenants are often appreciated for making improvements without asking for compensation.

We went back to the hardware store and, with help from a store representative, managed to find a near-identical color based on a photo of the porch before our paint job. I had to repaint it again, but thankfully, this color satisfied the management company, and the issue was resolved.

Understanding that we were navigating a different culture, where adaptations were necessary and integration a process, I also faced the challenge of finding employment. With two master's degrees, one in psychology and another in management, I had hoped for a well-paying job beyond minimum wage. These were great dreams, but they painfully crashed against the harsh rocks of reality.

My education here seemed irrelevant, and my work experience was of little interest to employers. To work as a psychologist, I was told I would need a doctoral degree, a seven-year commitment that was daunting and unfeasible, especially considering my visa only allowed me two more years in the country. The cost of education in America was astonishing, and this realization was deeply disappointing. My job search was increasingly pointing towards cleaning or fast food, options that did not excite me at all.

Every job I found offered only minimum wage, which hardly matched the living costs and prices of essentials. It was disheartening, a stark contrast to the achievements and capabilities I knew I had. In this new country, it felt as if I was invisible, as if I were a fresh high school graduate with no experience or education. This was not what I had prepared for. I was ready to work hard and build a career, but I wasn't prepared for this reality—a heavy burden many immigrants face.

One day, a friend of our sponsors visited us and mentioned that an acquaintance who owned an online language school was looking for Ukrainian language teachers. I was elated. She gave me the contact details; I reached out but got no response. I learned that in America, you often need to persistently follow up with employers to show your interest, a practice that contradicts everything I knew about job searching.

It felt like stepping into a world where black was white and white was black. My sense of direction and priorities were completely skewed. I followed up, and they responded, saying they would be in touch. Eventually, I got an interview, prepared a demo lesson, and performed excellently. But I was told I was chosen because our sponsor's friend had put in a good word for me. It was bewildering and somewhat unfair that getting a job often depended on recommendations. What about talented professionals, especially newcomers without a network of influential connections?

I was thrilled about this new job opportunity. It promised to pay four times the state minimum wage—an impressive salary that would allow me to work from home, adjust my schedule around my daughters' school timings, and spend quality time with them. I eagerly calculated my potential earnings, almost matching Artur's income.

However, it turned out I would have only one student, and the sessions would last just half an hour each. This revelation crushed all my hopes and expectations. Despite enjoying teaching Ukrainian and the satisfaction it brought, the preparation for each lesson took five to six hours to ensure it was enriching, fun, and educational—all packed into a mere thirty minutes. This was a huge disappointment and felt like a massive letdown.

That evening, I sat at the kitchen table, feeling drained, when Artur came in and immediately noticed my low spirits.

"What's wrong?" he asked, sitting down beside me.

"I just found out I'll only have one student," I sighed, staring down at my cup of tea. "Only half an hour each day, that's it. I was really hoping this would be a real job, something that would let me earn more to help the family."

Artur shook his head, gently squeezing my hand in sympathy. "I know how disappointing this is for you. You put so much effort into preparing, and I can see how much it means to you. But you're still just getting started. Maybe other students will come in time."

I nodded, trying to share his optimism, but the disappointment lingered. "It's just . . . it's hard when you build up big plans, only for everything to turn out so differently."

Artur smiled, giving my hand a reassuring squeeze. "You see it as a setback, but I see it as the first step. Every step takes us closer to what we want. Give it time. Things will work out."

His words brought me a sense of relief, even if the feeling of disappointment still smoldered within. I knew Artur was right, but it was hard to accept that the beginning of this journey could be so challenging, demanding such patience and resilience.

18

An Immigrant's Trial

From Dreams to Reality

As the teaching job provided negligible income, my job search continued, and one day our sponsors mentioned that the cleaning company they used was hiring. I reluctantly took a position cleaning homes, which was incredibly stressful for me. I had never expected to find myself in such a role, having been accustomed to a different lifestyle. Cleaning your own home is one thing, but cleaning for others felt very different and was a tough hit to my self-esteem.

The company was small, just the founder and one other employee, both of whom were wonderful women who excelled at their jobs. On my first day, they showed me the ropes, and I was eager to follow their guidance since I represented not just myself but the company's reputation. However, the physical demands of the job were punishing. My body ached tremendously after work; I would come home, lie down, and be unable to move, needing considerable time to recover and adapt to the physical strain.

They had promised me a certain wage, but instead, I was put on a prolonged trial period with nearly minimum wage pay. I also had to use my own car for travel between jobs without compensation for fuel, and sometimes the drives to clients' homes took as long as half an hour, which was costly.

Masha struggled with the idea of her mother cleaning other people's homes and toilets. She repeatedly asked me to quit and find another job, her frustration often spilling over in our conversations.

One evening, as I sank wearily into a chair, Masha sat across from me, a troubled look on her face. "Mama, I don't like that you're doing this," she began, her tone firm but tinged with worry.

I looked at her, understanding her concern but unsure how to explain. "Masha, it's just temporary. I'm doing this to help our family while I keep looking for something better."

She shook her head, clearly upset. "But, Mama, you're a psychologist! You can help people, heal their hearts and minds. Why should you have to clean other people's homes? Why should you be the one to . . . clean their toilets?" She looked down, almost embarrassed, as if saying it aloud made it all too real.

I reached across the table, taking her hand. "I know, Masha. I don't love it either. But right now, this is the work I've found, and it helps us have what we need. Here, things are different. It takes time to start over, even with experience and education."

"But, Mama, you could be doing so much more," she insisted, her voice wavering. "You always told me that being a psychologist meant helping people in the deepest ways. Now it feels like . . . they don't even know how valuable you are."

Her words hit me deeply, echoing my own feelings of frustration and loss. "I know, Masha," I said softly. "I thought I'd find a job where I could use my skills too. But sometimes, we have to take small steps before we can take big ones. This is just the first step."

She sighed, clearly still troubled, but then looked at me with that determination she always had. "I just hope that soon you'll find something where you can be who you really are. I want you to do what you love, Mama."

I smiled, squeezing her hand. "I want that too. But for now, knowing I'm doing this for you and Dasha gives me strength. We'll get there. We just have to believe."

Masha nodded, leaning her head on my shoulder. "I know you're doing this for us. I just wish it didn't have to be this way."

In that moment, I realized that, despite my current work, I was still shaping Masha's understanding of resilience. She was watching, learning from my challenges and persistence. And even though it wasn't the path I'd envisioned, perhaps it would lead to where we needed to go. Yet, even with her encouragement, some days were particularly hard, testing the very resilience I was trying to model for her.

There were days when I found myself scrubbing toilets used carelessly by elderly clients, often without even being provided gloves; I brought my own to protect myself. Walking through the luxurious homes of wealthy families with large dogs while having so little of my own served as a stark reminder of all that I had lost. After building a secure life and owning my own home, the reality of starting over, reduced to cleaning strangers' homes, was deeply wounding.

One day, I was tasked with cleaning a bathroom adorned with many small glass animal figurines, probably collected by the homeowner. In the process of dusting and cleaning, I accidentally chipped a small piece off one of the figurines. I was mortified. I knew I should confess, but shame overtook me, and I quietly returned the figurine to its place. This incident still haunts me with guilt for not having the courage to take responsibility—a trait I pride myself on, usually holding myself and my children to account for our actions.

The founder of the cleaning business was a remarkable and kind woman. She understood that I needed more time to complete tasks to the high standard I set for myself, which often meant taking longer than expected. My colleague, who had been with the company for about eight years, spoke Spanish, and I enjoyed learning a few words from her. With my arrival as a probationary apprentice, she finally had the chance to assert some authority, which she fully embraced. I often found myself nodding and hurriedly agreeing to redo tasks, even when I had followed instructions exactly but had not left the carpet pattern to her satisfaction.

The business owner often lamented the difficulty of finding new employees, criticizing people's reluctance to work. I lacked the courage to tell her that the reluctance was likely due to the wages not matching the physical demands of the job. My body struggled with the physical toll of the work, which required both speed and high quality, and I could not keep up with the pace set by those with years of experience.

This was a dark period for me. All my dreams and plans shattered in an instant as I faced harsh realities. Back home, we believed America welcomed intelligent and talented individuals. I had never considered myself unintelligent and had anticipated greater opportunities, but I found myself just another immigrant starting from scratch with only two years to somehow establish myself. It felt like being plunged into darkness, unable to see a way forward.

Artur was deeply distressed by my job. He, too, had never anticipated that I would need to earn money this way. It pained him that his income wasn't enough to allow me to stay home with Masha and Dasha, focusing on their education and managing our household. Despite his own exhaustion, he tried to help however he could, searching for other job opportunities for me, preparing dinner for when I got home, and spending time with the kids. It was rare to see him in good spirits during this time, adding to the strain we both felt.

One evening, as I came home, he was waiting for me in the kitchen, looking tired but determined. "I can't stand seeing you so exhausted," he began, his voice soft but weighted with frustration. "You shouldn't be working like this. It's not right."

I looked down, feeling the weight of his words. "Artur, we both know I don't want this either. But . . . what choice do we have?"

He reached out, gently taking my hand. "I know. I just . . . I wish my job here paid enough to keep you from needing to do this. You're more than capable of so much more. We both know it."

"I appreciate everything you do," I replied, giving his hand a reassuring squeeze. "But I can't just wait around. I want to contribute, too . . . even if it's in a way we never expected."

He nodded, a hint of sadness in his eyes. "It hurts to see you doing something so far from what you're meant for. I'd imagined you using your talents, helping people in ways only you can . . . not this."

I felt a sting of frustration mixed with gratitude. "I know. But right now, this is what we have. And maybe . . . maybe this struggle is just a step toward something better."

Artur took a deep breath, nodding as he pulled me into an embrace. "We'll get through this. Together. And I'll keep looking, for both of us."

Certainly, my husband had been the sole provider for our family for twelve years, doing everything he could for us. Suddenly, it felt like a part of his capability was taken away, and it deeply wounded his pride. This saddened me even more because I wanted him to be happy. I had genuinely believed that moving to America would bring us all happiness, living in a beautiful country full of opportunities, leaving the war and nightmares behind, hoping for better material and moral conditions. But reality was harsher than expected. We were just another immigrant family chasing happiness and stability, only to encounter new challenges.

One day, we went to a liquor store—these are separate establishments in our state. As I parked, I noticed a young man stumbling out of his car, visibly drunk and barely able to walk. I followed him into the store, horrified that the cashier sold him more alcohol. I voiced my concern, suggesting they call the police before he drove off and potentially harmed someone. After some reluctance, they took his license plate number and appeared to call for help.

Later, I shared the experience with our sponsors, who supported my reaction but cautioned me about confronting strangers, especially in America, where some people carry guns and might react unpredictably. Their warning struck me deeply. Where we came from, helping a stranger didn't carry such risks—here, even kindness required caution.

Another day, two utility workers came by, asking us not to be alarmed and, surprisingly, to please not shoot them while they inspected the yard. Artur and I exchanged a look, unsettled by this request. Why should inspectors have to fear doing their jobs? It felt surreal, leaving us questioning the culture of widespread gun ownership.

These realizations were sobering. In the span of a few weeks, we'd begun to understand how differently safety and freedom were balanced here. In this land of opportunity, there were also new fears—an unexpected cost to our new beginning.

19

Finding Comfort in Small Joys and Big Dreams

At last, we had the chance to go to the movie theater—a seemingly simple outing but one we had waited so long for. The war had taken such ordinary joys from us, and in Europe, language barriers made it impossible. Now, though, we could give our children, Masha and Dasha, this small celebration.

Artur and I worked to create unforgettable moments for them, hoping that these new, joyful memories might somehow replace the shadows of the past. We took them to zoos, children's centers, trampoline parks, museums, and every kind of attraction we could find. We worked hard to give them a chance to see a world that was beautiful and safe.

Of course, it took time. Time to live without fear, to stop flinching at every noise, to stop hearing explosions in the sound of thunder. But we did everything we could to ensure that our lives—and memories—became bright again and that our children felt protected.

Then came a day when, before the start of classes, children and parents visited the school to familiarize themselves with the schedule, classroom locations, and meet the teachers. It was very exciting and touching. The teachers were incredibly responsive, open and kind. This was very unusual compared to the former Soviet Union. We loved it. Masha was absolutely thrilled with the school, the teachers, everything around her, because she had only seen such a school in movies, and she had dreamed of having her own locker.

As we walked through the hallways, she couldn't contain her excitement.

"Mama," she whispered, her eyes wide with amazement, "There are so many kids here! Do you think one of them might be my new friend?"

I smiled, seeing her joy. "I'm sure you'll make friends very quickly. You're so friendly, Masha."

She nodded, almost as if convincing herself. "And the teachers are so nice too! They smile a lot . . . not like back home." She paused, glancing around the bustling hall. "I feel like I'm in one of those movies we watched!"

When we entered the school and she saw the wall with lockers beside it, she was just ecstatic, trying to guess which locker would be hers. "Mama! Look at all the lockers! Do you think I'll get one?" she asked, practically bouncing with excitement.

"I think so," I laughed, sharing in her happiness. "Just like in the movies, right?"

"Yes!" she beamed. "I can't wait to put my things in it, my books, maybe even a little picture . . . It feels like a dream."

Watching her, I felt a surge of pride and relief, grateful that she was beginning to find joy and wonder in her new surroundings. It was a very sweet moment, one that made all our sacrifices seem worthwhile.

I thought back to my own childhood, when I dreamed of dance and music lessons that we could never afford. I managed to take a few free piano lessons and learned Beethoven's "Moonlight Sonata," my father's favorite piece. Even though no one really listened, it was a small achievement that felt monumental to me. Years later, when Artur gifted me a white electronic piano here in the United States, I relearned the sonata, and the melody made me feel connected to my father and my roots.

There were other bright moments as well. Once, on my birthday, I came home to find a real piano—a gift I never thought possible, given our poverty. This took me back to when Masha was around four years old and noticed the music school beside her kindergarten for the first time. Curious, she asked what it was, and I explained it was a place where children learn to play musical instruments. She immediately declared she wanted to go there—not just to see the instruments but to play the violin. I was surprised to hear this from someone so young and assumed it might be a passing interest. But she kept asking, and after talking it over with Artur, we decided to give it a try.

We bought her a tiny violin, almost toy-sized, which was challenging to find, and she began her lessons, sticking with it for five years and loving it. But when COVID hit, the transition to online classes dimmed her enthusiasm. She eventually quit, and though we were disappointed, we supported her decision, believing that children should choose their own path, especially in something so personal.

To our surprise, some American schools offer an orchestra class where children play various musical instruments together. This is treated like any other school subject, which unfortunately we don't have in Ukraine. It would be wonderful if Ukrainian schools had this. Masha enrolled in this class, and I was thrilled about her desire to return to playing an instrument. She was especially inspired by the fact that all the kids would be beginners, not all of them even knowing how to play, which meant she wouldn't feel self-conscious about having forgotten how to play over time. She was also very anxious about her poor English, but she believed that the language of music is understood by all musicians, regardless of the language they speak.

We decided to buy her an instrument, a white violin. We've always bought her colorful violins; she's had pink, green, blue ones, and now a white one. We really tried to support her interest in this direction as much as possible. I was so happy because she was returning to this activity. She was doing wonderfully well. She has a great ear for music—she even composed her own songs and melodies, which was magnificent. Masha is an incredibly talented girl, and I am immensely proud of her!

Children's dreams were my salvation, even if they rarely came true. Now, when I think about my daughters, I want to give them more opportunities— not just to dream but to achieve even more. And so the day came when we went to Dasha's school and met her future teacher. At the time, she was starting kindergarten, which is a preparatory stage before first grade. We had high hopes for the schools, that the girls would start socializing with other kids, find friends, and succeed. Although I was very nervous, I was deeply concerned for them. I worried about Masha because at eleven years old, entering middle school, preteen and teenage girls each have their own character and their own struggles with adolescence. There could be abuse, and I feared she might be bullied, become an outsider, or just be unhappy. After so many years of suffering and horrors, she deserved to be just a happy child going to school, having friends. I was also very worried for Dasha because, unlike her sister, she didn't speak English at all. I tried to teach her basic phrases like "I want to eat," "I want to drink," "I feel sick," "I need the bathroom," so she could say something in an emergency. I really hoped everything would work out for my girls, that they would finally be happy.

Then came the end of August, and with it, the start of school. It was very tough—I had become so accustomed to always being with my children, always caring for them, being there. First the pandemic, the fear of dying, then the war and the constant threat to life. It was morally difficult to send them off alone, especially in a foreign country where they barely spoke the language, and it weighed heavily on me, making it hard to sleep in the days before school started. I couldn't imagine how it would go for them, and I was so nervous and worried.

One of those restless nights, as I lay beside Artur, he sensed my worry and gently asked, "You're worried about the girls too, aren't you?"

"Of course," I sighed. "They barely even speak the language. How will they communicate? How will the other kids accept them?"

Artur nodded silently, carefully choosing his words. "I've thought about that too. A new system, a new environment . . . everything's so foreign to them."

"Yes, and it's not just the system," I added, trying to put my fears into words. "In Ukraine, all the kids learn together in one class, and they know each other from day one. But here . . . Dasha doesn't speak English at all. And Masha . . . she's so hopeful about making friends."

Artur reached over, taking my hand in his with a comforting squeeze. "You know, they're strong. We managed, and they'll manage too. And schools here are different . . . I feel like the teachers are kinder and will help them adjust."

"Yes, you're probably right," I replied, feeling a little calmer with his reassurance. "It's just so hard to let them go into this unknown world. It feels like such a risk."

He smiled softly, trying to lift my spirits. "Maybe they'll surprise us. Remember how excited Masha was about her locker? For her, that was already like a dream come true. She may find friends before she even notices."

I smiled, feeling the tension ease a bit. "Yes, she'll have her own locker," I whispered. "Let's just believe in them and support them all the way."

It was an incredibly exciting first day of school. Masha was the first to start, with Dasha set to begin a few days later. She was both thrilled and nervous, wondering how things would go and how the other kids would receive her. The educational systems in Ukraine and America are vastly different. In Ukraine, students have forty-five-minute lessons with fifteen-to-twenty-minute breaks in between, giving them time to socialize. Typically, one class of about thirty students stays together for all subjects, creating a close-knit group of classmates. Here, however, my daughter found herself navigating a new environment where classes are longer, breaks are brief, and students move from one class to another, meeting new faces throughout the day. She had to adapt to this unfamiliar system on the fly, essentially learning to "swim in deep water" without external support.

It was very hard for me that they would be away from me all day. And I also disliked the fact that in America, the school day is very long, even for young children. In Ukraine, little ones study just a few hours, and parents who have the ability take their children home afterward. If there is no possibility to pick them up, children stay for additional time after school. It was very hard for me to send them off.

A few days passed, and Masha was content. She only disliked having to wake up at 6 a.m., which I also didn't like because her school bus came at 6:40 a.m. It was too early; I still don't understand why middle school starts so early, and why it is necessary at all. Why not start school just a bit later, giving parents a little extra time to sleep, especially those who go to work later?

Dasha's school started at 9 a.m., which was very inconvenient because I had to wake up early to drop off Masha, come back, wait, get Dasha ready, and drop her off too. Plus, their return times were staggered and inconvenient—Masha came home at 3 p.m. and Dasha two hours later. This schedule was very cumbersome for me. But school started, and on the first day when Dasha went to school, I had to put her on the bus. It was incredibly hard to let her go. When the bus door closed, I started to cry; it was very difficult to stop. She was so little, her first time going to school, and I was extremely worried about her. Unlike her sister, who could call or text me as she had a phone, my youngest had nothing. I was left completely in the dark for eight hours without my child, and it pained me deeply. I cried that whole day, filled with terrible anxiety and worry. It's morally hard to put your child on a bus and just watch it drive away. We are not used to this in our country; we typically take our children to school personally, as we don't have school buses, and it's different when you see your child being received by a teacher rather than just putting a small, vulnerable child on a bus alone.

In Ukraine, when children start attending kindergarten, they begin with just a couple of hours a day, accompanied by parents, and gradually spend more time there as they get used to the teacher, other children, and the environment, slowly integrating into the educational process. Here, the immersion is sudden and for a long duration, which I really disliked and found hard to accept.

A few days after school started, when I was waiting for Dasha at the bus stop, the bus arrived and she got off very upset. When I asked what happened, she said that the bus made very sharp turns in the morning. I had noticed this and discussed it with other parents whose children took the same bus. Dasha had fallen off her seat onto the floor during one such sharp turn, and the bus driver had yelled at her for "playing around" and not sitting properly. This upset me deeply, and I realized I should have spoken to the bus driver to stand up for my daughter. It weighs heavily on me that I did not defend my child.

As my children began attending school in person after years of online learning, they started getting sick more frequently, and we soon encountered another reality of America: the healthcare system. We had heard that it was both one of the best and most expensive in the world, but we were unprepared for just how costly it would be. Despite having basic health insurance through my husband's job, we paid a large amount each month, only to face additional fees every time we visited the doctor.

The financial aspect was only one challenge. Communicating effectively with doctors was another. I struggled to explain things as simple as air quality or nutrition for my kids in English, often using phrases that sounded clumsy and awkward. It was frustrating to feel intelligent in my native language but sound limited and simple in English.

I continued working at the cleaning company, a job I disliked deeply. I knew it was time for a change, and eventually, I left. Leaving was difficult—I felt as if I was somehow doing something wrong—but I also knew I could no longer stay. My mind had already started drifting to other dreams, especially the idea of opening a restaurant, inspired by my disappointment in the food quality here compared to Europe. Even the same products tasted different, which was an unpleasant surprise.

Whenever we cooked our traditional dishes and shared them with neighbors and sponsors, the response was overwhelmingly positive. They often told us they had never tasted anything better. Ukrainian cuisine, with its simplicity and freshness, offered a richness of flavors that made people feel connected to the food. In Ukraine, almost everything comes from local farms, and we prepare our meals from scratch, which makes them nutritious and satisfying.

The idea of sharing this part of my culture led me to think about opening a restaurant, or at least selling food from home as a starting point. But as I considered it further, I began to wonder if there might be a different path—a way to help others on a deeper level. Perhaps retraining as a psychologist would allow me to provide support in a way that resonates with my journey here. Although I didn't settle on a path immediately, these thoughts sparked a sense of hope. Every small step toward something meaningful made the dream feel more real, even if it took on a different shape. I reminded myself that new beginnings, however modest, could lead to a purpose that brings value—to my family and to those I hope to help.

20

Freedom's Complex Landscape

I continued working as a Ukrainian language teacher and was grateful for each student who came my way. One day, I gained a wonderful new student—a bright little girl from another state who wanted to learn Russian. Although I hadn't originally planned to teach Russian, I had known it since childhood, as it was a required part of life in the former USSR. So I agreed—and that's how I began offering Russian lessons as well. Our lessons became a bright spot in my week; she genuinely enjoyed them, and her enthusiasm was infectious. Each session was filled with laughter, jokes, and a lot of fun. Her ability to pick up new words was remarkable, and she made incredible progress. I cherished teaching her, and those lessons will always hold a special place in my heart, filled with love and warmth.

To earn extra money, I needed to find another job. By then, I had finally gotten my driver's license, and with our car registered, I could start work in delivery. I love driving, so working as a delivery driver felt like a great option—without the heavy physical demands of other jobs. That's how I began delivering food from restaurants and handling grocery orders from supermarkets.

Despite keeping busy with two jobs and adjusting to our new life, my thoughts were never far from Dasha and Masha. I was relieved to see Masha settling in well; she found a friend and seemed genuinely happy. But with Dasha, things were different. She started to change in ways I couldn't ignore. One day, out of the blue, she began to refuse to go to school. She would cry, pleading with me not to take her. Her mood, strength, and spirit seemed to drain away, and she began waking up screaming in the night.

At first, I thought she was simply adjusting, and I tried everything I could to help her settle into her new environment. But after a few weeks, it was clear: this was more than just adaptation. And yet, Dasha refused to tell me what was really happening. No matter how hard I tried to reach her, she held her pain inside.

One evening, as I was tucking Dasha into bed, she clutched my hand tightly, a look of fear in her eyes.

"Mama," she whispered, "I beg you, please don't make me go to school tomorrow."

I took a deep breath, heart sinking. "Dasha, I've noticed for a while now that something isn't right. I keep trying to talk to you, but every time you stay silent. I can't help you if I don't know what's wrong." I gently hugged her, feeling her small hand trembling in mine. "I thought it was just because you don't know the language yet, or maybe you're still getting used to the other kids. But I see now that something bad is happening, and I want so much to help you."

She looked away, visibly struggling with what to say. Finally, she blurted out, "It's my teacher. She . . . she makes me sit alone and read while everyone else plays." Her face twisted with pain as she continued. "Even if I don't know the words, she says I have to sit quietly and read."

"But, sweetie," I said, heart aching, "you're still learning English. Doesn't she understand that?"

Dasha nodded, eyes downcast. "She knows, but she doesn't care. And if anyone else talks in class, she yells at me for it." Her voice dropped to a whisper. "Sometimes she just glares at me . . . like she hates me."

I felt a surge of anger. "Dasha, you don't deserve to be treated like that. You're a kind, smart, and wonderful girl. No one has the right to make you feel scared."

She looked at me with pleading eyes. "Please, Mama, don't tell her I told you. She'll just get angrier and . . . make me sit out again when everyone's playing."

I wrapped my arms around her as she started to cry. "Please don't make her mad."

Her words struck me deeply, filling me with both sadness and anger. How could any teacher be so cruel, especially to a child who was new, vulnerable, and already dealing with so much with war? I knew I couldn't ignore this. The very next morning, I went straight to the school and arranged a meeting with the counselor, the teacher, and school representatives. I brought along my sponsor, who insisted on helping with language and other matters.

Sitting in that room, I felt a fierce desire to fight for my daughter Dasha. How could anyone treat such a young, beautiful creature, who has seen too much and is weary from the adult political games, in such a way? How can someone be a teacher if they clearly do not love children?

We had already faced issues with this teacher because she never responded to my emails except once, at the very beginning of the school year. She also ignored me at parent-teacher meetings, even laughing in my face when I suggested adjusting Dasha's hours to help her adapt or asked how she was doing in class. This dismissive and inhumane behavior was appalling.

At the meeting, it was very difficult for me to restrain myself, but since our sponsor was present, I felt it inappropriate to cause a scene. Of course, Dasha was accused of lying. It was suggested dismissively that since we were from Ukraine and she had seen war, we should perhaps see a psychologist. The meeting was very unpleasant, and I struggled to maintain my composure.

I was told to stop making things up and to let Dasha continue attending school, claiming that the teacher was wonderful and that my daughter should lie less. I asserted that my daughter would not return to that class and that we would either change classes or leave the school. I was told that it is not customary in America for children to change classes whenever they want, which was astonishing to me because in my home country children can change classes if they don't mesh well with the teacher or peers. I said we would then withdraw her from the school. They told me they would contact me within a couple of days, and that same evening, I received a message that Dasha could switch to a different class starting the next week.

I really didn't want to continue sending Dasha to that school, but our sponsors dissuaded me, saying that it's not customary to just pull a child out; you're in a different country, you need to follow the rules. However, I strongly wanted to take her out of that school. Changing schools wasn't an option because you can only attend according to your residential area. The only solution for me was to change our home, and I eagerly awaited the end of our first year's lease so I could find another place and switch schools.

As soon as Dasha began attending the new class with a new teacher, she immediately stopped being nervous. She began sleeping through the night without screaming, stopped crying, and started enjoying school. She always talked about how her day went and was delighted because she found a wonderful friend in class and the teacher treated her well. I don't know what caused the first teacher's behavior toward us, but it was abnormal and should never happen. It was outrageous, and unfortunately, this wasn't an isolated incident. I started to learn that such things happen in other countries too. But it's one thing when it occurs among children and entirely another when an adult, a teacher, humiliates a small child to the point of a nervous breakdown.

After weeks of fighting for Dasha's well-being, I was both relieved and exhausted. We had finally managed to move her into a new class where she could feel safe and happy, but the entire experience left a bitter taste. I felt like a stranger in a society that seemed, in many ways, so foreign to me. There were these subtle yet striking differences in mentality and the whole structure of life here. Just as I was grappling with the unexpected challenges at school, I was also facing a completely different reality in every other part of our lives.

I felt terrible. There was an incredible difference in mentality, in the entire structure of society that was utterly incomprehensible to me. The relentless pursuit of ratings everywhere is exhausting. Credit scores, driving scores, insurance ratings—it feels like soon there will even be a rating for the air we breathe. These ratings must be constantly built up and cannot be allowed to fall. This constant pressure is truly draining and unpleasant. Why do we impose these assessments on ourselves, and what for? It feels almost like a form of slavery.

Another aspect of cultural difference was the long waiting times in America. It's surprising how people can plan a wedding a year or more in advance. You might not even live to see the event! Young people fall in love and want to be together today, not in a year or two. We are used to things happening much faster in my country—whether it's document processing or simply moving forward with life. Here, it's all about waiting—waiting for work permits, which can take months. Surely, paperwork can be processed faster. Surely, life can be lived faster. Why not live today, here and now?

I also couldn't understand why healthcare was so unreasonably expensive, why higher education was so prohibitively costly. It felt like every aspect of life here came with some hidden cost. Everywhere, there seemed to be attempts to draw you into a subscription, a contract, or a recurring fee—often for things you didn't even realize you were signing up for. It created the impression that the system itself was designed to confuse and extract money in subtle ways.

Of course, dishonest people exist everywhere—we ourselves had been deceived back in Ukraine when selling our apartment. But that had felt like an unfortunate encounter with the wrong individuals. Here, it felt different—more widespread, more normalized, almost built into everyday life. That contrast was hard to ignore and difficult to adjust to.

To most people in Ukraine, America is the ultimate land of opportunity—a paradise on Earth. Moving here is seen as a blessing, a stroke of great fortune. Artur and I felt the same way, sharing in the idealized view shaped by Hollywood movies and American music, which made it seem like a place where any hard-working person could succeed. There's even a joke that once you live in America, you no longer dream of living in America.

Of course, every country has its strengths and struggles. But experiencing America firsthand has been a surprise, even a shock, in many ways. There's freedom here, but at times, it feels overwhelming. Trying to explain this concept of boundless freedom to Masha was challenging. I had to help her understand that people here live very differently—things we consider unusual or extreme seem ordinary here. Sometimes, I feel that this freedom exists to keep people focused on self-expression, distracting them from the realities around them—like high insurance costs, low-quality food, and other challenges hidden beneath the surface.

I shared my thoughts with Artur, mentioning how envious our friends and family were when they heard we'd moved to the U.S. For many Ukrainians, living in America seems like reaching life's pinnacle. But in reality, it hasn't been so easy. I cried more in a few months here than I did in years back home. I told myself it was all part of adjusting, but perhaps we're just too different—our cultures are worlds apart.

Trying to integrate into a foreign society only to realize partway through that you may not want to continue is heartbreaking. I missed home. Yes, home was now in ruins, but they were my ruins. I missed the convenience of managing everything online instead of waiting for physical mail. I found the relentless advertising and aggressive marketing overwhelming, and I realized that maybe, in some ways, we're just too different.

Living in America has changed how I see myself. I've grown more confident, realizing that I don't need to compare myself to anyone. I used to think everyone around me was smarter, that I fell short as a mother, a wife, a daughter. But here, in a foreign land, I came to see that people everywhere are simply human. We're all the same species, bound by similar hopes and fears. This insight has made me braver and stronger. I even found myself wanting to grow my hair long again—a small but meaningful symbol of healing from the war. Still, the war remains a part of our daily lives, with Danya and my parents still there, under the threat of constant shelling. We check the news every day, our hearts in our throats, as we hold close the friends and family still in Ukraine.

21

Navigating Highs and Lows

One night, I couldn't sleep—my mind was tangled in worry as heavy shelling struck the city where my parents and Danya lived. Residential buildings were hit, and many people had died. I spent the night on the phone with Danya and our loved ones, listening to each explosion, my heart sinking with each one.

"Danya, where are you right now?" I asked, my voice trembling, listening to his breathing as if that could somehow bring him closer to me.

"I'm home. Mom and dad are fine," he tried to sound calm, but I could hear the exhaustion in his voice. "It's noisy here, but we're okay."

In his words, I could hear the distant echoes of explosions he was trying to ignore.

"Danya, this is . . . it's terrifying," I whispered, barely holding back tears. "Every time I call you, I'm scared you won't answer."

"I know," he replied softly, "I think about that too. But, you know, we'll get through this. You need to hold on, too. Don't forget you have your own life, your future."

"How can I think about the future when you're . . . there?" My voice trailed off, frustration and helplessness overwhelming me.

"You have to," he said firmly. "We're holding on because we believe there's something worth surviving for. You need to keep going—for us."

His words felt like an order, but I knew this was his way of supporting me, giving me a spark of hope. I was stuck between two worlds—each day, I had to wake up, adapt to a new culture, try to fit into a new society, yet my heart and mind remained in Ukraine, with my family under daily bombardment.

The constant worry and exhaustion of these nights felt like a shadow over every aspect of my life, following me into each day. By morning, my body was weary, yet I had to gather the strength to carry on with my daily responsibilities. After that sleepless night, I had to drive Artur to the office early in the morning, completely exhausted. On the way back, I was pulled over by a police officer for speeding. I was shocked; I thought I'd get a simple fine, as I usually follow speed limits. But it turns out these cases go to court here. I was terrified—back home, a court summons implies criminality.

Artur supported me, but I cried a lot. I worried about my driver's rating dropping, insurance costs rising, and the fine itself, which I couldn't afford. A couple of months later, the court case went quickly. Despite my fear, the judge was humane and understanding; I received a small fine and was asked to take a driver's improvement course. The whole ordeal was unpleasant, but the respectful treatment helped, though I hope never to go through it again.

Balancing home life, children, and two jobs was an exhausting challenge. Coming home from work didn't offer a break; it felt like starting a second or third shift. There was so much to manage—cleaning, cooking, keeping order, spending time with the children, and taking them for walks—all of which demanded a tremendous amount of time and energy.

I was used to being a homemaker, keeping everything under control—the house clean, the children well-fed and groomed. Now, however, maintaining those standards was impossible. In our family, Artur had always focused on work while I managed the household and cared for the children. But under this new pressure, our usual setup only intensified the strain I felt. Although Artur helped as much as he could and tried to support me, neither he nor the kids were used to being so involved at home. Out of sheer exhaustion and frustration, I often snapped at them, which was emotionally draining.

I felt inadequate as a homemaker and mother, unable to engage with the children or prepare meals with the same care as before. This internal struggle was compounded by adapting to a new environment, dealing with the aftermath of war, and keeping up with the fast pace of life here. There was no time to adjust; everything had to be done immediately, leaving me feeling completely overwhelmed.

Another month of immigration passed. Trips to the ocean really pulled me out of this routine. Yes, they were rare, maybe once a month, but I eagerly awaited them. It was like a breath of fresh air, and it was amazing for me to go to the ocean in mid-autumn. The water was warm, and you could swim, lie on the beach, and sunbathe. Back in my country, it was already quite cold, and the first snow had already fallen. It was very unusual and surprising for me, absolutely thrilling. It was just wonderful.

After all the stress of those months, I found peace in an unexpected place—through my daughter's dance. Masha really wanted to continue dancing, which had always been such a huge part of her life. We went to a class at a dance club. I remember that first session. I waited for her and peeked into the room as they danced to loud, joyful music. The girls moved beautifully and in sync—it was very picturesque. I ended up crying heavily. I sat there, unable to calm down because I finally felt like I could breathe, stop fearing death for the moment, and appreciate that life goes on and is beautiful. It was comforting to realize that my children were safe and that life continues.

But I was constantly tormented by thoughts about what to do next, who to be. This restlessness haunted and tortured me; I couldn't sleep because of it. I didn't know whether to continue my education to become a psychologist or to start my own business. I was unsure where it would be more profitable, where I could quickly see benefits. I just didn't know who to be or what to do here. And this was very draining. I tried to find a job but couldn't. The only thing I managed to do was get my diplomas evaluated through a charitable organization. And that was it. It was very difficult.

I continued to look for a better job. I applied to work at the nearest supermarket and a delivery service. They promised one salary, but the offer that came was much less than promised, and it turned out to be a temporary, short-term hire, so I had to decline. I also went for an interview at a daycare center. But they barely listened to me; they didn't even look at me during the interview. Of course, they never called back, and there were many such interviews, even for jobs I didn't really want to take. So far, I hadn't managed to find any job other than delivery. But I had plans for the future; I really wanted to achieve something.

I truly cried more in those few months in America than I had in my entire life. Still, the sunshine saved me. The higher number of sunny days than cloudy days in Virginia per year is just incredible. The sun really does help; when you step outside and the sun is brightly shining, somehow life feels easier. The girls continued to go to school, and I began driving Masha because the bus came too early, and driving her gave her an extra thirty minutes of sleep in the morning.

This month was also Artur's birthday. When we moved from Ukraine, we all had to leave behind something important, something dear to our hearts. For my husband, it was his electric guitar. It was very hard for him to part with it. Yes, we gave it to a friend's son, but it meant a lot to him. On his birthday, I took him and our daughters to a music store and suggested we buy an electric guitar.

As we walked into the music store, Artur's eyes immediately landed on a beautiful electric guitar hanging on the wall. I saw a familiar spark in his eyes, but he quickly looked away, pretending not to care.

"Come on, Artur," I said, nudging him playfully. "It's your birthday. You deserve this."

He shook his head, trying to brush it off. "It's too expensive. Besides, I don't really need it . . ."

Before he could finish, Masha chimed in, tugging at his sleeve. "Papa, you miss your guitar! You always talk about it."

"Yes!" Dasha added, her eyes wide with excitement. "And you were so good at playing. We want to hear you play again!"

He looked at both of them, then at me, a soft smile breaking through his resistance. "But it's too much . . . really. We don't need to spend money on this."

I leaned closer, gently putting a hand on his arm. "Artur, we want you to be happy. You gave up so much already. This is something you deserve. And we're all here together to make it happen."

The girls nodded in agreement, their eyes pleading. "Please, Papa! It's your birthday! Just this once!"

He let out a sigh, finally letting himself smile fully. "Alright . . . if you all insist. But only because it's my birthday and you won't take no for an answer!"

We all cheered, and the girls hugged him, thrilled that he'd finally agreed. Watching his face light up as he held the guitar, I felt a wave of joy—moments like these brought a sense of normalcy to our lives despite the challenges we'd faced.

As we settled back into our routines, I noticed how these small celebrations lifted our spirits. Even Masha and Dasha seemed happier, and they were happy about friendships at school. Masha, in particular, grew close with a classmate. One day, the two of them decided to try a dance class together. While I waited for them, I struck up a conversation with the other girl's mother. She was warm and understanding, and we quickly got to know each other better.

She listened to me attentively; she was one of those people who, after hearing my story, suggested I write a book about my adventures. She was a remarkable, wonderful woman. It's rare for me to open up about my feelings and share what I'm going through because, perhaps due to my profession, I'm used to listening to people, even if it's just casual conversation rather than a formal consultation. I'm accustomed to being the listener. But somehow, I felt a strong urge to express myself during our conversation. She listened very attentively and offered support. At one point, I thought how great it would be to have such a wonderful friend with whom I could simply talk openly. It was a very pleasant experience, and I fondly remember that moment.

Meanwhile, we were eagerly anticipating Halloween. I worked with Artur to earn enough money to buy decorations for the street, to adorn our house, prepare for the holiday, and purchase costumes and candy buckets for Masha and Dasha. They were really looking forward to this celebration. Although Halloween isn't traditionally celebrated in our home country, in recent years we'd encountered a few isolated cases—like the time a neighbor's family once came over in costumes. Still, it was nothing like the scale or spirit of Halloween in the United States, and for us, it felt like stepping into a different world. We were excited to see the decorated houses and children in costumes, and to immerse ourselves in the entire festive atmosphere. It was exhilarating to dive into it and enjoy an unforgettable experience. I expected everyone to decorate their homes, but it turned out that on my street, I was the only one who did. Some neighbors came by and said, "Oh, it's so cool how you've decorated; thank you for creating the mood." I think I, the only Ukrainian around, decorated my home and prepared for this American holiday better than my American neighbors. It was a wonderful celebration.

On the night of October 31, we drove to the neighborhood where our sponsors lived so Masha and Dasha could go trick-or-treating. The homes there were beautifully decorated, everything was lit up, and the streets were full of children in costumes. We were all dressed up too—our kids, Artur, and I—and the festive spirit was truly contagious. It's such a fantastic holiday, primarily because it teaches not to fear all this—mysticism, ghosts, and the entire theme of death and beyond. I love that in the U.S. they turn all these monsters into something humorous, inflatable, and fun. Wandering around at night, collecting candies from neighbors, was an amazing experience, and we thoroughly enjoyed every moment.

22

The Price of Perseverance

I continued working in delivery, but soon the downsides began to show. One of the hardest parts was the rating system. When I received my first one-star review, it was painful and disheartening. I couldn't understand why—every order was delivered with care, on time, and exactly as instructed. But that one low rating meant a significant drop in pay, fewer orders, and all for reasons I couldn't control.

For just two or three dollars per delivery, I'd drive through any weather, wait long minutes while the food was being prepared, then carefully transport it, sometimes with one hand balancing the order while driving. And after all that, a bad review could be as simple as a customer's bad day. There's a saying, "If someone insults you without reason, go earn that insult." But here, I wanted to be judged on my work, not on someone's mood or a random whim.

The job also took me into neighborhoods I'd only seen in movies, places I never imagined really existed. It was heartbreaking to see people living in such conditions, and terrifying for me as a delivery driver. There was no expectation of tipping here, and some customers would even complain that their order wasn't delivered—just to get a refund. In these situations, I felt humiliated; I, with two degrees, was being accused of theft just to save someone a few dollars.

On some days, the weight of it all would hit me. Once, after a delivery in a dangerous area, I parked to send a message to my language students and just broke down. I was physically exhausted from job searching, my back constantly aching, and my nerves frayed. Occasionally, job offers would come in, but the pay was often even lower than delivery earnings.

Tipping is often viewed as optional by customers, but for us, it's a crucial part of our income. Companies shift this responsibility onto the customer, avoiding the cost of a livable wage and leaving us to depend on inconsistent generosity. Immigrants like me work tirelessly in these roles, supporting so much of daily life—home delivery, lawn care, fast food—all taken for granted by others. Without us, much of it would grind to a halt. We do this work for our families, but our efforts often go unnoticed.

The job left its mark—not only in the lingering smell of food in the car but in the exhaustion that seemed to deepen with each passing day. This was the price I paid daily just to make ends meet. Yet, I held onto the hope of finding a job that matched my skills. I applied for a research position and even traveled to another city for the interview. The process seemed to go wonderfully, and I was excited to use my expertise to contribute to their projects. But days passed without any response, and my follow-up messages went unanswered. It was disappointing, but I couldn't let myself dwell on it for too long—I needed to keep searching.

Yet, as the job search continued, I felt another challenge rising—one rooted in my own self-doubt. Insecurity doesn't develop overnight; it takes root in childhood, growing if those around us fail to believe in us. Over time, it becomes a quiet barrier, making it hard to trust in your abilities. Each interview seemed to chip away at my confidence, leaving me questioning whether I could truly succeed in this new environment.

This feeling of uncertainty made adapting to a new culture and language all the more challenging. It became especially apparent at Thanksgiving, where language barriers made communication difficult, and I realized just how much I still had to learn.

That month, we were invited to a Thanksgiving celebration. It was hosted by a wonderful family with grown children who also brought their own families. It was a great honor for us because we know Thanksgiving is a very intimate family holiday. We felt so welcomed and appreciated being included in their celebration. It made me, Artur, Masha, and Dasha feel part of the community, which was exactly what we needed at that time. Of course, there were awkward moments, especially when trying to speak another language. The sentences in my head sounded intelligent and complex, but all I could manage to say were a few simple words. Despite attending English courses, Artur and I still had much to learn. Yet, I enjoyed observing this family; they were so happy and such a large, joyful group. It's wonderful to have such a family, to have people who come to visit you on Thanksgiving. Sadly, many Ukrainians have lost loved ones in the war, and it was heartening to see that at least here, in the United States, people live lives far removed from war.

The following month was eventful, though not all events were positive. As New Year's approached, our country was bombarded especially harshly. We often stayed up at night due to the time difference, trying to stay connected with our family and friends back home. But despite everything, that month I saw a glimmer of hope for a bright career and future. I reached out to the state psychology board to inquire about what I needed to do to work as a qualified mental health professional here. They informed me that I could work in that capacity. I was so thrilled. I submitted the documents for the license as a trainee, and it was approved. I found a job surprisingly quickly. I passed the interview and was hired at a salary twice the minimum wage. I was so happy. It felt like finally, things were falling into place. Finally, I had an interesting job where I could think, apply my moral and intellectual qualities, make a difference, and help people. I was ecstatic, despite the fact that Artur and I were doing our English homework late into the night, since I felt my vocabulary was still not good enough. I was terrified to work in this profession, to communicate with people as a psychologist, because I realized that saying just "good" or "bad" wasn't enough in English. I had to sit and learn words that described emotions.

I was initially overjoyed about the new job opportunity, but it quickly turned into a challenging ordeal. The job involved working with homeless individuals and troubled families, primarily in the most dangerous neighborhoods. There were times when I was genuinely afraid to step out of the car because people with weapons were around. The job required me to spend three hours at a time with clients, three to four days a week, which felt like practically living at the client's place. The fear was overwhelming, and it was a struggle for me to cope.

Working with homeless individuals and troubled families required not only physical stamina but also resilience. Each day felt like a new test of my strength, as lingering fears from the war surfaced and grew more intense.

When I tried discussing this with my mentor or supervisor, seeking a different assignment that didn't involve such risky neighborhoods, I explained that my psyche wasn't ready for this after experiencing war. It was too dangerous. I was worried about my car, the only one I had, and fearful of stepping out when people with guns were nearby. I dreaded spending three hours in the homes of troubled families, especially because some individuals had mental illnesses and could be aggressive. The job felt perilously unsafe, and I wasn't prepared to risk my life or my children's future. The response I got was blunt: Either work or leave. Despite my fears, I chose to stay.

I cried a lot during this period. It was tough and frightening, and despite every human instinct to overcome fear, I couldn't shake mine. Each day, the dread only grew. Artur was deeply concerned.

One evening, as I sat on the edge of the bed, exhausted and struggling to hold back tears, he placed a hand on my shoulder, his face clouded with worry.

"I can see how much this job is affecting you," he said gently. "You're scared every day, and it's not worth it. Maybe it's time to quit."

I shook my head, frustration mingling with helplessness. "I wish I could, Artur. I hate this job—it terrifies me. But . . . where else would we get the money?" I hesitated, the weight of the reality settling over me. "This job pays more than delivery, and even then, it's barely enough."

He sighed, looking torn. "I know. I hate that we're in this position. But your safety, your peace of mind, that matters too. I wish I could do more."

I took his hand, trying to smile through the tears. "We'll manage. Somehow. Even if it means doing both jobs. It's not fair, but I'll keep going."

Although I had a decent number of clients, many would cancel last minute. I could arrive early on a weekend morning, only to have clients decide not to hold their session. Even with a full schedule, I wasn't working as much as I'd hoped, and I still needed to do delivery work just to make ends meet. It was extremely difficult, and some days, it felt almost impossible.

I was also torn between my family and work. I had a lot of work and was hardly ever home. I worked in delivery in the mornings and visited clients in the evenings. The worst part was that I still couldn't make enough money, and there was always housework waiting for me when I got home. Masha and Dasha found it very hard without me; they were not used to me being absent. They were used to always being with me, and my absence was emotionally tough for them.

One morning, as I hurried to drive Masha to school, I slammed my toe against the door frame, breaking my toe. The pain was sharp, and though I limped and held back tears all day, I still had to work. That evening, exhausted and worn, I opened our mailbox and found a substantial medical bill for the children, who had both been sick twice that month. The sight of it crushed me. It felt so unfair that, while others lived their lives, built careers, and enjoyed the comfort of their homes, we were starting over in a new country with nothing. If only there had been no war—we could have stayed in our cozy apartment, driving our own car, traveling, and focusing on Masha and Dasha's happiness.

On days when physical pain mingled with emotional exhaustion, I sometimes found solace in Ukrainian music. One afternoon, as the lyrics echoed, "Someday the day will come when the war will end," a surge of emotions overwhelmed me—both despair and a glimmer of hope. My deepest wish is for the war to end, for our soldiers to come home, and for our children to never again feel the terror of hiding from soldiers. That longing for peace mixed with my frustration, and I realized just how much of my resilience was tied to these hopes—how they kept me pushing forward through every hardship.

Instead, on weekends and evenings, Artur and I would find ourselves working deliveries together because I was too afraid to go alone. I hadn't recovered from the war; everything still frightened me. Our car became a makeshift home for the kids, with blankets, toys, and cartoons so they'd be comfortable, even on Christmas, when we couldn't afford to take time off. There were Sundays when I'd wake at five in the morning, starting early, only to sit in silence for hours, waiting for an order.

In those quiet, early mornings, I couldn't help but reflect on everything we'd been through. The constant struggle, the uncertainty, and the sacrifices weighed heavily on me. But even in those moments of doubt, there was a part of me that refused to give up. I held onto the hope that, one day, all this effort would lead us to a better life—a life where my children could feel secure, where our hard work would be rewarded, and where I could finally feel a sense of belonging and peace.

I did not know when that day would come, but I reminded myself that perseverance is the price we pay for the future we dream of. And for now, that hope, faint yet steady, was enough to keep me going.

23

The Burden of Uncertainty

Each morning begins with checking the news about my country, focusing on where my family and friends live. I hope, just once, that the night was peaceful. But more often than not, it wasn't. Videos with sounds of explosions still haunt us, triggering memories we try to keep at bay. When thunderstorms roll in, the children are terrified. They end up sleeping in our bed, seeking comfort, and sometimes Masha hides in the bathroom, afraid the thunder might shatter the windows like an incoming missile.

One night, I found her there, huddled in the corner with her arms wrapped around her knees. I gently knocked on the door, trying not to startle her.

"Masha, sweetheart, it's just thunder," I said softly. "You can come out; it's not dangerous."

She shook her head, casting a nervous glance at the window. "But what if it breaks the glass? What if it comes in?"

I knelt beside her, wrapping an arm around her shoulders. "The thunder won't break the windows, I promise. You're safe, Masha."

For a moment, she seemed to relax, but then another rumble echoed, and she pressed her hands over her ears. "But what if it comes here, like before?"

I held her closer, stroking her hair. "There's nothing here like what we were afraid of at home. We're far away now; this is just thunder and rain. Nothing's coming for us."

As her breathing slowed and her grip loosened, I was reminded of how fragile this newfound sense of safety could be.

She looked up at me, uncertain, but stayed put. I stayed beside her, whispering reassurances until, little by little, she loosened her grip on herself, though she still wouldn't leave the bathroom.

At times, the urge to return home is overwhelming—a longing so strong it feels like I could drop everything and go. Sometimes we regret leaving Ukraine, and other times, our children, especially my oldest, are plagued by nightmares of war. Masha wakes up in the middle of the night, crying, caught in dreams of being back in Ukraine under artillery fire. Even with the help of a psychologist, this trauma lingers; it's a part of us that will stay for a long time.

Occasionally, we watch a Ukrainian show called *Super Mom*, where mothers compete for the title. Whenever the women mention the war, Masha and I break down in tears. All of it—every sound, every image—is still so vivid in our minds. And I wonder, how long will it take for my children to start forgetting?

Living without a sense of home is deeply unsettling. Where is home now? It's gone; it was taken from us. It feels unfair to have been decent, honest people who lived with hope and love, only to be unwillingly turned into refugees forced to start from scratch. We're ready to work hard, to rebuild. But too often, we're treated as though we're third-class citizens, judged as if we've achieved nothing with our lives—as if we're somehow lazy.

In these moments of quiet comfort, I sometimes think of our cat, Yubi, who endured her own journey to find a safe and loving home. She went through hell in Ukraine to get to us, enduring terrifying hardships just to join our family. Once a battered, exhausted kitten on the streets, she had broken legs and deep scars—signs of the long suffering she had endured. A charitable rescue organization saved her, and that's where we found her. Without those trials, she might still be a street cat, struggling daily for food and shelter, surviving alone.

It's the same with people; sometimes, you have to wade through a lot of trouble for something good to happen. When you look back, you realize that without that hell, you wouldn't have what you have now. If I hadn't argued with my parents, I never would have left. I never could have left them and gone away. And if not for the war, I never would have ended up in the U.S.

Reflecting on these changes also helped me understand why I'd always been so focused on learning. My life had been a series of courses, degrees, and certificates, and only here, in America, did I realize the reason behind it all. It was tied to my childhood, and to my fear of making mistakes. As long as I was learning, no one could judge me—I was simply a student. I realized that I knew how to do so many things, but always with a hint of imperfection. I could bake beautiful cakes, but not well enough to make a living from it. I loved surprising people, but as long as I was "just learning," no one could criticize me.

Letting go of certain expectations from my parents was another hard-won lesson, but it was essential. I finally took a step toward reconciliation, sending them a message on Christmas, wishing them well. They responded, thanking me, but even that small exchange left me feeling torn—caught between the desire to rebuild and the painful weight of the past.

Not long after that, the emotions came crashing down. One day, I found myself sitting in the car, feeling overwhelmed. There I was, sitting in a parking lot with my face in my hands, crying as everything hit at once. I'd been counting on a paycheck from my new job, but it was delayed until the following month. By then, I was working three jobs—something I'd never imagined—yet still feeling like I was barely moving forward. The lack of stability, both financially and emotionally, was hard to bear.

Adding to the frustration, my car's seat belt had started to jam, and every time I tried to buckle up, it felt like another reminder of the struggle. I'd get in, try to buckle, get out, and repeat the process each time I went out for a delivery. It was a small issue, but somehow it seemed to capture how exhausting everything had become.

Then there was the uncertainty at home. The house we rented was put up for sale, which meant constant viewings with strangers walking through, disrupting what little sense of peace we had. Artur, working from home, tried to manage it, but it was unsettling. We had no idea what would happen—whether the new owner would allow us to stay, raise the rent, or ask us to leave altogether. The uncertainty loomed over us like a constant cloud, making us wonder if we would ever find a stable place to call home.

An agent came to us, and he was a very unpleasant man. He constantly lied and deceived. He would smile, look you in the eyes, then turn away and do his own thing. We had agreed that visitors who came to view the house would either remove their shoes or wear shoe covers, and that someone from our family would always be home. We insisted that no visits could occur without us present. However, people still entered without removing their shoes. Artur had to keep asking them to do so. Our key was used by anyone who wished. It was all very frustrating and disagreeable.

When I called the agent again and asked him to remove the lock with our key from our door, since the house had been sold, he said it could hang there a few more days. We argued, and I said I would not allow anyone into the house anymore, especially since pre-sale inspections were pending. He immediately came and removed the lock. His constant lying was very irritating and unpleasant. It's very uncomfortable when people enter, look around the house, and even inspect the contents of your fridge and rummage through your cabinets and belongings. It's simply awful. You don't feel like you're at home. You don't feel safe.

Despite this weight of loss and uncertainty, there were still moments that reminded us life could be beautiful, even here. This month, we celebrated Masha's birthday at a children's entertainment center. Despite everything, we wanted her to feel like a regular kid, with friends to invite and joyful moments to look forward to. The room resounded with excited chatter, children's laughter echoing against the bright walls. Balloons in every color filled the air, while the scent of freshly baked cupcakes and sweet frosting wafted from the table, adding to the sense of celebration.

Among the guests was a girl from China, Masha's closest friend, even though they only shared one class. She and her family had recently moved to the U.S., and her father, who spoke very little English, was an incredibly kind man. We communicated through a phone app, typing into Google Translate.

At one point, he handed me his phone with a translated message: "I want to say sorry for my country's support of Russia in this war. I hope you don't hold this against us personally. We are so sorry for what your family has gone through."

Touched, I typed back: "Thank you for saying that. We know not everyone in a country agrees with its leaders. We are just grateful to have met kind people like you here."

He smiled, nodding with understanding as he read the translation, and typed back, "If there is anything we can do to help your family here, please let us know. We are happy to be your friends."

His words warmed my heart, and Artur nodded with a grateful smile as we took turns typing short messages. Despite our different languages and backgrounds, a sense of mutual respect and kindness made us feel like we'd known them for much longer than just a brief time.

Some people, no matter how briefly they touch our lives, leave a lasting impact. This family was one of those blessings. They even invited us to a Santa breakfast at their church during Christmas. Seeing my daughter with a true friend brought me so much joy, and we were delighted to make new friends ourselves. I will always remember them with special warmth.

Our sponsors invited us to a Christmas party, a gathering filled with warmth, laughter, and the rich aroma of holiday treats. The room buzzed with children, sweets, and laughter as Masha and Dasha eagerly dove into the festive spirit. We baked a Grinch-themed cake, and the air filled with the smell of chocolate and spices as children's voices blended into cheerful chaos. Strings of twinkling lights wrapped around the room, casting a warm, golden glow that softened every shadow, making even the simplest moments feel extraordinary. As I stood amid the joyful scene, I found myself drawn to the familiar scent of our sponsor's perfume—a fragrance that somehow felt safe, stable, and peaceful. Just being near her, surrounded by that scent, brought memories of our first days here, of the kindness and comfort we felt staying with them.

Moments like these make us feel truly alive, as if we're not just surviving each day, but really living. In the midst of all our struggles, these gatherings are a precious reminder of joy and community, a reprieve from fear and tension. They ground us, helping us hold onto the beauty we find along the way.

This season, Artur and I worked hard to make Christmas magical. We wanted Santa to bring something special this year, so we got the children big playhouses and a mountain of gifts—more than Santa had ever brought before. We bought an artificial Christmas tree and decorated it with beautiful ornaments, trying to create memories they'd cherish.

Dasha, meanwhile, had become enamored with the Grinch. She had Grinch pajamas, a big cuddly Grinch toy, and watched the cartoon on repeat. One evening, I came home from work to find her lying in bed in her pajamas, engrossed in her favorite movie. The warmth of her little body against mine and the soft glow from the screen created a cozy cocoon, where for a moment, the outside world felt far away. It was a simple, beautiful moment that soothed my soul—a brief escape where all that mattered was being with her, sharing that small joy.

The same month included a concert by Masha with her school orchestra. We bought the most beautiful dress from the store. She went to the concert, and I was immensely proud of my child. As the music began, my heart swelled with emotions, and I couldn't hold back the tears. Artur noticed, gently reaching over to take my hand.

"Why are you crying?" he whispered softly. "Everything's good."

I smiled through my tears. "I'm just so proud of her . . . She's so strong, despite everything she's been through."

He squeezed my hand, his own eyes softening. "She's incredible. And so are you, you know? You're handling everything so beautifully."

Hearing his words, I felt a deep sense of peace and pride—not only for our daughter but for the strength we'd found as a family. I wiped my tears, feeling reassured.

It's moments like these when you forget everything else and realize you're on the right path. You have wonderful children. You're doing everything right. As a mother, you're managing well. We bought flowers for Masha's teacher and for her. It was a beautiful moment, the kind you want to live forever.

24

Fighting for Peace and Place

January turned out to be the most challenging of my emigration experience, marked by an unforeseen event that deeply upset me and was emotionally trying. Recently, Masha had been coming home from school very distressed, telling me about how one of her friends started ignoring her and persuading other children to do the same. As a psychologist, I tried to help her. We agreed that she should immediately inform her teachers about these incidents.

However, the abuse continued to the point that she would call me in tears from school, pleading to be picked up.

"Mom, please come get me," Masha sobbed over the phone. "I can't take it anymore... My only friend is Yinqi, the girl from China, but I only see her during the first class. She's my only refuge. The rest of the time, it's unbearable."

"Sweetheart, what happened?" I asked, already getting ready to leave.

"That other girl—my former friend, who found a new best friend—they both ignore me now," Masha continued, trying to hold back her tears. "She tells other kids not to play with me, points at me, and laughs. She says horrible things about me all the time, Mom. I just can't stand it anymore."

I had to leave work and rush to her, which was incredibly hard. I decided to address the problem as we would back in our country. I chose not to make it a public school-wide issue and instead solve it quietly between us, the parents. I respected the mother of the girl involved, viewing her as rational, fair, and sensible. When we spoke, I explained the situation, hoping for understanding.

"I just wanted to talk with you about what's been happening between our daughters," I began carefully. "Masha has been really hurt. She says that your daughter has been asking other kids to ignore her and making hurtful comments."

She paused before responding, her tone firm. "Well, I don't know what Masha's been telling you, but my daughter says it's the other way around. She says that Masha is the one who's been causing trouble."

"I'm truly sorry you're experiencing this," I replied, genuinely feeling sympathy for her. "But I think you might want to speak with the teachers. They've witnessed some of the bullying themselves, and they can tell you what they've seen."

"Fine," she replied curtly. "I'll do just that."

Unfortunately, despite my hopes that this conversation would bring some resolution, the situation did not improve. The conflict only escalated, and one day Masha came home in tears, her white pants marked with shoeprints where she had been kicked by this girl and her new friend. This was the last straw for me. When Masha reported the incident to a teacher, the teacher dismissed her, saying it wasn't her problem.

I didn't call the school; I went there the next day and insisted I would not leave until the issue was resolved. I was prepared to fight for my child and told them they could call the police on me, but I wouldn't leave until actions were taken. I was taken to the administration where I explained the situation to an administrator who was surprisingly unaware of it, despite my numerous discussions with the school counselor. They had merely taught Masha to ignore the problem. I argued that this was an unacceptable strategy for such cases and questioned why they were teaching her to ignore such behavior. Other children had approached her, saying they were simply afraid to associate with her because the girl instilled fear in them and prohibited them from talking to Masha.

Finally, steps were taken. The administrator sent a message to the girl's mother detailing the incident and stipulated that her daughter must keep a certain distance from mine. Letters were sent to all teachers ensuring the girls would sit separately and have no contact. Some action, at least, was finally undertaken.

While I thought I might finally find some peace, my work challenges quickly reminded me that this peace was elusive. My job with the homeless brought new anxieties. I had to transport clients in my own car, which felt unsettling. I tried to help one woman, but she declined, saying our program didn't offer enough benefits for her needs. It was disheartening; I believed she had a real chance for a better life.

In another case, a client complained about me before we even met, assuming I was rude. Some clients simply didn't want to meet, and one canceled after I'd traveled across the city to see them. This work required ten to twelve hours a week with each client, feasible only for those genuinely seeking change. Worse yet, the job felt unsafe: A colleague had recently been hospitalized after being attacked by a client. After much inner struggle, I decided I couldn't keep going. Leaving brought relief, though I wished I'd done it sooner.

The whole experience left a lingering sense of injustice. Though I hold a foreign diploma and experience, I am still a psychologist. But here, licensing means lengthy retraining, creating what feels like artificial barriers that limit immigrants to low-paying, high-stress jobs. The pay, too, was less than expected. I earned almost nothing but stress, worry, and a mental map of areas to avoid.

In yet another line of work, I faced moments that felt all too familiar. One day, while I was picking up a delivery at an upscale country club, the restaurant manager looked me over with barely concealed disdain, remarking that I was "obviously from the delivery service." But that wasn't the end of it. Coffee would spill on sharp turns, orders got mixed up due to incorrect addresses, and I was even accused of "forgetting" items that I hadn't packed. Despite my two degrees and professional background, it felt as though I was being reduced to a caricature, as if I might have eaten someone's meal on the way to drop it off. Many of the orders were either heavy or plainly unpleasant, and yet, the daily challenges far outweighed any compensation.

As I reflected on all of this, I realized that these experiences—these layers of misunderstanding and judgment—formed a kind of quiet but relentless struggle of their own. Whether it was facing dismissal, bearing judgment, or simply navigating the unseen walls between me and where I wanted to be, each moment seemed to whisper a reminder: My place here was still something I would have to fight for.

25

The Hidden Cost of Dreams

I was thousands of miles away when the news came: A massive snowstorm had engulfed my homeland, and my father, who was working in transportation, was stranded in his car, trapped beneath layers of snow. For three days, he'd been living there with no gas, no heat, and no hope of immediate rescue. Danya told me that the battery had died, that my father had no way out. And for the first time in a year and a half, I picked up the phone and called him through a messaging app. He answered, and we had a surprisingly warm conversation.

"Papa, are you okay? I've been so worried. Three days in the cold—how are you managing?" I asked, my voice full of concern.

He let out a soft sigh. "It's tough, but don't worry, everything will be fine. I'll get through this," he said, trying to reassure me.

"I just feel so helpless, knowing you're there alone," I said, feeling the weight of the situation. "I wish we could do more from here."

"You have enough on your plate. I'm glad we're talking, that's all that matters," he replied. "And you? How are you all doing over there?"

I told him about our life, and he listened quietly, then said he had hoped we were living much better, that our lives were more settled. It was a therapeutic call, difficult in some ways, but I was glad we finally talked. Fortunately, on the fourth day, the rescue service reached my father. They dug him out, and he made it home safely.

Around that time, I decided to write to my mother. I told her I was sorry for how things had turned out, to which she immediately responded that it was okay, this is life, and everything was fine. I was surprised because I hadn't expected her to respond at all, and it had been very difficult for me to make the decision to write. On one hand, I was very reluctant and angry; on the other, I wanted to mend the relationship to heal the rift in my soul. Relearning how to communicate with my parents was quite hard. I did this secretly from Artur because he would have been against it. I didn't even know how to tell him. I felt uncomfortable admitting that we had reconciled because he was worried that a relationship with them might hurt me again. He was just looking out for me. It was very unpleasant, almost as if I was hiding something terrible from him, and I felt very guilty about it.

These hidden emotions reminded me of other feelings I had struggled with—feelings I'd had back in Ukraine. When I was there, I used to feel frustrated with people who left the country. It seemed unfair that some stayed behind to face danger while others started new lives abroad. Now, I realize I have become one of those people I once judged. Despite the outward appearance of well-being, life here is unexpectedly challenging, often more about "seeming" than "being." From afar, it looks like a shimmering soap bubble—beautiful yet fragile, and, up close, often empty.

This country is known worldwide for its healthcare, quality of life, and high standards, yet there are hidden challenges: educational gaps, gun control issues, high costs, and a difficult path for immigrants. Here, the system often requires immigrants to start over—going through lengthy retraining instead of simply validating their credentials. It seems as if the process is deliberately slowed, keeping immigrants in a supporting role while prioritizing jobs for citizens.

And who fills the many essential roles? Immigrants. Those perfectly manicured lawns, the food on tables, and much of the hard labor that sustains daily life come from immigrant hands. This work is essential, yet undervalued. Many immigrants work long, grueling hours to support their families, often cleaning, delivering, or doing manual labor that rarely earns the respect or compensation it deserves.

It's undoubtedly easier to be born here, go through the local education system, work eight-hour days, and earn a stable income. But coming here with nothing and striving to build a life is incredibly hard and deserving of respect. This struggle is far different from what one imagines from the comfort of a settled life back home. The process of integration is demanding, and the hidden costs—mental and emotional strain, cultural isolation, and the constant micro-adjustments—are profound.

Every country has its pros and cons, and the immigration journey is always challenging. But it's hard to convey just how undervalued and unappreciated efforts to succeed feel. Immigrants should receive more recognition and fair pay for their contributions, as the true cost of building a new life here goes far beyond what people see.

The last month of winter came with its own challenges and small joys. Dasha's birthday was approaching, and we put in a lot of effort to celebrate it at a children's entertainment center, inviting her school friends to join. The day was wonderful; seeing Dasha's eyes light up, surrounded by friends and laughter, filled us with happiness. We were happy because our children were happy.

Later that month, Masha hosted a pajama party with neighborhood girls. The house buzzed with giggles and whispered secrets as they huddled together in blankets and pillows. It was a magical night; the girls were thrilled, and we all felt the warmth of their joy. Moments like these remind me of the beauty in the everyday, the joy of childhood under a peaceful sky, and the comfort of knowing that, despite everything, our children can laugh, play, and feel safe.

Meanwhile, our house was sold, and the rent was raised for the next contract. We decided to look for another place to live, partly because I wanted to change Dasha's and Masha's schools and partly because I didn't like the house we were in.

"Maybe it's time to find somewhere else," I said to Artur one evening. "The rent is going up, and honestly, I'd like the girls to be in different schools."

He nodded thoughtfully. "It's getting expensive, and if a new place means better schools for them, maybe it's for the best."

"I know it's not ideal to move again, but it feels like the right time," I replied, already imagining a new start for our family.

With that decision, we paid our taxes, received a small refund, and planned to use it to help with moving expenses. I began searching for houses, excited about the possibilities. But soon after, I got sick and couldn't work for a week. That week off made Artur and me realize how vulnerable we were financially. If one of us couldn't work for a short time, we'd lose nearly a quarter of our income. It became clear we needed a savings buffer before taking such a big step.

It was hard for me to accept, but eventually, we decided to stay in the same house. I wrestled with this choice for over a month before finally informing the management company that we would not be moving. It wasn't an easy decision, but I knew it was the responsible one—for our family, for our stability, and for our peace of mind.

26

Steps Forward, Glances Back

Leaving my teaching position wasn't easy. I had one student left, and preparing for each lesson took far more time than a half-hour class could justify. I loved teaching, but I knew it wasn't sustainable. I had to trust my instincts and let it go. Teaching Russian stirred mixed feelings in me. In the shadow of war, my mother tongue has painful associations in Ukraine, where it's now seen as a symbol of unwanted history and loss.

I questioned myself: Could teaching Russian somehow betray my values? Was I contributing to a legacy I wanted no part of? These thoughts lingered as I prepared each lesson, casting a shadow on my love for teaching.

But in time, I came to see that my relationship with Russian ran much deeper than its political associations. It was more than the language of headlines; it was the language of my earliest memories, my family, and my hometown Bakhmut, with its rose-lined alleys and quiet streets. Russian was woven into the fabric of my childhood. For me, it was not a language of conflict but one of home. The memories it held were peaceful, joyful—even though the streets I once knew now lie in ruins, a place I would give anything to visit just once more.

In the eastern region where I grew up, Russian was a constant presence—on television, in schools, in music, in every part of daily life. Since Soviet times, it was spoken by nearly half the country, and for us, it wasn't a choice but a part of who we were. Eventually, I realized that teaching Russian was less about the politics others had attached to it and more about honoring my past, my roots, and my memories.

Additionally, in March, my mother sent me a huge message that was totally unexpected. She wrote such a heartfelt apology. It was a detailed, extensive message that deeply moved me. She touched precisely on all the points of my childhood traumas and the grievances I had. She voiced everything, and I never thought I could ever hear something like that from her. It was incredible. It was a significant gesture, which I, of course, appreciated greatly. It was powerful. This, of course, made me very happy. It gave me strength. I told Artur about the lengthy apology letter, and he was concerned that our renewed communication might again cause me pain. But her words brought a sense of warmth and healing, reigniting our longing for a place that feels like home.

Soon after, Artur and I found ourselves seriously considering a return to Europe. We couldn't settle on which country would suit us best, so we constantly reached out to friends who had moved there, asking about life, opportunities, and the conditions they faced. The idea of moving to Europe consumed us. Although we knew it would require significant savings, the possibility of being closer to our homeland and its familiar way of life felt essential to us.

Having grown up in the years following the collapse of the Soviet Union, we carry a set of values and perspectives that often feel out of place in the U.S. We long for a lifestyle rooted in our own culture, a place where the nuances of our mentality and upbringing feel natural. We pray for peace back home, dreaming of a day when we can return with our children, Masha and Dasha, to a life that feels truly ours.

Before the war, I had my life in Ukraine planned down to the smallest details: kindergartens, schools—I knew where my child would go. Everything was prepared, from the best pediatricians nearby to the right speech therapy groups. That stability felt unshakable, yet it was lost in an instant, leaving me to adapt and survive in an unfamiliar place.

And now, with my children far from their birthplace, it breaks my heart that all our memories remain only in our minds. Childhood photos, family mementos—everything from our past—was destroyed when my hometown was reduced to rubble. My parents' home, which held generations of memories, was lost, leaving nothing to show my children, nothing tangible to pass on. Losing these physical reminders feels like losing a piece of ourselves, a part of our history that we can never reclaim.

During this time, I felt utterly drained—not just physically, but emotionally, as fear crept into every corner of our lives. I worried constantly: about being stopped by the police again, the risk of hitting a deer on the road, or the possibility of wrecking our only car. The endless hours spent driving were filled with these anxious thoughts, and it was exhausting to carry that weight of fear day after day.

Compounding this was the frustration of feeling capable yet invisible. I knew I had the skills and experience to excel in my profession, but opportunities seemed perpetually out of reach. I applied to a few universities for an assistant professor position in Russian, hoping to share my knowledge and passion. After a long wait, one replied with a rejection; the other simply never responded. I had the education, the drive, the dedication, yet I wasn't even given a chance to prove myself. I knew I could have made a difference, but no door seemed willing to open.

When people would ask, "How are you?" I might say "fine," but my hidden tears often told another story. Simple things continued to sadden and trigger me. I had once dreamed of taking Masha and Dasha to Disneyland, and here I was, in a country that had one—yet it was just out of reach financially. Balancing work and home life was an ongoing struggle, and even after months, it still felt overwhelming. I'd hear others boast about how quickly their children adapted, speaking perfect English within a few months and even forgetting their native language. Listening to those stories weighed on me, adding to the feeling of being worn out, trapped in a cycle of trying to keep up in a world that often felt like it was moving too fast for us.

Even Dasha would sometimes break down unexpectedly, her tears flowing as she sat down, crying over all she missed from her life in Ukraine—her toys, her room, her friends. One evening, as I held her close, she looked up at me, her eyes filled with confusion and sadness.

"Mama," she whispered, her voice breaking, "Why did Russia do this to us? What do they want from us? Why would they take everything away?"

The question hit me like a wave, and I struggled to hold back my own tears. "I don't know, my love," I replied softly, pulling her into my arms. "Sometimes . . . people make terrible choices because they want control over things that aren't theirs. And it's not fair. You didn't do anything to deserve this."

She looked up at me, her brows furrowing as more tears welled up. "But why us?" she continued, her little voice trembling. "Why do I have to lose my room? My toys? My friends? Why did we have to leave everything?"

I stroked her hair, feeling the ache of her words, knowing there was nothing I could say to make this hurt less. "I wish I could tell you it makes sense, Dasha. I wish you could be in your own room, with your own things, where you feel safe. You should have had that."

Her small hands clutched at my shirt, and she buried her face into my shoulder. "Mama . . . what if the war comes here, too?" She pulled back just enough to search my face, her eyes wide and fearful. "What if we have to leave again?"

The innocence of her question, mixed with the weight of her worry, left me speechless. I took a deep breath, steadying myself for her sake. "Sweetheart, I don't think the war will come here. We're safe right now. And I promise, I'll do everything I can to keep you and your sister safe, no matter what."

She looked at me, uncertain, and whispered, "You promise?"

I nodded, my heart breaking as I held her tighter. "I promise, my sweet girl. We'll make a new home here, a place where you feel safe. And if ever anything changes, we'll face it together, just like we have before. But for now, you don't have to worry. We're okay here."

She sniffled and leaned back against me, holding on tightly. "I just want my home back, Mama. I want things to go back to how they were."

"I know, Dasha," I whispered, my own tears slipping down. "I want that too, more than anything. And one day, we will have a home again, a place where you feel safe, where we can make new memories together."

In these tearful moments, holding Dasha as we mourned the life we'd left behind, I realized that adapting was something we simply had to endure—not just physically, but in every part of our hearts—as we navigated the loss and longing woven into our new reality. For Dasha, for both my daughters, I would keep going. We would find hope and make new memories, even if it felt impossible now.

By the time I began writing this book, I didn't even know why I started it. Initially, it was simply a way to express myself, to vent. I really enjoyed it. But then, I felt a strong desire to create something useful for others, something that would make readers feel they're not alone. That there are people who make mistakes, who feel similar emotions, who face similar situations. I wanted this book to offer help. If it can help even one person, then it's all worth it.

I believe not allowing yourself to be who you are is a sin. This book has pulled me through many difficulties. I've long envied people who are deeply passionate about something, like a computer game or a hobby. I dreamed of finding such a passion. I tried installing games, but none appealed to me. I tried various hobbies, but nothing stuck, nothing captivated me. Then one day, everything clicked, and I eagerly awaited the end of the day to finish all tasks, spend time with Masha and Dasha, and finally continue writing this book. It's wonderful when you find yourself, when something engrosses you completely. It's marvelous.

But there were good moments, too. While working, I'd play Ukrainian songs loudly, feeling connected to a part of my homeland. I am immensely proud to be Ukrainian; it's the best place I could have been born, where I spent most of my life. Masha, too, found her own way to stay connected—she played modern songs on the violin with her teacher, pieces by artists like Adele and Michael Jackson. Waiting outside, I'd watch other teachers hum along and even dance a little. It was refreshing to see people enjoying what they do, so full of life and energy.

Also my brother, Danya, quit smoking, and my parents were incredibly proud. My mom even called to share how wonderful it was. I wanted to tell her, "Mom, I quit too. Sixteen years, a pack a day." But I held back; she'd never known I smoked. It had been my quiet rebellion, a personal escape.

Yes, I smoked—starting at fifteen, heavily and with real attachment. While I avoided drinking, smoking became my crutch, the hidden anchor in my routine. Every moment seemed to bend around that next cigarette.

After sixteen years, I finally quit. A line from a book haunted me: "You never know which cigarette could be the one to start the irreversible." It terrified me. The first days were brutal, but I took it as a challenge—one evening without smoking, then one morning, then a day, then another. I gained weight, felt lost without my old comfort, and nearly went back a few times. But by some miracle, I've been smoke-free for years now. And though tough days bring temptation, each day it gets a little easier.

Easter arrived, and with it, a warm invitation from our sponsors to join their holiday gathering. The yard buzzed with the sounds of children's laughter as they dashed around, eagerly hunting for colorful eggs hidden in every corner. Watching them—eyes wide with excitement, clutching their baskets, and shouting gleefully each time they found an egg—we felt an undeniable sense of joy. Masha and Dasha joined in, racing with the other children, their giggles and bright eyes blending into the cheerful chaos of the day. It was one of those rare, uncomplicated moments where everything felt light and whole.

Artur stood beside me, watching the scene with a quiet smile. I leaned over and whispered, "Look at them. They're so happy, just running, playing . . . like we're all back in some simpler time."

He nodded, his gaze soft. "Yes, it's easy to forget that life can be this simple, right? Just kids, laughter, a few hidden eggs."

I sighed as we watched Dasha proudly show Masha an egg she'd just found. "Sometimes I feel like all of this isn't really for us, but for them, so they can forget the rest of it all for a while and just . . . be children."

Artur put his arm around me, nodding. "It should be that way. These moments—maybe they're for us, too, to remember that they need to be happy, that they deserve this."

We shared a quiet smile, grateful to have been included in this day, grateful for the sight of our children carefree and laughing, even if just for a little while. And in that brief moment, it felt like hope, like we were given a glimpse of something lasting.

In these small celebrations, I found a reminder of resilience, a sense of strength in the simplest of joys. There will be hard days, there will be moments of doubt, but if our children can laugh like this, if Masha and Dasha can carry these memories forward, then perhaps—just perhaps—everything we're working for will be worth it in the end.

27

Crisis, Courage, and Continuance

May greeted me with a creative crisis, and I found myself at a loss. I was tired of fighting for a place under the sun, for a better life. I was just tired. Sometimes, it felt like my book was needed by no one, that it was all utter madness. But I was reinvigorated by a book by Steve Harvey titled *The Most Important Slap in Life, or Revelations of a Man Who Turns Words into Money*. I listened to the audiobook while working in delivery. I finished it in one day. It inspired me tremendously. It was the slap I needed at that moment. I lived through Steve's failures with him and admired his ability to keep moving forward regardless of the obstacles. I continued writing this book with renewed zeal, hoping to become a motivational force for you. It was not Steve's successes but his failures, his honesty about his downfalls, that inspired me. And that is priceless.

This push made me rethink my strength and determination to stand up for what's right—not only in terms of personal ambition but also in the everyday struggles that life throws our way. This time, I had to show resilience in the fight for my daughters' health. That same month, Masha and Dasha came down with fevers, and we found ourselves back at the doctor's office. I had hoped for a bit of understanding, some support in allowing them the time to rest and recover. Instead, it was the all-too-familiar struggle of pleading for just a few extra days. This time, it was Masha with a high fever on a Friday, yet the doctor insisted she would be fine to return to school by Monday. Frustration bubbled up as I argued, seeing how frail she was, and sending her back so quickly felt not just unreasonable but inhumane.

In our country, children are given time to fully recover before returning to school. Here, it seemed the goal was less about healing and more about getting them back to school as quickly as possible. Monday arrived, and her fever persisted, forcing us back to the doctor to finally obtain the note. Soon after, the bill arrived—a hefty charge for what felt like an unnecessary second visit.

I decided to fight the charge. It was not just about money; it was the principle of it. I called the pediatric office, explaining my refusal to pay for their oversight. I described how the doctor ignored my concerns and reminded them of basic guidelines from the World Health Organization, which suggest that children with high fevers should not be rushed back to school within two days. Other children could catch the illness, and the sick child simply wouldn't be well enough.

The conversation with the office dragged on for over an hour. They repeated the same line—"but you came back for a second visit"—without acknowledging why. My nerves frayed as I demanded they acknowledge their responsibility. Finally, I threatened legal action, stating this was about the moral boundaries they were crossing, not the money. Only then did they say they would "look into it" and call me back, which of course, didn't happen.

Days went by, and I had to reach out again. They finally agreed to review it but only after more delays. I reminded them that a trainee had witnessed the original conversation, confirming my request for a few recovery days. Eventually, they relented and canceled the second charge.

This ordeal was eye-opening, revealing a different world where medical bills come with an expectation to negotiate—a concept foreign and frustrating to me. Back home, it would be unthinkable to haggle over healthcare, let alone have fees vary wildly from one doctor to another without reason. I felt disheartened. All I needed was a simple doctor's note, not a battle over basic care.

This sense of loss and dislocation deepened one afternoon as I sorted through our old photographs. As I sat on the couch, scrolling through photos on my laptop, the familiar images of our home and city, of our life before, filled the screen. Memories of Dnipro. Suddenly, I felt the tears coming, and I couldn't stop them.

Masha noticed first, quietly sitting down next to me. "Mama, why are you crying?" she asked softly, glancing at the photos on the screen.

I tried to smile through my tears. "I just . . . miss it all, Masha. Our home, our city, everything we left behind."

Dasha came over, her brow furrowed. She looked at the screen and then back at me, confused. "Are those pictures of our old house, Mama? Is it still there?"

I nodded, brushing a tear from my cheek. "Yes, it's still there. It feels so close . . . but it's not really."

Masha's eyes filled with tears too as she reached over to hug me. "I remember my room. It was so cozy. I miss it so much," she whispered, her voice trembling.

Dasha, feeling the weight of our emotions, sniffled and looked at me with big, sad eyes. "Mama, can we go back there? I miss my toys and my friends."

At that moment, Artur walked in, seeing all three of us holding each other with tears in our eyes. He came over and gently put his hand on my shoulder. "It's hard, isn't it?" he murmured, his own voice thick with emotion. "Leaving everything we knew, everything we built . . ."

I looked up at him, nodding, barely able to speak. "I wish we could just go back."

Artur took a deep breath, kneeling down beside the girls. "I know it's tough, and I miss it too. But we had to leave so that you both would be safe. Sometimes life gives us hard choices, and we have to find new ways to feel at home."

Dasha looked up at him, her eyes wide. "But what if we can't ever go back, Papa? What if our house is . . . gone?"

Artur wrapped an arm around her. "We carry our home with us, Dasha, in our memories. One day, maybe we'll go back. But until then, we'll make new memories here, together."

I took a shaky breath and hugged them all close. "Yes, we'll make new memories. And we'll keep our old ones safe in our hearts."

Late at night, when everyone else was asleep, I lay alone with my thoughts, the memories of a life left behind pressing down on me. Overwhelmed by an ache I could hardly put into words, I suddenly remembered Google Maps. It struck me that perhaps this virtual window was now the only place where Bakhmut still lived on, untouched by destruction. I typed in my parents' old address. There, on the screen, my childhood home appeared—intact, as if frozen in time. The familiar streets, the tree-lined sidewalks, the small flower shop on the corner . . . everything looked untouched, still standing, though I knew the reality was so different.

With a trembling hand, I clicked to "walk" down the streets I once knew by heart. Each turn brought back a memory, a small fragment of a life that now felt distant yet excruciatingly vivid. I passed by the playground where Masha used to play as a little girl, her laughter mingling with the echoes of my own childhood. I could see her running, carefree, as if nothing could ever take this life from us. And in that moment, I saw myself there too—young and full of dreams, the same streets carrying both my past and hers. In this city of my childhood, where life once felt secure and predictable, I could almost hear Masha's laughter merging with my own younger self's joy.

I clicked down another street and found myself facing my old school. My mind filled with images of classrooms and friends, of Danya as a small child, looking up to me with wonder in his eyes. I remembered his small hand gripping mine tightly as we walked to school together, our laughter bouncing off the walls of the buildings that had shaped us. I saw myself growing up there, my brother taking his first steps, my parents walking beside me. These moments played out like scenes from a film, each one tinged with an unbearable sweetness and an even deeper pain. Every corner, every tree held a memory of a life that felt impossible to reclaim.

As I continued, I virtually passed the cafés where Artur and I had spent countless hours, sipping coffee and sharing dreams that once seemed limitless. There was the bakery, too, where the warm scent of fresh bread filled the air, comforting and grounding. I could almost feel Artur's hand in mine as we walked those streets, newlyweds filled with hope, planning the future that awaited us in our hometown. It was where our life together began, where we built dreams, and where we welcomed Masha into the world, believing that this city would shelter us forever.

But the reality was stark, cutting through my memories like a knife. I knew that Bakhmut no longer existed in this way. The city was reduced to ruins, not a single building left standing, its streets now silent, its spirit lost. No soul remained to walk those familiar paths or to share the laughter that once filled the air. It was a city emptied of life, its people scattered, and its buildings turned to rubble. Bakhmut was now a ghost, lingering only in the memories of those of us who had once called it home.

I felt an overwhelming ache in my soul, as if every precious moment of my past was being wrenched from me again. The weight of loss pressed down, heavy and relentless, as the life I'd lived there played out in my mind—my childhood, my family, my dreams, all taken from me by a force beyond my control.

I felt my eyes fill with tears once more. Alone in the quiet, I buried my face in my pillow and wept, mourning not just a city, but a part of myself, a piece of everything I had ever known and loved.

And yet, even in that dark hour, I found a small comfort. Though the city no longer existed in reality, it lived on in my memories, in the stories I carried with me. Bakhmut would always be a part of me, woven into the fabric of who I was, bound to my heart in ways that nothing—not time, not distance, not destruction—could ever erase.

But soon after, reality struck harshly. I learned that the very city where my parents, my brother, and many friends still live had been heavily shelled. Residential buildings burned, lives were lost. I frantically tried to contact my family, reaching out every moment I could, yet no one responded. I was left with a growing fear of what might have happened and how I could bear the unimaginable if they were gone.

During these times, I also began to notice something striking here in America: Many homes display the American flag proudly, celebrating patriotism. I respected that deeply. Yet I noticed some flags had modified colors, blended with shades from the countries of origin of those who lived there. At first, I didn't quite understand; after all, I wouldn't want another country's colors added to the Ukrainian flag. But then, I started to see the symbolism in these hybrid flags—a blending of their roots with a new identity here. They reflect a merging of worlds, an expression of belonging yet longing, a way of carrying pieces of their culture within their new one. It gave me a new perspective: Perhaps everything has a right to exist, even if it looks different than we're used to.

Once, during a lecture at a university, a professor praised Ukraine but lamented the impacts of globalization, calling it a negative force. At the time, I didn't fully understand his sentiment—I thought there was nothing wrong with international connections. But now, after months in America,

I feel a profound longing for my homeland. I see now that it's a gift to have your own culture, songs, traditional clothing, food, history, and the strength of a whole nation. It is incredible. I miss these things deeply and hold a powerful love for my country.

And so, our first year in the USA came to an end—a country of possibilities, where dreams are both realized and shattered, a land where hope and human flaws coexist in plain sight.

Yes, I still feel the weight of guilt as a mother, stretched between work, writing, and the needs of my children Masha and Dasha and my husband. Late at night, after work, I sit with this book, pouring into it what I hope will be useful for someone else walking a similar path. Perhaps for someone, it will ease the journey of immigration, or help them face war, or simply offer a lifeline in moments of self-doubt. Life, after all, is a series of challenges and growth. What matters is not stopping but moving forward, through every stumble.

I'm deeply grateful to America for the opportunities it has provided: for the peace, for the distance from war, for a new space to realize myself. I'm thankful for the kindness of people, for the chance to understand their culture, and for the freedom to build a new life. America opened its doors and gave us the chance to begin again, and that is a gift I hold close.

I wonder how many times a person can break and still rise again. I've been shattered more than once, yet here I am, piecing things together, writing this book, hoping it can help someone else. In life, we fall without instruction, often fearing we'll sink even lower. How much easier it would be if we knew that falling was just a part of finding our footing again. I wasn't taught how to fall, but I've learned this: We only reach as high as we dare to try.

I dared to write this book, to open myself up. I'd love to end it with a fairytale finish—winning the lottery, becoming a bestseller, achieving some remarkable success. But instead, I'll end with this: a first year in a new country, a year full of trials, and an open ending, where the next step is unknown.

What comes next is uncertain—whether this book will become a bestseller, whether I'll put down roots in this country, find a new home in Europe, or, perhaps, one day, see peace and return to Ukraine. But one thing is certain: I am moving forward, and I have grand plans for this life.

Part 4

ROOTS OF RESILIENCE

Ukraine, 2014

To understand resilience,
one must first understand where it was planted.

28

The Beginning of the End

The world became fully aware of the conflict on February 24, 2022, but for many Ukrainians, the war truly began in 2014. For me, that year marked the start of a slow-building tragedy, deeply reshaping life in my hometown of Bakhmut, on the eastern edge of the country. We lived with the uncertainty, fear, and daily instability of a conflict largely unnoticed by the rest of the world. Only in 2022 did the full scale of the war draw global attention, highlighting the hardships we had endured for nearly a decade. My city had faced immense struggles for eight long years before the world recognized this devastating reality.

As these national events unfolded, our lives in Bakhmut were gradually enveloped in an invisible storm—a storm that would soon reshape everything. The sounds of distant conflict grew closer, and each day brought new reminders of the danger encroaching upon us.

Today, not a single building in my town Bakhmut has survived intact. The country calls my city a fortress. It bore the brunt of the attack and was wiped off the map for its bravery. A ghost town. No one lives there anymore. Only in the hearts of its seventy-eight thousand former residents will it live on forever. Bakhmut is no more. I can never return and wander its streets, reliving memories of my youth. I can never return to my ancestral home. It has been destroyed and burned, along with my childhood photos and keepsakes.

But why did no one talk about the war when we were bombed and shelled starting in 2014? We had a military conflict that continued unabated until 2022. But it wasn't called a war; it was an "anti-terrorist operation" that lasted eight years. Seriously? Was this not a full-scale invasion? Just an invasion on a smaller scale? The same weapons were used, the same bombs dropped, the same horrors inflicted.

It all began with a prolonged political crisis sparked by Ukraine's decision to reject an association agreement with the European Union, as the country's leadership chose instead to strengthen ties with Russia. For many Ukrainians, especially those who held pro-European views, this decision was a deep disappointment—a step backward from democracy and the progress we hoped for. This rejection felt like a betrayal, especially to younger Ukrainians who looked to the EU as a symbol of openness, prosperity, and respect for human rights. We saw our place within it as guaranteeing a brighter, freer future, something generations had longed for.

Outrage and disappointment quickly led to peaceful protests, later known as Euromaidan—named for their location in Kyiv's Maidan Nezalezhnosti (Independence Square). These demonstrations weren't just about the EU agreement; they were a call for change, demanding government accountability, transparency, and a commitment to European values. The protestors wanted a Ukraine that stood against corruption and embraced the ideals of democracy and human rights.

What began as peaceful mass protests soon escalated into intense and often radical demonstrations across the country, lasting nearly four months. Protesters gathered in freezing winter conditions, enduring harsh weather and an increasingly hostile government response. Violent clashes eventually erupted between protesters and police, leading to tragic bloodshed and the deaths of over a hundred people. We honor these victims as the Heavenly Hundred. They sacrificed their lives for the hope of a better future. May they rest in peace.

After months of turmoil and mounting pressure from the opposition, Ukraine's president, Viktor Yanukovych, finally signed a crisis resolution agreement. But then, to the shock of the entire nation, he fled the capital the very same day. He simply ran away. Imagine the disbelief we felt—our leader just left us, abandoning his post at the most critical time in recent memory. I couldn't believe it; how is it even possible for a president to flee the country?

In that moment, we were left without clear leadership, facing immense uncertainty and a power vacuum. This event marked a turning point, setting off a chain reaction that would change the course of our country forever.

In the chaotic aftermath of the political crisis, Russia took advantage of Ukraine's instability. Crimea, strategically located on the Black Sea, was quickly occupied. Once a beloved vacation spot for both Ukrainians and Russians, the peninsula—with its beaches, vineyards, and history—suddenly became the subject of an international dispute. Russia deployed troops, held a questionable referendum, and claimed the territory almost without resistance. It was a bloodless invasion—no bombs, no battles, no visible opposition. The world watched in shock as Crimea's status changed overnight. The annexation of the peninsula happened almost silently, while we were left to face a far more brutal reality.

While the world was absorbed by the news of Crimea's quiet annexation, our lives in eastern Ukraine were crumbling under the sounds of explosions and gunfire. The same forces that had crossed into Crimea without firing a shot were now attacking the towns and villages of Donbas. This eastern region of Ukraine, rich in coal and minerals, had long been known as the "industrial heartland" of the country. It was our home—a land of mines and factories, where life was defined by the labor and pride of its workers.

In February 2014, as tensions escalated in Crimea, armed conflict erupted in our towns. Pro-Russian groups declared "independence," rejecting our government and sowing chaos. As the conflict intensified, Ukrainian forces launched what was called an "anti-terrorist operation," a desperate attempt to protect us and maintain the country's sovereignty.

Bakhmut, one of the cities in Donbas and my hometown, found itself at the heart of this conflict. Once a peaceful city, known for its salt mines and vineyards, it turned into a war zone in 2014. Blockades were set up at the city's entrances, making it impossible to leave; those who tried to were shot on sight. Each day, the sound of gunfire grew louder, closer, while our army, fighting valiantly, was stretched to its limits.

The world around us had turned into a nightmare. Explosions, the roar of tanks, and gunfire became our everyday reality. Like all of Donbas, Bakhmut was under constant shelling. Roads that once connected us to nearby towns now led only to death and destruction. Communities were shattered, lives lost. The government refused to acknowledge the full scale of the catastrophe, leaving us feeling as though our suffering was invisible.

While Crimea was annexed almost without a sound, we continued to struggle for survival. Every day, we looked into the face of war's horrors. In this forgotten war, our home, our identity, and our future were at stake. All we could do was hold on.

Days turned into nights, and the distant sounds of war had become an unsettling lullaby—a grim reminder of the world outside. But that night was different. It was as if the air itself was holding its breath, awaiting the arrival of something terrible.

It was 4 a.m. Artur and I were fast asleep, our little Masha curled up between us, just two years old, peacefully dreaming. Only the night before, we had made plans for the next day, clinging to the illusion that tomorrow would come as usual. The silence was shattered by a sudden explosion, so close it felt as though the walls themselves were trembling. The deep rumble of tank fire and the crack of gunshots echoed around us, filling the air with a brutal symphony of violence. The blasts seemed to reverberate in my chest, a suffocating pressure that made it hard to breathe, each shockwave pressing down as if the very air had turned against us. Every noise was amplified in the darkness, the roar of planes overhead, the whistling descent of shells, the ground quaking beneath us—it was as though the world itself had come undone.

I woke up, my whole body trembling, seized by a fear unlike anything I had ever known. Artur's grip tightened around my hand, his body tense as we huddled together, hoping the walls would hold. I looked at him, desperate to understand what was happening. His voice was steady but laced with tension.

"Don't move . . . stay right here," he whispered, nodding toward the window. "Please, don't go near the glass."

I could hardly breathe, terror gripping my throat.

"Artur, what . . . what is this? Are they . . . are they already here?" My voice cracked, as though the war itself stood just outside our door, close enough to touch.

He pulled me closer, holding me tightly, trying to calm me. But I could feel his own fear, a silent tremor that filled the room.

"I don't know," he replied, his voice hoarse, raw with worry. "But we can't take any chances. We have to stay here. Together. Don't leave my side, okay? Let's just stay close . . ."

The Beginning of the End

I held Masha against me, trying to hide my terror, but it was like the world had shattered in an instant.

"Artur . . . what if . . . what if a shell hits our building? We're on the fourth floor—what if it collapses?" My chest tightened, the fear crushing me.

He looked into my eyes, a mix of desperation and determination in his gaze. "We'll get through this," he murmured, almost as if saying it too loudly might break the fragile hope we clung to. "We just have to make it through tonight . . . together. Only together."

I didn't understand or know much about weapons by their sounds. It was all new to me. Artur and I were very frightened. I couldn't imagine what to do next, how to live, how to stock up on food and other necessities. And it was terrifying, holding my little daughter, Masha, just over two years old, in my arms while war raged outside, and not understanding why it was happening. How could something like this even be possible? At that moment, it felt like it would never end. It was terrifying. The shooting didn't stop until dawn. Helicopters and planes flew overhead. They fired with all sorts of weapons. It was simply hell.

We gathered, dressed, and sat huddled in the corner of the room. We were completely at a loss about what to do in such a situation. I was shaking uncontrollably. I couldn't calm down. I didn't understand what was happening to me. Why was my whole body trembling? Masha was scared. I tried to comfort her, but it was hard to do so. To calm a child, you need to be calm yourself. But I was shaking, crying. I was frightened by the gunfire, the volleys around us. We didn't understand what was happening. We didn't know what to do. Naturally, I couldn't calm anyone else because I needed calming myself. At that moment, we were unaware that we needed to stock up on food and water, withdraw cash from our cards to have on hand. We were completely unprepared for war.

Our mobile connection was down. We couldn't contact anyone. We were simply terrified. As it turned out, a war had erupted, one that our country refused to acknowledge. They called it merely an anti-terrorist operation. Planes flew overhead, bombs exploded, tanks rolled by. There were soldiers everywhere. It was like waking up in the middle of a war movie, unable to understand when it would end or how you could escape back to reality. Our world had collapsed in an instant. All our plans, all our hopes for the future, had crumbled. We were left alone amid the war.

We sat without water because the pipes were damaged. Of course, store shelves were bare as people had panicked and cleared out the supplies. In their panic, people had withdrawn all the cash from ATMs, and banks weren't refilling them because it was too dangerous. It was frightening to go outside. The streets had become unsafe. But Artur continued to go to work, and I cried every time because I was not sure he would return home from work. I was terrified. Occasionally there were breaks and the shooting would stop. We tried to use these breaks to gather food and water. People slowly began to adapt to the war, setting up basements to hide in. My parents lived in the house opposite mine at the time. We tried to devise some kind of plan, but we simply couldn't come up with one.

At that time, Artur and I didn't have a car, and we didn't even know where to run if there was a direct threat. Social media was rife with speculation and falsehoods. Every day they convinced us that there would be a massive shelling and no one would survive. Day after day, we simply existed. It took us a long time to understand what had happened, what was happening. And what the aggressors wanted was unclear.

We heard only horrors about what was happening in neighboring cities, about what their soldiers were doing, how they were tormenting women, children, even elderly men, how people were simply surviving on the streets, cooking whatever they could find because, well, everything had stopped. Life just ended in a moment. Store shelves were empty, pharmacies empty, no products were being transported because it was unsafe to travel on the highways. Nothing was left, the city had died out. No supplies. And you just feared dying. And you didn't know from what you might die. From starvation, dehydration, or from someone just shooting you on the street.

Unspeakable horrors were unfolding in our region, in the neighboring towns. This plague was approaching ever closer, and we were simply waiting in terror for its arrival. We had no means to leave; we had neither transportation nor the financial means to do so, as buses and trains were not operational. The only escape was by car. Military skirmishes were a daily occurrence. The city was bombarded every day. At that time, we lived near a military base, so we could hear the attacks on our unit, the bursts of automatic gunfire, as our soldiers managed to hold their ground.

While the main nightmare was in the neighboring city, they managed to push closer and closer to us. The panic was horrendous. Stores were completely empty, there was no shelter, nowhere to go. Our building didn't even have a basement; we had nowhere to hide. In case of shelling, all we could do was stay inside our homes and pray that it wouldn't reach us. The most terrifying part was not understanding what was happening and why. Why the sudden onset of war, why we were being killed, why was all this happening? Why were our acquaintances, our friends, our relatives dying? Some died because they went to defend their homeland, others while trying to leave the city limits, and they were simply shot on the roads, along with their children. These are horrific things.

It felt as though, from their side, there were not soldiers, not people, but simply beasts devoid of any feelings or compassion. It was simply genocide. And the whole world remained silent. Everyone was more concerned about Crimea being taken, a peninsula where no one was harmed, but no one cared about our part of the country being obliterated along with its people. We were completely bewildered.

During each bombardment, I would shake violently. I was terribly cold, and I was gripped by an unbearable fear. Especially in the evenings, when the shelling occurred, I would always put Masha to bed. Artur was perplexed and asked why every time the shelling started, I put Masha to bed. I said I didn't know. But after some time, I realized why I was doing it. I thought that if we had to die that day, perhaps it would be easier for her in her sleep. This is something no one should ever have to experience. It was terrifying.

At that moment, my best friend was my cousin, Tanya. She was more than a friend to me; she was everything. We had become close when I was fifteen and she was sixteen. We bonded over small rebellious acts, like when she taught me to smoke, and we became inseparable. We talked every day, shared everything in our lives, and over the years, we truly became best friends. Later, we even had our children just a few months apart.

But our relationship wasn't always easy or simple. We often fought because of our different perspectives on life, yet none of that mattered—we were still close. She was my closest confidante, a steadfast presence. Even during the darkest moments, she had been there, a source of strength when the world felt unstable. Her decision to leave meant losing a part of myself.

When Tanya decided to leave the city and move to the aggressor's country, I felt completely betrayed. It was as if my world collapsed. Her departure felt like abandonment, especially since we lived only a few kilometers apart in Bakhmut. And then, out of the blue, she called me one evening and said, "Tomorrow, I'm leaving to live in Russia."

I was shocked. "Are you serious? Just like that? You just call me in the evening and tell me you're leaving tomorrow? As if that's . . . normal?"

"I didn't want you to find out this way . . . but I had no choice," she said. "We've made our decision, and there's no going back."

"How could you keep this a secret and then just tell me the night before? You knew what this means to me. You know this feels like betrayal," I said, feeling the words burn as I spoke.

"I know, but we've decided. I need to be with my mom, with my family . . . I just . . . I can't stay here anymore."

"Family?" I said. "What about me? Do I not count anymore? We lived so close, we were always together! And now, just like that, you're throwing it all away?"

"It hurts me too. Do you think this is easy for me? I just . . . please, forgive me," she whispered.

"Forgive you?" I replied, disbelief flooding my voice. "You ask for forgiveness after dropping this on me? You don't even give me a chance to understand . . . Do you really think this is something I can just let go of?"

I couldn't understand why she would leave me here, especially at a time like this. The pain, resentment, and anger I felt were overwhelming, amplified by the fact that she was moving to Russia. I knew she was going to be with her mother, who had been living there for years, yet knowing didn't lessen the sting of her choice.

Her absence left a hollow ache in my life. Back then, we didn't have the easy, instant connections we do now—no video calls, no messaging apps to bridge the distance. We relied on costly international calls and the occasional SMS, words weighed down by the expense and distance between us. She had left just as the war began, before the darkness truly settled over our world, and from the safety of her new home, it was as if she doubted the depth of my suffering, questioning the reality of the devastation around me. That disbelief pierced me more deeply than I could have imagined.

Our relationship had never been simple, but even with all our complexities, losing her like that tore a wound through my heart. I couldn't picture my life without her presence. And yet, there I was—left behind, trying to find a way forward through the emptiness she had left.

As I stood alone amid the ruins, I realized that war wasn't only taking away homes, lives, and futures—it was shattering bonds that had once felt unbreakable. The losses stretched far beyond the physical world, etching deep scars into my heart and soul.

29

Living Under Siege

On April 12, 2014, the aggressor reached our town. From that moment, we began living under occupation, a dark cloud descending over us as they took control. Fear crept into our homes, growing heavier each day.

Armed soldiers patrolled the streets, often drunk, carrying weapons they wielded recklessly. Simply going to the store became a terrifying ordeal; these men could fire without a second thought, regardless of who stood in their path—a child, a woman, an elderly person. Nowhere felt safe. In a small town like ours, the smallest details spread quickly, turning quiet anxiety into something more oppressive.

Horrors befell women and children, and in a town like ours, large enough to house many but small enough for rumors to fly, stories spread quickly. People spoke in whispers of homes broken into, of tanks crushing civilian cars, of stores looted for every last bit of food. Any resistance felt pointless, crushed before it began. Many tried to protest, but in the end, it all seemed futile. The violence around us, chaotic at first, soon became a systematic tightening of control. They were firmly in power, and it was terrifying.

As if living in constant fear wasn't enough, they stripped us of any remaining sense of control. Then, came the so-called vote. We were to "decide" whether to live under their rule, to become part of their invented republic. But there was no choice. Soldiers roamed the streets, rounding people up, dragging them from their homes. They kicked down doors and forced everyone to the polls, ensuring no one could refuse. At each voting site, soldiers loomed with automatic weapons, their eyes fixed on us to make sure each vote aligned with what they wanted, not with what we truly felt.

It was a time of relentless fear, moving so quickly that we hardly understood what was happening to us. We couldn't grasp it fully. Back then, we didn't understand the stages of shock or trauma. We didn't know how to help ourselves or our child. We did whatever we could to survive, believing, praying, that one day our country would recognize what was happening and come to save us. But no one came. No one rushed to help. We were left to endure it all on our own.

People still tried to escape, to break through the surrounding chaos. Some managed to do so, slipping past the soldiers and risking everything. Convoys of cars leaving the city were often targeted, and many of these desperate attempts ended in tragedy. Yet a few did make it through, and with every escape, there was a small flicker of hope for those of us who remained.

But for us in the East, the most painful realization was not just the war at our doorstep—it was the growing distance from our own countrymen in the West. It was as though we were living in entirely separate worlds. Life continued for them, seemingly untouched. They knew of the "anti-terrorist operation" unfolding in the East, but for many, it was just something happening "over there," a vague, distant conflict.

And then, the judgments came. They blamed us, saying it was our fault, as though speaking Russian made us responsible for the horrors we faced. Housing prices in the western regions soared, and those who tried to move found themselves unwelcome. Rentals were denied, and people were told to "return to their territories." This quiet but bitter divide, drawn along language and regional lines, revealed an underlying fracture in our country. It was deeply painful to feel like strangers in our own land, to reach out for solidarity only to find ourselves pushed away.

Yes, we tried to resist. People fought back however they could, some like partisans, sabotaging when possible, using whatever means they had. In whispers and behind closed doors, they found ways to poison soldiers, to disrupt the enemy's plans. Everyone who could, everyone with even a little power to hinder, took the risk.

And then, finally, after what felt like an eternity, we saw a light—a glimmer of freedom. In early July, to our immense relief, our soldiers arrived to reclaim the city. The sounds of gunfire and explosions filled the air as they fought to free us. We trembled, we huddled in fear, unable to process it fully. Only later did we understand what was happening: Our military had come to save us. Our city was free again, but the scars of occupation remained.

We were exhausted, but we did what we could to support our soldiers, bringing supplies to hospitals, sharing food, gathering clothes, even washing their uniforms. It felt like our duty, a way to heal the wounds that had been inflicted on our home. But even though we had reclaimed Bakhmut, neighboring towns still suffered under occupation, and our city stood as a fragile island of freedom in a sea of violence.

At that time, my husband's parents were in a nearby town, one still untouched by occupation, though another just beyond theirs was not so fortunate. Despite the danger, Artur and I made these perilous journeys to see them, navigating through checkpoints and patrols where men were sometimes pulled right from their cars and drafted on the spot. Each trip felt like a gamble with fate, yet each time, I found myself behind the wheel of my father's car, loaded with essentials for Artur's parents. We argued endlessly about the risks, especially with Masha in tow, but I couldn't refuse my in-laws.

"Artur, I can't do this anymore," I said, gripping the steering wheel as we rattled along the road back. "Can't you see how dangerous this is? We're not only risking our lives, but Masha's too."

He sighed heavily, rubbing his face with his hands. "I know, but they're my parents. They need us. What if things get worse tomorrow, and they can't reach us on their own?"

"And what about our daughter?" I burst out, feeling despair and anger boiling inside me. "Every time we go, I promise myself it'll be the last, that we won't put Masha at risk again. But then we go again, and I'm terrified at every checkpoint, every stretch of this damned road."

Artur fell silent, his face darkened. Finally, he said quietly, "Do you think I'm not scared? Every time, I fear for all of us. But how can I leave them?"

"I'm not asking you to abandon them, but maybe they can manage without us for a while? Or we could find a way to help them without putting us all in this danger?" I whispered desperately.

"I'll try to figure something out," he replied at last, staring ahead with a look of anguish. "I just don't know what the solution is."

As much as we wanted to believe in a solution, each trip back felt even more harrowing than the last. As we drove along the highway bordered by open fields, the landscape could suddenly erupt with explosions as artillery fire struck nearby. Anti-aircraft missiles and GRAD rockets slammed into the earth around us, and I would push the gas pedal to the floor, silently promising myself it would be the last time we made this journey. Yet, despite my fears and the gnawing guilt, I found myself returning to that road again and again, unable to escape this terrifying cycle that put our child at risk.

Even in the moments when we weren't on the road, stability felt like a distant hope. At that time, we were renting an apartment, trying to carve out a semblance of security amid the chaos. One evening, the phone rang unexpectedly. The owners were on the line, their tone cold and matter-of-fact.

"We're coming back to the apartment," the man said abruptly. "We lost our jobs because the city we work in is now occupied. We have no other place to go."

I froze, clutching Masha close. "What do you mean, we have to leave tonight?" I gasped, my voice a mix of shock and desperation. "We have nowhere to go on such short notice."

"We don't have a choice," he replied, his voice devoid of sympathy. "You have four hours. Make sure the apartment is empty by the time we arrive."

They hung up, leaving us stunned and scrambling. We had to move out quickly, finding ourselves on the street in the evening with a small child and our belongings. Miraculously, we immediately found another apartment and moved in. It was a huge shock, in the unstable wartime environment, to be kicked out at any moment because, during a war, many things we hold dear, like a lease agreement, lose their significance.

In our new apartment, we set up the bathroom because everyone said it was safest to wait out the shelling there. Our bathroom was stocked with food, water, blankets, and pillows for about three days, prepared for enduring the shelling. The new house had a basement where neighbors had set up a little shelter, but we stayed in our bathroom. It was then that I began to experience panic attacks, but at the time, I didn't understand what was happening to me; I just felt awful, as if I was going to die. And all this happened amid strong, continuous shelling. Yes, there was almost constant gunfire; it's one thing when the shots are very far away, and you know it's at the outskirts or at a checkpoint between military forces, and it's another when it hits the city. Each time, I would tremble, I was very cold, I was terribly frightened, I felt I was going to die.

Every day, I begged Artur not to go to work, to stay home. He worked as a programmer, and he could have stayed home to work. But at that time, it wasn't common practice, and everyone was still expected to go into the office. Each morning as he prepared to leave, I would plead with him to reconsider.

"Artur, please, can't you just stay home today?" I asked, my voice trembling as I clung to him at the door. "It's too dangerous. What if there's shelling while you're out?"

He gave me a gentle, reassuring smile. "I know you're worried, but if I don't go, they might let me go," he replied quietly. "We need the income, now more than ever."

"But what good is that if . . ." My voice broke, and I couldn't finish the sentence.

"I'll be careful," he promised, squeezing my hand. "I'll come back. I always do."

Each day, I watched him leave, waving goodbye with a heavy heart, not knowing if he would make it home safely. The fear was constant, gnawing at me every moment he was gone. What if there was shelling while he was returning? What if he got caught in the crossfire on his way to work? These were terrifying times.

Artur worked for the country's largest bank, and there was just a branch in our city. Due to the situation, they offered employees to move to the main office in the center of the country. But we had no means to go there; we couldn't afford to rent a place. And we had heard terrible accounts from people who had left, about how scary it was to say where you were from while in your own country. Just scary to say that you were from the eastern part. That you might be beaten. That you might be attacked. Horrible things. And as the conflict escalated, men were mobilized from all over the country. The western part of the country blamed us for their men dying. It was all our fault. The conflict within our country flared up intensely.

We lived through a year of war, which was incredibly hard and complex. Every day brought uncertainty, and invariably, nothing good was expected to happen. If you survived the day, it was just another day lived in fear. Each day tested our endurance, pushing us closer to breaking, but nothing could prepare us for what happened next. Exactly one year later, on February

13th, another shelling occurred. The aggressor targeted a school and a kindergarten with an incendiary system, killing children.

The entire city, in a huge procession, came out to bury the children. It was horrifying. People were fearless. We took to the streets, and the entire city accompanied these children on their final journey. That was the breaking point for me.

That evening, as I held Masha close, whispering promises of a new beginning, Artur sat beside me, his face shadowed with grief and exhaustion. I looked at him, my heart heavy with a decision that felt inevitable.

"Artur, we can't stay here anymore," I whispered, my voice barely audible. "This place has taken too much from us. I can't bear to lose anything else."

He looked down, nodding slowly, then asked, "Where would we go?"

"To Dnipro," I said firmly. "It's in the center of the country. Your bank's main office is there, and you could go to work without fearing for your life every day."

Artur looked down, processing everything, then reached out and took my hand. "I'll find out about a transfer to Dnipro first thing tomorrow," he replied, determination in his voice.

I nodded, feeling a glimmer of hope. "It's our best chance to give Masha a safe life."

There was no more room for doubt. This place had stolen too much from us, and we couldn't bear to lose any more. That night, we made our decision: We had to escape—if not for ourselves, then for her.

30

Battling Fear and Finding Hope

When we first told our parents about our plans to move to the center of the country, they advised us not to mention where we were from. Bakhmut had been our home, a place filled with vibrant streets where laughter echoed from children playing in the parks, and the aroma of fresh bread from the local bakery wafted through the air. I could still envision the sun filtering through the leaves of the trees in my favorite park, creating a warm and cozy atmosphere for Masha and me. But now, those streets lay in fear, each corner a reminder of what we had lost, a deep sense of grief engulfing me as I navigated through the debris of my former life.

"Please, don't say anything about Bakhmut," my mom said, her voice filled with anxiety.

"Why not?" I asked, not understanding her concern.

"People will judge you. They'll think you're trouble," my dad added, looking at me with care.

"But it's the truth," I insisted.

"The truth doesn't matter if it makes things harder," he said, pointing out how much we had already been through.

They feared that revealing our origins might only bring more challenges in our new surroundings. Despite our hesitation, I made the initial trip to Dnipro with my father, who drove me as I searched for a place we could call home. Masha was with us, and at one point, we nearly fell victim to a housing scam. Thankfully, I recognized the signs and managed to avoid it. But I remember standing in that office, overwhelmed with anger and frustration, shouting at the people who tried to take our last savings. "How could you?" I demanded. "I've been living in hell, in war, for over a year, with a small child, and yet here you are, trying to swindle me out of everything." Their indifference felt inhumane. We returned home, unsuccessful and disheartened.

The contrast between our world and theirs struck me deeply. Just 180 miles away, life carried on peacefully. Arriving in this new city, we were met with bustling streets filled with honking cars and people rushing about, their lives seemingly untouched by the chaos we had fled. Bright shop windows displayed an abundance of goods, a stark contrast to the empty shelves back home. The vibrant lights of restaurants and cafes created an atmosphere of celebration, one that felt almost mocking as we grappled with our fear and uncertainty.

Artur was determined, and he went back alone to try again. The rental prices for people from the East were double, and some of those who realized where we came from refused to rent to us at all. Against the odds, he found us an apartment, and we began our preparations to leave.

"I can't believe we're really doing this," Artur said, looking at me with concern.

"I know it all seems scary," I replied, trying to reassure him. "But this is our chance to start over."

"If it weren't for you, I would never have had the courage to take this step," he admitted. "I'm glad you voiced it. I was afraid for so long, but now that we have an apartment, it's becoming a reality."

"We can handle this," I said, feeling hope beginning to stir within me. "It's like a new life on another planet, but we'll be together."

"Yes, together," he confirmed, and there was a note of determination in his voice.

I had never imagined leaving my hometown; I had envisioned my entire life there. Yet here we were, forced to let go. The apartment we rented was furnished, so we couldn't take much with us. Our journey was an evacuation—no more than a couple of bags, and everything else had to be left behind. Toys, dishes, linens, furniture—all the things we had gathered together over the years. Our refrigerator, washing machine, even my piano, a precious gift from my father, had to stay. I never thought I would have to part with it. And so, with only a few bags and Masha in my arms, we left.

It was terrifying. Part of me wanted to stay, to hold onto my home despite the danger, but the fear of what might happen left us no choice.

My parents and Danya stayed behind in our small town, while we began a new chapter in the center of the country. It was the first of many fresh starts. I tried to accept that everything we had was gone, and I needed to build our lives anew.

Arriving in this new place, we felt completely alienated. The streets, the people, the very air felt foreign. Everything around us seemed indifferent, going about its routine, while we felt like strangers passing through. The reality of our displacement began to sink in, leaving us with an overwhelming sense of loneliness. As I stepped outside for the first time, a wave of panic washed over me. It felt as if the world had turned its back on me, and I was just a ghost wandering through this unfamiliar place. The sounds of laughter and celebration around me only deepened my sense of isolation, reminding me of the warmth we had lost. Every evening, returning to our small apartment felt like a retreat into a shell, where I could hide from the chaos of the world outside.

Adapting seemed impossible. Everything around us was baffling: this city, this region, lived its own life, full of celebrations, fireworks, late-night outings, and parties. People here had everything—comfortable homes, furniture, beautiful decor—while we had nothing and were forced to start from scratch. Restaurants bustled with birthday festivities, all while our people were dying.

As days went by, a deep sadness took hold of me. The happiness around us only amplified my despair, and it wasn't long before depression began to creep in, making every day feel heavier. Panic attacks became a constant presence, making any attempt to blend into this society almost unbearable. We enrolled Masha in daycare, and during a medical check-up at the clinic, a woman noticed the daycare group number on our medical card. She leaned over to whisper, "Oh, we're in the same group. Can you believe it? Newcomers from the eastern part of the country are joining us now." She didn't realize she was speaking about me. I turned to her, feigning surprise, and replied, "Really? That's quite the news." It was a nightmare.

Later, when the doctor saw our address, he asked immediately, "When are you going back? When will you leave?" I simply replied that we'd gladly return if the war ended. We were strangers everywhere, even in our own country. Hated, unaccepted—it was profoundly difficult to adjust to this life. Shopping became a torment—seeing fully stocked shelves while knowing that, just a few towns over, my parents would celebrate if they managed to find a pack of pasta in nearly empty stores. Walking through the aisles, I was bombarded by the sights and smells of abundance, a cruel reminder of the scarcity my family faced back home.

And then there was the growing resentment between us and the residents of Dnipro from the western part of the country. Once, as I sat watching Masha play with other children at a playground, a mother approached me. Having learned that we were from the east, she began yelling, accusing me of being the reason her husband might be drafted into the war while people like us weren't fighting. "Why did your husband move to the center of the country instead of going to the front, while mine might be taken?" She was almost ready to physically attack me. It was terrifying, deeply disturbing. She poured out all her anger and fears onto me, blaming me for anything and everything. It was horrific. The accusation hung in the air, sharp and piercing. I stood frozen, feeling the hostility radiate from her. It was terrifying to be seen as a scapegoat for someone else's fears, and in that moment, the weight of my existence in this new place became painfully clear.

As time went on, the war settled into an illusion of ceasefire. The aggressor managed to create two so-called people's republics, and although our city remained under Ukrainian control, the shelling continued despite attempts at peace. Gradually, we began to visit our parents again, and sometimes they came to us. Stores in their area started to carry more goods, and transportation slightly improved. But to see each other, we had to pass through checkpoints and endure frightening inspections, proving we weren't traitors, only family visiting family. It was all incredibly hard and terrifying.

My panic attacks never left me; they only deepened as time went on, and with them came a heavy wave of depression that I couldn't quite understand. This made everything seem worse. Slowly, a paralyzing fear took root within me, growing until I was too afraid to even step outside, too terrified to go to the store. Agoraphobia crept in, and my condition deteriorated. This went on for a year, and truly, I felt as though I were losing my mind. I don't know how Artur endured it all, how he stayed by my side and didn't give up on me. I lived in a constant state of bleakness, devoid of joy. I managed the basics—taking care of Masha and the household—but it took everything I had.

I was constantly on the edge of tears, often thinking I might not survive. It never even crossed my mind to seek psychological help. I went to various doctors, and each prescribed antidepressants, but they only seemed to worsen my condition, amplifying my fear of medication. My appetite vanished, and over time, I lost half of my body weight—shedding 123.5 pounds in the process—and transformed from a plump young woman to someone incredibly thin. Strangely, this change gave me a small spark of joy; it was one of the things that helped me slowly recover. Yet, the fear that I might relapse never left me, haunting me with an endless cycle of anxiety.

The mental strain was only worsened by the weight of our financial situation. Living in a big city proved to be much more challenging than life in our small town, and each month brought new struggles just to get by. The cost of living here was far higher, leaving us to make difficult choices as the days ticked down to payday. I vividly remember the evenings when we had to resort to frying bread, the simplest meal we could manage, because our funds were so tight.

Desperate to ease this burden, I began searching for work, but each application ended in rejection. Time and again, I faced the harsh reality that my origins played a significant role in their decisions. Each "no" felt like a weight added to my already heavy heart. Realizing I needed a new direction, I decided to return to school. Even though I already held a degree, I chose to pursue a path in IT, hoping it would offer the stability we so desperately needed. With that decision, I embarked on a new chapter of my education.

For the first time in what felt like ages, I sensed life beginning to return to me. The desire to adapt and rebuild sparked within me, fueled by the knowledge that Masha deserved a childhood free from the shadows of our struggles. Every three months, we made the trek to visit my parents and Artur's family. Yet, each trip filled Masha with dread, and I often found myself regretting putting her through such uncertainty. During that time, the aggressor focused on establishing the so-called people's republics, and while ceasefires were frequently declared, they were often broken, leading to continued shelling. But through it all, we learned to navigate our new reality.

I came to understand that we had to persist, to rebuild our lives piece by piece. For the first time, I could look in the mirror without feeling disgust; instead, I saw a disciplined, slender figure staring back at me, a reflection that felt strangely empowering. With newfound resolve, we began to venture out more. Our first trip to the circus was unforgettable—a rare moment of unfiltered joy that reignited a spark in our hearts. Dining out together felt like a luxury; I remember the sensation of feeling almost like a princess, marveling at the beautiful dishes presented before us. Sitting there with Artur, we savored that brief escape from our harsh reality.

Despite the darkness that had enveloped us, I began to see glimmers of light breaking through the clouds of despair. Each small step we took felt monumental, a testament to our resilience. I realized that while our past may forever be a part of us, we had the power to shape our future, to rebuild our lives, and to nurture hope in our daughter's heart.

31

Battles Within and Beyond

It had been three years since the war began, and two years since we had moved to the central part of the country. Life in Dnipro was quieter than in the east, where my parents still lived under the constant threat of bombardments. Yet even here, the weight of the war never truly left us. Conversations with friends, walks through the neighborhood, even ordinary errands felt tinged with the unspoken tension that had settled into everyone's lives. Artur and I often found ourselves discussing the fragility of life over late-night tea, wondering what kind of future we were building for Masha. We began contemplating the idea of giving her a sibling, a sister or brother—someone who would be by her side in this world of uncertainty, someone to share her life with, to hold onto.

It felt strange, almost paradoxical, to think about bringing new life into such a tumultuous time. Yet, perhaps that very chaos stirred a desire in us to defy it, to create something pure and hopeful. I'm not sure why, but it felt right, even natural, to consider a child amid all this uncertainty. I suppose there's something primal, a subconscious survival instinct, that drives people to create life in the face of death, as if to say, "We will endure, no matter what."

During this time, I also got a small tattoo on my arm that read "Leave fear." The words were a reminder to myself, a sort of silent prayer, that I could overcome the weight of anxiety pressing down on me. I was still haunted by the possibility of my previous conditions returning—the panic attacks, the waves of despair that seemed to have no end. This tattoo was my shield, a symbol of the strength I was trying to muster every day.

Looking at Masha, I felt both fear and hope. I wanted her to have a sister or brother not only for company but as a shared anchor—a family she could lean on when life seemed unbearable, someone who would understand the unique experience of growing up during these turbulent times.

Despite the uncertainties around us, we did our best to live a normal life. We settled into a new routine, finding solace in small rituals that made the days feel predictable, even stable. I focused on completing my programming course, using it as a way to prepare for the future and to give our family a sense of security. Artur was busy with work, often coming home late, yet he made sure to spend as much time as he could with Masha, reinforcing the normalcy we were trying so hard to cultivate.

Then, just as I finished my training and started the nerve-wracking process of job hunting, I discovered I was pregnant. The news hit me like a wave of relief and excitement, quickly followed by a surge of protective instincts. Suddenly, our home felt fuller, brighter, as if the walls themselves held a new warmth. I was filled with the strange, beautiful knowledge that I was carrying another life, a gift I had long hoped for, despite the circumstances.

That evening, I shared the news with Artur. Tears filled my eyes as I tried to find the right words, a mix of joy and fear stirring within me.

"Artur," I whispered, my voice shaky, "there are two hearts beating inside me."

He looked at me, his face breaking into a joyful smile. He reached out, pulling me into a warm embrace.

"Why are you crying?" he asked gently, his hand resting on my shoulder.

I took a deep breath, wiping away my tears.

"I'm just . . . scared," I admitted, my voice barely above a whisper.

He held me a little tighter, resting his chin on my head.

"We'll face it together," he said, his voice steady and reassuring. "This is our blessing, and we're ready for it."

In that moment, my fear softened, replaced by a quiet, shared hope.

I hesitated before sharing the news with my prospective employer, uncertain about how they would react. But when I finally told them, they surprised me with understanding and support, assuring me that they would hold my position and wait for me to return to work after the birth. It felt like a small victory, a confirmation that life, despite everything, was moving forward in the right direction.

As we prepared for the birth of our second daughter, Masha turned six. She was growing fast, her curiosity blooming, and it warmed my heart to see her excitement about becoming an older sister. She often asked questions, her eyes wide with wonder as she tried to imagine what life would be like with a baby in the house.

One evening, as she was gently cradling one of her dolls, she looked up at me with a small, thoughtful frown.

"Mama, do you think she'll want to play with me?" she asked, her voice filled with anticipation. "Will we share toys and be best friends?"

I smiled, reaching out to gently tuck a loose curl behind her ear.

"I think she'll love playing with you, Masha," I said. "And when she's big enough, I know she'll look up to you and want to be just like her big sister."

She beamed, her eyes sparkling with excitement.

"I'll teach her how to play with all my toys," she declared proudly. "And I'll share my favorite ones with her!"

"You'll be the best big sister," I whispered, hugging her close.

She hugged her doll a little tighter, already practicing her new role. The anticipation of welcoming another child filled our home with a sense of purpose and joy, as we all prepared to embrace this new journey together.

Two months later, our wonderful new baby girl, Dasha, arrived. The moment I held her for the first time, I felt both joy and a rush of responsibility—a familiar and yet different kind of love that expanded my heart. Our family felt complete, but life quickly shifted into a new rhythm. Artur was busier than ever, working long hours to ensure our family's stability, and I was home with Masha and the newborn. The reality of juggling a newborn's needs with a young child's demands, all while managing household responsibilities, began to take its toll. I felt stretched thin, often running on little sleep and many unfinished tasks, and my worries weighed heavily on me.

On top of this, my parents were still in a dangerous situation in the east, their safety always on my mind. Every phone call with them was both a relief and a source of stress, as I was constantly afraid of the day they might stop coming. The unrelenting pressure built up inside me, and in the quiet hours of the night, I found myself stress-eating, trying to fill an emptiness that only seemed to grow. My weight started to creep up again, and with it came a haunting sense of despair, like a shadow from the past pulling me back into the depths of depression.

But the true turning point, the moment that shattered what little stability I had left, came during a routine check-up when Dasha was six months old. The doctor examined her quietly, his expression growing serious as he looked over the results. I sat in the sterile, silent room, holding my breath.

He turned to me, his face grave.

"I'm afraid I have some difficult news," he began, his tone cold and clinical, as though distancing himself from the impact of his words. "Dasha has a congenital heart defect. It's . . . significant. She will need surgery."

The words hung in the air, hitting me like a blow to the chest. I felt my voice catch in my throat.

"Surgery?" I managed to whisper, my hands trembling as I clutched them together. "But . . . she's so little. How . . . how serious is it?"

He paused, his gaze softening just slightly.

"We'll need to monitor her condition over time," the doctor said, looking at me carefully. "Dasha is six months old now, and we'll need to wait another six months to see how her heart develops. Most likely, she will still need surgery."

I felt myself spiraling, a crushing weight of fear and helplessness pressing down on me. My voice broke.

"How . . . how can this be?" I managed to ask, my voice trembling. "She's a healthy girl, with no signs of heart problems."

"Did I . . . did I do something wrong?" I choked out, barely able to get the words past the lump in my throat. "Is this . . . my fault?"

He shook his head gently, reaching a hand toward me, though he kept a professional distance.

"No, this isn't your fault," he said softly. "These things happen. But the sooner we act, the better her chances."

My vision blurred as tears filled my eyes. The room felt stifling, and my mind raced with questions, but none that I could put into words. I was free-falling, lost in a void of panic and despair, every beat of my heart echoing with guilt and terror for Dasha's future.

The weight of the diagnosis pressed down on me, making it difficult to breathe, to think. I couldn't see a way forward, and the practicalities of the situation only added to my desperation. Surgery was essential, but the cost was staggering. I had no idea where we would find the money, no idea how we would manage, and every solution I imagined felt inadequate.

I visited numerous clinics and consulted various doctors, who advised us to wait six months and then redo the heart ultrasound to decide the next steps. Those six months felt eternal, stretching out like decades, each day marked by an unending stream of worry. Every milestone with Dasha—her first smiles, her first babbling sounds—was tinged with fear, as I anxiously watched for any signs of discomfort or struggle. I was desperate for her to reach her first birthday, counting down the days until we could redo the ultrasound and, I hoped, hear better news.

During this time, I was constantly in tears, my mood depleted and my mind too consumed to focus on anything else. Even the ongoing war, which had once been my greatest fear, seemed distant and blurred by comparison to this all-consuming worry for my child. It was as if the world around me had faded, leaving me alone in my own isolated nightmare.

On top of it all, I felt the weight of what I suspected was postpartum depression pressing down on me, pulling me deeper into despair. With two young children to care for, a husband working long hours, and no family nearby to lean on, I was completely overwhelmed. Depression, panic attacks, the relentless news of the war, and the terrifying diagnosis for Dasha created a relentless storm that I felt powerless to escape. I found myself replaying the doctor's words in my mind over and over, his voice echoing in my thoughts, fueling my darkest fears. There were moments when I felt like I didn't want to go on, when the weight of it all seemed too much.

But even in my darkest moments, I knew I had to keep going. My children had no one but me, and that knowledge, more than anything, kept me moving, even if only one difficult step at a time.

My wisest decision ever was to finally seek a psychologist. For so long, I had resisted the idea, convincing myself that I could manage on my own, that I needed to stay strong for Masha and Dasha. But as the weight of my struggles grew, I knew I couldn't keep going like this. I was running on empty, my days filled with a constant hum of anxiety and despair.

By chance, while taking Masha and Dasha to the playground—an important daily ritual for me, one of the few outings that grounded me—I struck up a conversation with another mother. She spoke warmly of a psychologist who had helped her daughter overcome a fear of flying, and something in her words resonated deeply. I hesitated, feeling a mix of hope and apprehension, but I asked for the psychologist's number. I thought, maybe, just maybe, this could be the help I'd been needing but had been too afraid to ask for.

When I called, the psychologist explained that she specialized in working with children, and for a moment, my hope faltered. I felt foolish, embarrassed for even reaching out, but something in her voice told me to hold on a little longer.

"I usually work with children," she said gently, sensing my hesitation. "But tell me, why did you call?"

I took a shaky breath, struggling to put my feelings into words.

"I . . . I don't know if I can keep going like this," I admitted, my voice barely above a whisper. "It feels like everything is slipping away. I'm so tired . . . and scared."

There was a pause on the other end, and I worried I had said too much. But then her voice softened, filled with understanding.

"I hear you," she said kindly. "And if you're ready, I'd like to help you. We can work through this together."

A rush of relief washed over me, and in that moment, I felt a glimmer of hope—fragile, but real. And so began a new chapter in my life—one that would slowly lead me from the shadows of my struggles and into a space of understanding and healing.

This incredible woman, Marina, became the very center of my universe, filling a void that I had carried for so long. She gave me what I so desperately needed—gentle, warm interactions and the nurturing support I had been missing, as if she were family. Every session with her felt like a gift, and I clung to each word, each piece of advice, as though they were precious lifelines. I poured myself into the homework she assigned, completing each task with all the honesty and diligence I could muster, because she was truly my last hope.

Marina was the first person in my life to look into my depths and see something beautiful, to tell me things about myself that I could barely believe, much less accept. Her words were gentle yet powerful, peeling away layers of pain and fear that I had thought were permanent. Each time she praised me, a part of me felt like it was being reborn, like someone was gently breathing life back into my soul, healing the parts of me that had long been neglected.

After each session, I left with a sense of purpose, a renewed strength to face another day. The darkness that had consumed me started to lift, and with time, my panic attacks grew less frequent, like shadows retreating before the dawn. I felt hope where there had been only despair, and I realized just how transformative true compassion and understanding could be.

I will always carry an immense gratitude for Marina in my heart. She had the courage to take on an adult client outside her usual scope, to meet me in my darkest hours, and to guide me back to life. In her, I found not only healing but inspiration. She showed me the incredible impact of helping others, and I knew then that I, too, wanted to be that source of hope for someone else—to become a light in the darkness for those who felt lost, as I once had.

When Dasha turned one, we finally went for the ultrasound. I remember every detail of that day—the sterile scent of the clinic, the coldness of the exam room, the rhythmic beeping of medical equipment. My hands were clammy as I held Dasha, and my heart raced with a mixture of dread and hope. The doctor conducted the ultrasound with calm precision, his face unreadable, and I held my breath, afraid of what he might find.

After what felt like an eternity, he finally turned to me, a small smile breaking through his professional demeanor.

"Her heart . . . it looks completely normal," he said softly.

I stared at him, barely able to believe his words. "Are you sure?" I asked, my voice shaky. "Can you . . . please, can you check again? Just to be certain."

He nodded reassuringly, glancing back at the screen as he reviewed the results once more. After a moment, he looked back at me with the same warm smile.

"Yes, I'm sure," he said gently. "Dasha's heart is healthy. She doesn't need surgery."

A wave of relief washed over me, but I was still overwhelmed, trying to grasp this sudden change. "How . . . how is this possible?" I whispered. "Just six months ago, you said she'd need surgery."

The doctor's expression softened, and he placed a comforting hand on my shoulder.

"Sometimes, as children grow, their hearts can develop fully on their own," he explained. "It's rare, but it happens. In cases like this, the heart just needs a bit of time to fully form. Miracles do happen."

Tears streamed down my face as I hugged Dasha tightly, overcome with gratitude. "Thank you . . . thank you so much," I whispered, my voice breaking.

In that moment, it felt as if the entire world had shifted. I felt almost weightless, as though I could breathe fully for the first time in a year. Tears filled my eyes, and I hugged Dasha tightly, feeling a tidal wave of relief and gratitude. It was nothing short of a miracle, a gift I hadn't dared to hope for. I cried tears of pure joy, letting out all the fear, the sleepless nights, the relentless anxiety. That moment was beyond words, a happiness I could scarcely describe.

This experience, and Marina's steady support, changed me. I continued therapy with her, determined to build a life filled with purpose and meaning. Over time, I realized that the path I had initially chosen in IT—driven mostly by financial concerns—was not truly mine. Watching Marina work with such patience and understanding, I saw the transformative power of her role in my life. Her compassion and skill gave me a glimpse into what it means to truly help someone heal, and I felt a growing desire to offer that same kind of support to others.

My heart lay elsewhere. The struggles I had faced, and the healing I had experienced, ignited a deep desire within me to help others who felt lost and hopeless. I knew I had to follow this calling. Marina didn't just help me find myself again—she inspired me to become someone who could guide others through their darkest moments.

With renewed courage, I made a decision that surprised even me: I would pursue a second degree, this time in psychology. I enrolled in university, driven by a commitment to be a source of hope for others, especially those who, like me, came from the eastern part of our country, enduring the horrors of ongoing war and loss. I wanted to guide them through their own darkness, to offer the kind of help that had once saved me.

Thanks to Artur's stable income, we were able to manage comfortably, and for the first time in years, life felt like it was finally falling into place. My depression lifted, little by little, like fog clearing after a long, dark night. I began to reclaim my health, shedding the weight I had gained, not just physically but emotionally as well. With each step, I felt a little stronger, a little more myself.

I made small but meaningful changes in my life: I started saving money, quit coffee and smoking, focused on nourishing my body and mind. I was finally living the life I had yearned for, the life I had fought so hard to reclaim.

Looking back, I saw how far we had come, how many battles—both internal and external—I had faced. And though the scars remained, they were now reminders of resilience, of a strength I hadn't known I possessed. I was no longer just surviving; I was living, with a heart full of gratitude and a newfound purpose.

And so, as I closed one chapter of struggle and fear, I began another, filled with hope, healing, and the promise of brighter days ahead.

32

The Cycle Restarts

It's strange how quickly life can shift from ordinary to unimaginable, how a single phone call can redraw the contours of your world. This time, a phone call from my mother shattered the calm of the day. Her voice, trembling with fear, told me that during a check-up, the doctors had found a tumor in Danya's esophagus. Sixteen years old, and life was already testing him so mercilessly.

"They said . . . they said it could be cancer," she whispered, her voice breaking. I could feel her fear reaching across the distance, wrapping around me.

I struggled to find words, my own heart pounding. "Mama, we don't know that yet. Let's stay calm. Have they done any more tests?"

She sighed shakily, as if grasping for strength. "They're not sure. They need more scans. I . . . I thought, maybe if we brought him to your city, if you could help us find another doctor . . . maybe someone will say something different. Maybe . . ." She trailed off, her voice filled with a quiet desperation.

"Yes, absolutely. Send me everything you have, all his documents, and bring him here. We'll find the best doctor, Mama," I said, trying to sound as steady as possible. "We're not giving up. There are always options, always someone who can help."

There was a long pause before she finally whispered, "Thank you. I just . . . I don't know what we'd do without you."

My heart ached hearing the helplessness in her voice. "We're in this together, Mama. Danya's strong, and we'll face this as a family. He's going to be okay."

As I hung up, a sense of urgency settled over me. I knew I would do everything possible to ensure my brother got the help he needed, but the weight of what lay ahead pressed heavily on my chest.

I rushed to consult a specialist in my city, carrying my brother's records as if they were fragile, as if by some miracle I could protect him by holding them close. The doctor studied the scans and reports with a deep, focused silence, his face an unreadable mask. And then, breaking that heavy stillness, he reached out, took my hand gently, and looked into my eyes.

"I'm so sorry," he began, his voice low, filled with a sadness that echoed in my own heart. "Your brother has esophageal cancer."

The words hung in the air, striking me like a physical blow. I felt the room spin, my vision blurring as disbelief washed over me. Cancer? At sixteen? My mind scrambled to reject his words, yet they settled like a stone in my chest, cold and unmovable.

Somehow, I stumbled out of the hospital, numb and reeling, and called my mother. My voice barely held steady as I told her they needed to come to our city, where he could receive better treatment. It was the only clarity I had amid the shock—a fierce determination to get him the help he needed.

We made arrangements. I would go to the regional children's hospital, register my brother, speak with the doctors, and prepare everything for their arrival. The next day, accompanied by my younger daughter, Dasha, I made my way to the hospital while Masha was at school. My hands were trembling, but I tried to hold myself together for Dasha's sake. I held her tiny hand tightly, as if hoping that her innocence and simplicity could shield me from the weight of what was happening. How I wished all of this was just a bad dream from which I would soon wake up. A deep fear had settled within me, leaving nowhere to hide, yet I kept walking, repeating to myself that I had to stay strong, that I simply couldn't give up. After reviewing his records, they looked at me gravely, saying surgery was needed immediately. We agreed on the date, and all I could do was wait for my family to arrive.

When my parents and brother, Danya, finally arrived, we faced the harsh, sterile reality of the hospital together. Danya was admitted, and additional

The Cycle Restarts

tests were run. The doctors confirmed the need for surgery to remove the tumor but couldn't yet say whether it was malignant or benign. We clung to hope, each of us trying to mask our fear for his sake, but the weight of uncertainty pressed down on all of us.

On the day of the surgery, as Danya lay on the gurney, ready to be wheeled into the operating room, he looked up at me, his young face already marked with fatigue. "I'm scared," he whispered, his voice trembling, "but I trust you."

I felt a surge of fierce protectiveness and leaned down to squeeze his hand. "We'll be here the whole time, okay? Right outside, waiting for you. You're so strong, and you're not alone."

He gave a small nod, and I could see the glimmer of courage in his eyes, despite his fear. I held his gaze, silently willing him strength, as the nurses prepared to take him away.

And so the waiting began. We sat in agonizing silence, each second stretching unbearably, weighed down by fear and helplessness. I stared at the closed door of the operating room, trying to hold back my thoughts, which inevitably returned to the worst-case scenario. "What if something goes wrong? What if . . ." I shook my head, trying to silence these thoughts. "He's strong. We'll all get through this," I repeated to myself like a mantra, trying to quiet the pounding of my heart that echoed in my temples. Each second of waiting felt like an eternity. All I could do was sit, silently pray, and hope that everything would end well.

Finally, the surgeon came out. The tumor had been successfully removed, he told us, but it had been sent off for analysis. We were left to wait once more, our hearts gripped in a vise of dread and cautious hope.

Days later, the news arrived: The tumor was benign. I felt a surge of relief so powerful that I could barely breathe. Danya would be okay. The nightmare we had been living in for weeks was finally over. I clutched him close, overwhelmed by gratitude, and in that moment, it felt as though life had returned to us.

But some memories are etched in pain, impossible to forget. Bringing Dasha to that hospital, watching as she tried to understand why her uncle was there, and witnessing the suffering etched onto the faces of other children—it was an image that would stay with me forever. I saw children, barely able to walk, pale and fragile, clinging to life with heartbreaking strength.

Parents stood outside, their faces lined with exhaustion and sorrow, crying or nervously smoking, desperately seeking solace in a moment of reprieve.

It's a scene filled with so much raw fear and aching hope. My heart broke not only for my brother but for every child there, every parent who carried that weight. I found myself wishing fervently, helplessly, that no child would have to suffer like this, that they could grow up healthy, happy, untouched by illness. My thoughts became a silent prayer for all the children in the world—to be strong, to heal, to live the joyful lives they deserve.

After such a difficult period, all I wanted was a little stability—a chance to finally exhale, to feel the ground steady beneath me. By February 2020, it seemed that life was aligning at last. We were slowly returning to ordinary life—Dasha had just started preschool, and we had saved enough for a down payment on a mortgage. And though memories of hospital corridors still surfaced anxiously in my mind, it felt like we had crossed an important threshold.

Finally, we were on the verge of buying our own home, a step that felt like a promise of safety and stability. But just as everything was starting to fall into place, the coronavirus pandemic struck, and once again, the future was thrown into uncertainty. It felt like a cruel pattern: As soon as life began to improve, another disaster loomed. Whether it was war or a global crisis, it seemed as if the universe was warning me not to settle, not to relax.

As the pandemic intensified, schools and preschools shut down, pushing everything online. Suddenly, both of my children were at home in our small, two-room apartment. Fear gripped me; I worried about getting infected and the possibility of leaving my children motherless. Death was no longer an abstract concept but something ominously close. I began obsessively washing groceries, laundering clothes daily, and disinfecting everything in sight. The confinement of lockdown was suffocating, and without even the relief of a simple walk outside, each day blurred into the next. Masha's online lessons only added to the stress, and I felt the weight of it building inside me.

One afternoon, as I scrubbed down the kitchen counters for what felt like the hundredth time, Masha looked up from her tablet and sighed.

"Mama, do you think we'll ever go back to school?" she asked, her voice carrying a mix of hope and uncertainty.

I stopped for a moment, forcing myself to set the sponge down and meet her eyes. "Yes, Masha," I said, smiling softly. "One day, things will be normal again. We'll go outside, see friends, and even have fun at the playground."

She tilted her head, as if trying to imagine it. "I miss my friends."

"I know, sweetie. I miss a lot of things too," I admitted. "But we have each other, right? And we'll make the best of it."

Dasha piped up from the couch, clutching her beloved stuffed unicorn. "Mama, can we have a tea party?"

A tea party. Such a simple, innocent request. Yet, in that moment, it reminded me of the world they needed me to create for them—a world filled with small joys and warmth, even amid the heaviness that lingered around us. "Of course, my love," I said, scooping Dasha into a hug. "Let's make it the most magical tea party our unicorn friend has ever seen."

And so, for a little while, we transformed the living room into a haven of make-believe and laughter, sharing pretend tea and cookies with stuffed animals lined up around us. In these tender moments, I found glimpses of strength, a reason to keep pushing forward. I wanted to protect their innocence, to fill their days with love, despite the deep uncertainty that had become part of our lives.

But as the days turned into weeks, the weight of it all began to settle on me, pressing harder than before. Overwhelmed, I found myself falling back into unhealthy habits, stress eating to cope with the endless tension. I gained weight and quickly grew to loathe myself for it, haunted by fears of slipping back into depression and the panic attacks I had worked so hard to overcome. The cycle felt relentless, as though I were spiraling with no way out.

But I knew I couldn't fall back into that dark place. Determined not to lose myself, I continued working with my psychologist, Marina, the woman who had been my lifeline. She was more than a therapist; she was my guide, my healer. She helped me see life from a new perspective, challenging me to transform my fear into growth. Instead of succumbing to despair, I began focusing on self-development. I continued my education online, immersing myself in university courses and taking self-improvement classes that helped me rebuild my confidence and resilience.

This time, I was determined to move forward, not merely survive. Slowly, I began piecing life back together, allowing myself to believe in a future where stability was possible.

Shortly after, however, we contracted coronavirus. It was a brutal illness that lingered for weeks, but we endured it together. When we finally recovered, Artur and I decided to buy our first car. It was old, and we knew every bump and squeak in its frame, but to us, it felt like freedom. We didn't care about its age; we were simply happy. With a car and our two beautiful children, we were carefully reconstructing our lives—piece by piece, like a puzzle—and hoping the final picture would be one we loved. As the pandemic began to recede, life gradually resumed a familiar rhythm. We ventured out in our little car, no longer confined to trains, and visited family. We found joy in small, everyday moments that felt like precious gifts.

That spring, we took a trip to the sea. We wandered through a zoo, walked along the shoreline, and embraced the simplicity of those moments. My studies were nearing completion, and my master's thesis was becoming an engaging project. Seeing some of my work published in academic journals filled me with pride. Through it all, Marina was there, guiding me with unwavering support. She often joked that my life experiences made me a "natural psychologist"—that I could relate deeply to others' pain. It was true; my life had been shaped by so much sorrow, but I'd reached a point where I could use it to help others.

In the meantime, Artur and I continued our search for a permanent home. When no suitable place turned up, we decided to purchase the apartment we were renting. Taking on a mortgage felt like an enormous leap, but it also gave us a sense of security we had longed for—a place where no one could evict us, where we could truly settle. We took on the renovations ourselves, learning through countless YouTube tutorials, each small improvement making the place feel more like home.

As we tried to build a new life, Artur and I found ways to simply live. We took Masha to another city for a concert by her favorite Ukrainian artist. Watching her light up with joy was a reminder that, amid the chaos, these were the moments that mattered. We held on to each other and found ways to thrive. Toward the end of 2021, I suggested we buy another car on credit. We planned to give our old car to Danya, so he could gain independence

The Cycle Restarts

and confidence. Soon enough, we bought our "little bluebird"—our cherished car, now a part of our lives in America.

As I held my psychology degree in my hands, a wave of accomplishment washed over me. That evening, sitting beside Artur, I felt the weight of everything we'd been through, and the joy of having reached this milestone.

"Can you believe it?" I said, smiling. "After all these years, I finally did it."

Artur reached over, taking my hand in his. "I never doubted it, even for a second," he replied softly, his eyes filled with pride. "You're incredible. I've seen you push through things that would have broken most people."

I squeezed his hand, feeling a warmth spread through me. "Thank you," I murmured, trying to hold back tears. "I couldn't have done it without you."

He smiled, pulling me into a gentle hug. "So . . . what's next?" he asked, a glimmer of excitement in his voice. "Do you think you're ready to take on this new career?"

I took a deep breath, the thought both thrilling and a little daunting. "Yes," I said, nodding. "More than ready. It's time to stop just surviving and actually live—make a difference."

He leaned back, grinning. "Then let's make this our best chapter yet. And let's get that mountain trip planned. I think we all deserve a bit of an adventure, don't you?"

I laughed, the joy of that moment filling me. "Absolutely. Let's take Danya and show him the world we've fought so hard to build."

In that moment, everything felt right, as if we were truly on the brink of something beautiful. My life, it seemed, was just beginning.

But only a month later, the war reached our doorstep. The invasion swept through the heart of our country, touching central cities and even the capital, shattering any remaining illusion of safety. And this—this moment of upheaval and heartbreak—is where this story began, where this book began. A cycle so cruel and familiar: war, displacement, starting over from nothing. This was the moment that compelled me to capture it all—to record the pain, resilience, and fragments of hope amidst the ruins, so that this story, our story, would not be forgotten.

To those who have ever had to rebuild from ashes, I offer this story as a testament. There is a part of us that endures, an ember that no hardship can extinguish. And as I write this final page, I find a quiet strength within—a knowledge that, if we must begin again, I will be ready.

www.ingramcontent.com/pod-product-compliance
Lightning Source LLC
Chambersburg PA
CBHW032021230426
43671CB00005B/161